ESSAYS ON LITERARY THEORY AND CRITICISM

Essays on Literary Theory and Criticism

By

Abraham Mathew

CYBER TECH PUBLICATIONS
4264/3, Ansari Road, Daryaganj, New Delhi-110002 (India)
Ph.: 011-23244078, 011-43559448 Fax: 011-23280028
E-Mail: cyberpublicationsdelhi@yahoo.com
Website: www.cybertechpublications.com

Essays on Literary Theory and criticism

Abraham Mathew

First Edition 2011

Asian Offset Printers

Published by

G.S. Rawat for Cyber Tech Publications

4264/3, Ansari Road, Daryaganj, New Delhi-110002 (India)

Ph.: 011-23244078, 011-43559448 Fax: 011-23280028

E-Mail: cyberpublicationsdelhi@yahoo.com

cyberpublications@gmail.com

Website: www.cybertechpublications.com

Contents

	Preface	*vii*
1.	Literary Theory and Criticism: An Overview	1
2.	Major Schools of Criticism	26
3.	Gender Criticism	54
4.	Reader-Response Criticism	92
5.	School of New Criticism	109
6.	New Historicism	150
7.	School of Russian Thought	160
8.	Psychoanalytical Criticism	188
9.	Modernism and Postmodernism	200
10.	On Language	226
11.	Role of Theology	252
	Glossary	272
	Bibliography	273
	Index	286

Preface

> "The higher we soar the smaller we look to those who cannot fly."
>
> —*F.W. Nietzsche*

It is pertinent to note that `literary theory' is the theory of the interpretation of literature and literary criticism. Its history begins with classical Greek poetics and rhetoric and includes, since the 18th century, aesthetics and hermeneutics. In the 20th century, "theory" has become an umbrella term for a variety of scholarly approaches to reading texts, most of which are informed by various strands of Continental philosophy. To being with, one of the fundamental questions of literary theory is "What is literature?", though many contemporary theorists and literary scholars believe either that "literature" cannot be defined or that it can refer to any use of language. Specific theories are distinguished not only by their methods and conclusions, but even by how they define a "text." For some scholars of literature, "texts" comprises little more than "books belonging to the Western literary canon." But the principles and methods of literary theory have been applied to non-fiction, popular fiction, film, historical documents, law, advertising, etc., in the related field of cultural studies.

As the name of the present title suggests, we have compiled here highly useful and vital information on literary theory and literary criticism. The well-researched readings are grouped under the following chapters—Literary Theory and Criticism: An Overview; Major Schools of Criticism; Gender Criticism; Reader-Response Criticism; School of New Criticism; New Historicism; School of Russian Thought; Psychoanalytical Criticism; Modernism and Postmodernism; On Language; Role of Theology; Glossary and Bibliography etc.

Definitely this will enlighten students, researchers and teachers of English literature alike.

With the sole aim of furnishing authentic information, we have drawn upon authoritative works of many scholars in the field. We have tried to acknowledge them amply in references and bibliography. If any name is left, it is unintentional. We express our gratefulness to these scholars. My teachers, colleagues and friends have contributed a lot in completing this work by way of guidance, inspiration and assistance. I am extremely grateful to them also. Last but not the least I am thankful to my publishers for publishing this work in superb way.

—Abraham Mathew

1

Literary Theory and Criticism: An Overview

"When you go into an orchard and see lots of sticks and stones under a tree you know that the tree has borne some fruits. This little observation should be consolation to those who tend to get discouraged under criticism. No one bothers much about throwing verbal brickbats at people who are doing nothing. The more active and fruitful your life the more you will receive criticism."

Here in the present book, we intend to put light on literary theory and criticism. In fact, it is the theory which moulds the shape of literary activities.

First we would describe the evolution and development of literary theory in historic perspective.

It is pertinent to note that `literary theory' is the theory of the interpretation of literature and literary criticism. Its history begins with classical Greek poetics and rhetoric and includes, since the 18th century, aesthetics and hermeneutics. In the 20th century, "theory" has become an umbrella term for a variety of scholarly approaches to reading texts, most of which are informed by various strands of Continental philosophy. To being with, one of the fundamental questions of literary theory is "What is literature?", though many contemporary theorists and literary scholars believe either that "literature" cannot be defined or that it can refer to any use of language. Specific theories are distinguished not only by their methods and conclusions, but even by how they define a "text." For some scholars of literature, "texts" comprises little more than "books belonging to the Western literary canon." But the principles and methods of literary theory have been applied to non-fiction, popular fiction, film, historical documents, law, advertising, etc., in the related field of cultural studies.

Basically, some scholars within cultural studies treat cultural events, like fashion or football riots, as "texts" to be interpreted. By this measure, literary theory can be thought of as the general theory of interpretation. Since theorists of literature often draw on a very heterogeneous tradition of Continental philosophy and the philosophy of language, any classification of their approaches is only an approximation. There are many "schools" or types of literary theory, which take different approaches to understanding texts.

It is remarkable the practice of literary theory became a profession in the 20th century, but it has historical roots that run as far back as ancient Greece (Aristotle's *Poetics* is an often cited early example) and ancient Rome (Longinus' *On the Sublime* and Horace's *Ars Poetica*), and the aesthetic theories of philosophers from ancient philosophy through the 18th and 19th centuries are important influences on current literary study. The theory and criticism of literature are, of course, also closely tied to the history of literature. The modern sense of "literary theory," however, dates only to approximately the 1950s, when the structuralist linguistics of Ferdinand de Saussure began strongly to influence English language literary criticism. The New Critics and various European-influenced formalists (particularly the

Russian Formalists) had described some of their more abstract efforts as "theoretical" as well. But it was not until the broad impact of structuralism began to be felt in the English-speaking academic world that "literary theory" was thought of as a unified domain. In the academic world of the Great Britain and the United States, literary theory was at its most popular from the late 1960s through the 1980s.

During this span of time, literary theory was perceived as academically cutting-edge research, and most university literature departments sought to teach and study theory and incorporate it into their curricula. Because of its meteoric rise in popularity and the difficult language of its key texts, theory was also often criticized as faddish or trendy obscurantism. Some scholars, both theoretical and anti-theoretical, refer to the 1970s and 1980s debates on the academic merits of theory as "the theory wars." By the early 1990s, the popularity of "theory" as a subject of interest by itself was declining slightly (along with job openings for pure "theorists") even as the texts of literary theory were incorporated into the study of almost all literature.

As of 2004, the controversy over the use of theory in literary studies has all but died out, and discussions on the topic within literary and cultural studies tend now to be considerably milder and less acrimonious. Some scholars draw heavily on theory in their work, while others only mention it in passing or not at all; but it is an acknowledged, important part of the study of literature.

The intellectual traditions and priorities of the various kinds of literary theory are often radically different. Even finding a set of common terms to compare them by can be difficult. For instance, the work of the New Critics often contained an implicit moral dimension, and sometimes even a religious one: a New Critic might read a poem by T.S. Eliot or Gerard Manley Hopkins for its degree of honesty in expressing the torment and contradiction of a serious search for belief in the modern world.

Meanwhile a Marxist critic might find such judgments merely ideological rather than critical; the Marxist would say that the New Critical reading did not keep enough critical distance from the poem's religious stance to be able to understand it. Or a post-structuralist critic might simply avoid the issue by understanding the religious meaning of a poem as an allegory of meaning, treating the poem's references to "God" by discussing their referential nature rather than what they refer to. Such a disagreement cannot be easily resolved, because it is inherent in the radically different terms and goals (that is, the theories) of the critics. Their theories of reading derive from vastly different intellectual traditions: the New Critic bases his work on an East-Coast American scholarly and religious tradition, while the Marxist derives his thought from a body of critical social and economic thought, and the post-structuralist's work emerges from twentieth-century Continental philosophy of language.

To expect such different approaches to have much in common would be naïve; so calling them all "theories of literature" without acknowledging their heterogeneity is itself a reduction of their differences. In the late 1950s, Canadian literary critic Northrop Frye attempted to establish an approach for reconciling historical criticism and New Criticism while addressing concerns of early reader-response and numerous psychological and social approaches. His approach, laid out in his Anatomy of Criticism, was explicitly structuralist, relying on the assumption of an intertextual "order of words" and universality of certain structural types.

His approach held sway in English literature programs for several decades but lost favour during the ascendence of post-structuralism.

For some theories of literature (especially certain kinds of formalism), the distinction between 'literary' and other sorts of texts is of paramount importance. Other schools (particularly post-structuralism in its various forms: new historicism, deconstruction, some strains of Marxism and feminism) have sought to break down distinctions between the two and have applied the tools of textual interpretation to a wide range of 'texts', including film, non-fiction, historical writing, and even cultural events.

Another crucial distinction among the various theories of literary interpretation is intentionality, the amount of weight given to the author's own opinions about and intentions for a work. For most pre-20th century approaches, the author's intentions are a guiding factor and an important determiner of the 'correct' interpretation of texts. The New Criticism was the first school to disavow the role of the author in interpreting texts, preferring to focus on "the text itself" in a close reading.

Different Schools

We have furnished below are some of the most commonly identified schools of literary theory, along with their major authors. In many cases, such as those of the historian and philosopher Michel Foucault and the anthropologist Claude Lévi-Strauss, the authors were not primarily literary critics, but their work has been broadly influential in literary theory.

(a) Darwinian literary studies - situates literature in the context of evolution and natural selection

(b) Cultural studies - emphasizes the role of literature in everyday life

(c) American pragmatism and other American approaches

(d) Comparative Literature - considers literatures from different languages, nations and cultures

(e) Deconstruction - a strategy of close reading which draws out "undecidable" interpretive decisions, rendering intelligible what the text does not itself think but nevertheless allows to be thought

(f) Feminism - which emphasizes themes of gender relations

(g) Formalism

(h) German hermeneutics and philology

(i) New Criticism - which looked at literary works on the basis of what is written, and not at the goals of the author or biographical issues

(j) New historicism - which examines a text by also examining other texts of the time period

(k) Postcolonialism - focuses on the influences of colonialism in literature, especially regarding the historical conflict resulting from the exploitation of less developed countries and indigenous peoples by western nations

(l) Post-structuralism - criticism of structuralism

(m) Psychoanalysis (see psychoanalytic literary criticism) - Explores the role of the subconscious in literature including that of the author, reader, and characters in the text

(n) Queer theory - examines, questions, and criticizes the role of gender identity and sexuality in literature

(o) Reader Response - focuses upon the active response of the reader to a text

(p) Russian Formalism

Literary Criticism and Literary Thought

Remarkably, literary criticism is the estimation of the value of a particular work or body of work on such grounds as: the personal and/or cultural significance of the themes and the uses of language of a text; the insights and impact of a text; and the aesthetic production (or, performance) of the text; particularly as these areas are seen to be mutually dependent, supportive or inflective. The word 'criticism' has ordinary-use negative connotations, and to an extent that is right: for literary criticism is part of the disciplining of discourse generally and of what is considered literature in particular.

One patrols the boundaries of good writing, admitting or excluding, determining what should be thought about a text, and why, what personal and cultural value should be placed on it. Judgments of value are not simple, however. They require that one consider what constitutes value, what the personal and social value of literature is, what the value of 'the aesthetic' is. And they require that one interpret the text. As texts judged to be of high literary value tend to be marked by complexity and even ambiguity, and to yield diverse interpretations, judgment may ultimately require a theory of interpretation, or at least careful attention to the question of what constitutes, guides, and legitimates interpretation.

Theory is the process of understanding what the nature of literature is, what functions it has, what the relation of text is to author, to reader, to language, to society, to history. It is not judgment but understanding of the frames of judgment. Theory, however, particularly as "a theory of A," tends to operate within a frame of values and expectations itself. Full understanding requires one think as fully as possible about the sets of expectations, assumptions and values of theory and theorizing, and this (always incompletable) exercise.

In the present book we have tried to present Literary theory and literarycriticism in all dimensions. Different schools of literary theory and criticism are given elaborate treatment in succeeding chapters.

As is being observed, no doubt 'Literary theory' has undergone drastic changes in the past century and here we will make an attempt to understand some of the influences that have altered the critical landscape. The change that has taken place in literary theory is not novel to this discipline alone, nor is it to be explained by any one phenomenon. The influences of modernism and post-modernism are accurately reflected in the changes that have taken place in literary theory. To introduce the ideas of modernism as an influence on academia is to introduce a host of difficulties which are only exaggerated by the term post-modernism. The factors that have brought about what we call modernism are legion and cannot be attributed solely to either a change in philosophical thought or in sociological "development."

There is a reciprocal relationship between these two phenomena. And both are necessary in order to understand the current situation. Before proceeding it may be helpful to examine what is meant by the terms modernism and post-modernism. These are notoriously elusive terms which at times appear somewhat arbitrary as they often overlap and at times lack clear distinction. One of the difficulties encountered in elaborating on these terms is that there is no clear disjuncture between these two time periods or paradigms in thinking.

Although many try, it is difficult to say exactly when modernism began and ended and when post-modernism has taken over. They are rather like rivers fed by many smaller streams so that while post-modernism may be said to be a late twentieth-century phenomenon, the ideas and sociological changes that have contributed to its rise may be traced back much further.

It is pertinent to note that, Modernism began with the rise of rationalism, in which man is viewed as the starting point for knowledge, and with the belief that truth can be ascertained chiefly through the scientific method. As a result of urbanization and the economic reordering of society there is a bifurcation between what is seen as public or social and what is held to be private. Increasingly, religious truth claims, individual morality, and meaning (whether it be that of a text or of life in general) are relegated to the latter, undergoing the same kind of privatization as capitalism has brought to property rights. Third, modernism shows a strong inclination toward individualism with its emphasis on freedom and the "existing" individual.

'Post-modernism' is in many ways, a reaction against modernism. Post-modernism is characterized first by a rejection of foundational truth or ontological essentialism. Language is the primary means by which this belief is established as language is believed to be a social construct. Second, its individualism is pitted against any authoritarian structure or worldview that would stand over the individual. Third, post-modernism differs from modernism in the degree to which pluralism is experienced by the average person. As these phenomena have influenced culture, what people view as plausible has clearly changed.

It is remarkable that most significant change that has occurred in the field of literary criticism and hermeneutics is in where the locus of meaning is perceived to inhere. In the disciplines of literary criticism and hermeneutics (when hermeneutics principally referred to the methods and rules of interpretation) it was originally assumed that meaning resided with the author. Thus the purpose of interpretation was to discern the author's intention which would unlock the textual meaning for all times.

After Lessing, however, a new-found distance between the present and the past caused interpreters to focus more concertedly on the text itself, because the author was no longer deemed accessible to the interpreter. The shift in the locus of meaning continued under the influence of cultural pressures and meaning came to be seen as inhering in the reader. Gadamer attributes to him the differentiation of understanding and misunderstanding, in which the interpreter is seen to begin the process within his or her own misunderstandings.

In other words, the interpreter brings to the text his own set of presuppositions which causes him to misunderstand the text. The hermeneutical method was intended to secure a right understanding of the text from preconceived understandings or misunderstandings. Thus there is a recognition that the mind does not necessarily act as a mirror reflecting exactly what is in the text. Schleiermacher's position is epistemologically more sophisticated than those preceding him. From this perspective the discipline of hermeneutics gradually moves from a methodological approach to the text toward the modern conception that hermeneutics is what happens when we interpret a text or how one comes to understanding.

Notably, story of modern hermeneutics begins with Edmund Husserl and his phenomenological approach. Following "Descartes' dream" of absolute certainty in knowing, Husserl focused on things as they show themselves. The philosophy of this movement was to "let things appear as they are" or to refrain from reading our presuppositions into a text. The purpose of Husserl's "phenomenological reduction" is to focus on what is immediate to experience, "Everything not 'immanent' to consciousness must be rigorously excluded."

In this approach the meaning of the text has been fixed by the language and exists in an "idealist" sense. In an attempt to go beyond Husserl's essentialist approach, his pupil Martin Heidegger posited an existential theory of hermeneutics in *Being and Time*. Heidegger rejects the notion of objective historical knowledge, instead man finds himself "thrown into" the world in which language, culture and the institutions of life are givens.

We cannot simply "bracket off" our pre-understanding in order to gain a transcendent, objective standpoint. Pure objectivity can never be gained by the subject. Heidegger's rejection of the subject-object, "I-it" duality leads him to the position of *denying that meaning is fixed in a text* which would be to affirm its objective reality. Thus meaning is not something objectifiable but is as elusive as Being itself. Heidegger's *Dasein* or Being examines the situation of Being from within, not outside of, history. Being for Heidegger is the historically conditioned individual which is aware of itself and the passage of time.

As Being exists in time its understanding is conditioned on previous understanding. Thus the interpreter finds himself in a hermeneutical circle in which prior understanding is always "read into" the process of understanding. Heidegger describes the circularity in the process of reasoning about Being in the following: "Phenomenological Interpretation must make it possible for Dasein itself to disclose things primordially; it must, as it were, let Dasein interpret itself."

Although he thoroughly grasped the situation of pre-understanding, because he failed to understand the primacy of language in producing, not just expressing, meaning, Terry Eagleton calls his approach a "hermeneutic phenomenology." It was one of Heidegger's students, Hans-George Gadamer, who first presented an adequate view of linguistics in hermeneutical theory. Gadamer makes a nice transition figure between hermeneutics and literary theory for he was also a student of Rudolf Bultmann. Like Saussure and Wittgenstein, Gadamer argues that there is no thought prior to language. It is language that both makes possible and limits our understanding. "Gadamer would say," according to Brice Wachterhauser, "that it is only through language that we have a world." In order to understand a text we need a fusion between the horizon of our world and the world of the text. This is a creative or dialectic fusion which produces a new meaning. "To understand it does not mean primarily to reason one's way back into the past, but to have a present involvement in what is said." Gadamer represents a movement away from author-centered interpretation but there remains, however, a two-way process between text and interpreter in which the latter's questions are informed by the former.

He explains in the following what is meant by a "fusion of horizons": One intends to *understand the text itself.* But this means that the interpreter's own thoughts too have gone into re-awakening the text's meaning. In this the interpreter's own horizon is decisive, yet not as a personal standpoint that he maintains or enforces, but more as an opinion and a possibility that one brings into play and puts at risk, and that helps to truly make one's own what the text says. While Gadamer moved the locus of meaning from the author somewhere between the text and the reader, on the American scene in the early to mid-twentieth century we see the rise of a school focused solely on the text with New Criticism. Gadamer's own theories bear a number of similarities to the approach of New Criticism.

I.A. Richards represents somewhat of a transitional figure to this movement. Eagleton comments that Richards "had naively assumed that the poem was no more than a ../graphics/cleardot medium through which we could observe the poet's psychological processes: reading was just a matter of recreating in our own mind the mental condition of the author. Indeed much traditional literary criticism has held this view in one form or another."

With New Criticism we find the ascendancy of a more text-focused hermeneutic where the author's intention, even if it could be discerned, is irrelevant to the work at hand. The text is all that is and all that is important. In text-centered literary criticism William Wimsatt and Monroe Beardsley are key figures. It is their famous article on the "Intentional Fallacy" that secured the death of authorial intention.

In fact, they argued that the psychological processes of the author are inaccessible to the interpreter. We are locked out of the mind of the author and have only the text and it is this that should be examined, not the author. As they wrote, "the design or intention of the author is neither available nor desirable as a standard for judging the success of a work of literary art." They continue in the same article by saying, "The poem is not the critic's own and not the author's (it is detached from the author at birth and goes about the world beyond his power to intend about it or control it). The poem *belongs to the public*" [italics mine]. What is important to the New Critics is the verbal context as it now stands instead of the historical context in which it was first spoken.

This may very well be a false dichotomy as it is unclear how the verbal context can have meaning apart from the historical context. But it is apparent that the wheels were in motion that transported meaning from the author's mental processes to that of the reader's, and the text from the public domain to the private. It is Wimsatt and Beardsley who also bear the brunt of the later "reader-response" critics' ire. In another article on the Affective Fallacy, they argued against taking into consideration the affect which the text has on the reader saying that when this is done, "the poem itself, as an object . . . tends to disappear" making what was public verse into private verse.

There are definite similarities between New Criticism and German Neo-orthodoxy. The text is severed from its past and the interpreter stands at the far end of a yawning chasm with only the text in hand. It was Karl Barth who sought to free the meaning of the text from being corrupted by past understanding by positing an existential immediacy in which the Word is revealed to us through the word (recall Heidegger's "Being" revealed through the medium of language). Rudolf Bultmann then carried Barth's project to its radical extreme by severing all connections with the past in an attempt to secure meaning as suprahistorical. It is this mindset that is behind his demythologizing program which seeks to demonstrate "the independence of faith from history".

Gadamer, on the other hand, sought to make immanent again the meaning by grounding it in language and Being. But if Gadamer moves us toward a text-centered hermeneutic, he also opens the door for the next movement in literary theory which is "reception theory." For Gadamer, because *Dasein* encounters the text in one's own world, the foundation of understanding is always shifting. *Dasein* is historically situated, which means that, "Our rational ability to make such judgments does not rest on some deep, permanent structure, transcendental reason or human nature, but rather it depends on our changing self-understanding."

These insights open the door for a new attentiveness to the reader's contribution to the hermeneutic process. Eagleton notes that there has been, "a marked shift of attention to the reader over recent years. The reader has always been the most underprivileged of this trio [author, text, reader]—strangely, since without him or her there would be no literary texts at all."

Whereas the New Critics sought to secure the text objectively with verifiable results in the critical process, reader-response critics opened the door for the reader to focus on his or her mental processes in the act of reading. Following the German tradition, a more moderate proponent of this type of criticism is Wolfgang Iser. Iser says, "The phenomenological theory of art lays full stress on the idea that, in considering a literary work, one must take into account not only the actual text but also, and in equal measure, the actions involved in responding to that text."

He goes on to say, "The convergence of text and reader brings the literary work into existence." Although Iser brings the reader more fully into the interpretive process, he does not find the locus of meaning to inhere in the reader. Similar to Gadamer's approach there is a free-play or creative act between the author and the reader with the reader supplying the gaps in understanding generated by the text.

A more radical approach to reader-response criticism in the tradition of neo-pragmatism and conventionalism is that of Stanley Fish.

His assertion is that the reader manufactures the sense or meaning of the text. Meaning no longer inheres in the text, but is fully located within the reading community. Thus the reader's presuppositions are not something to be overcome, they are inescapable. The "interpretive community" is a reading public that shares a strategy or approach to interpretation. The text is not an object that can be approached and examined from the outside. There is no metanarrative; there is no truth or story that will encompass and make sense of all other narratives. There are only ungrounded language games and ungrounded interpretive communities. Indeed, a narrative is nothing without the reader.

Fish rejects the idea that there are any right methodologies for interpretation; methodologies just are and they determine the interpretive results. He says that, "The meaning of an utterance, I repeat, is its experience—all of it—and that experience is immediately compromised the moment you say anything about it."

Many trace the rise of modernism in philosophy to Descartes' process of radical doubt. His intent was to place knowledge on a secure foundation. To do this he methodologically is called into question everything he felt he knew and discovered that almost everything could be questioned. Descartes ended his doubt, or found bedrock on the tenuous foundation of his own consciousness. His own inner cognition was the only thing of which he could be certain. *Cogito ergo sum* (I think therefore I am) is his final declaration. While his intention was to find certainty in knowing, Descartes radically changed epistemology by introducing his methodological doubt, a process which did not always end where Descartes had ended. Though few agreed with Descartes' assertion, none were left unaffected by it. His cogitation began a shift in the way people perceived and experienced reality. The modern paradigm brought with it a search for objectivity established on the tenuous foundations of the individual consciousness. Descartes prompted both the relentless pursuit of the "objective" as well as planting the seeds of its demise.

Kierkegaard perceptively identifies this subjective turn as early as 1843 in his publication of *Fear and Trembling*. To quote him

> Descartes has not cried 'Fire!' and made it everyone's duty to doubt, for Descartes was a quiet and lonely thinker, not a bellowing streetwatch; he was modest enough to allow that his method was important *only for himself* [italics mine] and sprang partly from his own earlier bungling with knowledge. ("Thus my design here is not to teach the Method which everyone should follow in order to promote the good conduct of Reason, but only to show in what manner I have endeavored to conduct my own . . ."). (P. 42)

Whereas Hegel would later attempt to encompass all of reality in his system, according to Kierkegaard, Descartes' intentions were much more modest. The shift in epistemological method and certainty is at the heart of what is referred to as modernism and post-modernism.

The Enlightenment project sought to replace divine revelation with human reason. Empiricism and scientific method were seen as the proper means of gaining access to truth, which is considered knowable within this paradigm. The human individual took center stage. In the post-Descartes world, however, knowledge was perceived to be an increasingly subjective endeavor, which is ironic as he sought to ground knowledge objectively. Lesslie Newbigin sees the Enlightenment mentality as a relentless pursuit of the critical method who says - . "But the critical method must ultimately destroy itself. You cannot criticize a statement of what claims to be the truth except on the basis of some other truth-claim which — at that moment — you accept without criticism. But that truth-claim on which your critique is based must in turn be criticized".

Whereas rationalism has reigned supreme from Descartes' time to our own, it has not been without its detractors. The Romantic movement in English and German literature is one of them. Reacting against the sterility and mechanization of all of life including that of religion, as evidenced by Deism, the Romantics sought to affirm the dynamic nature of the universe against the cold, rational system.

Romanticism reemphasized the central place of the individual and sought to free the unconscious mind. Existentialism is another form of rebellion against rationalism and it shares a number of similarities with Romanticism. Frederick Copleston assesses the situation nicely when he says, "Hegel sought to capture all reality in the conceptual net of his dialectic, while existence slipped through the meshes."

Existentialism reacted against any kind of a universal system or ethical absolute (especially Hegel's metaphysical system) that stands above the individual. Rollo May summarizes it aptly as follows

> Existentialism means centering upon the *existing* person; it is the emphasis on the human being as he is *emerging, becoming*. The word "existence" comes from the root *ex-sistere*, meaning literally "to stand out, emerge." Traditionally in Western culture, existence has been set over against essence, the latter being the emphasis upon immutable principles, truth, logical laws, etc., that are supposed to stand above any given existence.

In fact, after existentialism existence gains primacy over essence with the emphasis placed primarily on the individual actualizing his or her existence through choice. Truth is experienced as an inward passion or the recovery of Being as opposed to an immutable principle. As Kierkegaard put it, "An objective uncertainty held fast in an appropriation-process of the most passionate inwardness is the truth, the highest truth attainable for an existing individual." I would argue that to the extent that existentialism has succeeded in overthrowing the universal or "essence," the demise of the idea of "absolute truth" has been the result. However, the loss of essence eventually results in the loss of existence with its resultant "unbearable lightness of being." Being no longer has meaning. This state naturally leads to philosophical relativism a condition which is exaggerated by the theories of language that follow. Gene Edward Veith rightly concludes, "Existentialism is the philosophical basis for postmodernism."

Further, Stanley Fish, as a post-modern literary theorist, also reflects a dependence on existentialist thought including that of Gadamer in his writings. While his emphasis on what a text does versus what it means may be primarily indebted to pragmatism, the idea of "meaning as an event," is thoroughly existential. Fish reflects the existential priority of the human consciousness as it brings to prominence the existing individual with its focus on experience. Often he characterizes meaning as an experience in opposition to an essence or truth located outside of the individual reader. "In the procedures I would urge, the reader's activities are at the center of attention, where they are regarded not as leading to meaning but as *having* meaning."

But much of Fish's theoretical position can be seen as reactionary when viewed against the backdrop of philosophical modernism, by which we mean the Enlightenment project with its quest for absolute certainty and scientific objectivity. In Fish's thinking, as well as that of most post-modern thinkers, objectivity is an illusion brought about by the Enlightenment for which Descartes often takes the blame. Existence stands over essence and then essentialism or foundationalism, as Fish would call it, loses its independence and becomes dependant on the individual's experience. Fish claims that his formalist predecessors assumed that there were "observable facts that could be described and interpreted."

But he argues that what counts as a fact is in itself determined by the presupposition of the interpreter thereby invalidating the entire procedure. In an article published a few years later, Fish gives up on evidence altogether including evidence that might support his position, "But it is the very possibility of providing such evidence that is denied [in this paper]. . . . I cut myself off from any recourse to evidentiary procedures."

At this point one wonders what is the purpose of publishing papers if it is not to propound opinions and arguments, which amounts to the same thing as giving evidence. It is Fish's opinion that objectivity is an illusion, but as with making a claim to relativism, anytime one argues for a position he then stakes a claim to knowledge and anytime one stakes a claim to knowledge a claim to objectivity or truth is implicit. One of the most serious consequences of Fish's interpretive community theory is that it severs communication across cultural and historical boundaries. This is a result of his anti-essentialist position. Fish claims that "intention and understanding are two ends of a conventional act, each of which necessarily stipulates (includes, defines, specifies) the other."

What this means is that without being part of the interpretive community in which the act is done, spoken, uttered we have no access to its "intention" nor do we have "understanding." Thus we are sealed off from the utterances of history, bound to interpret them based on our cultural assumptions and unable to penetrate into the mindset of the past.

Remarkably, this is a radical reduction of worldview that Fish would have us confined within. The results of such a theory leave closed the possibility of enlarging one's understanding based on the presuppositions of a foreign culture, with the possible exception of actually being a part of that culture. While his determinism maintains that we can understand only what our culture makes available, any broadened perspective is then by default already encompassed within the assumptions of our interpretive community. Fish claims that "communication only occurs *within* a community." The question then becomes how to join that community in order to communicate.

Fish is in agreement with Wittgenstein as far as using proofs appropriate to the language game being played and in realizing that one must understand the activity of life or context in which the language game is played. In other words, one must understand the form of life, the general activity, in order to understand the language game.

The problem with this theory is that it proves too

much. It proves that anyone who is a member of the same interpretive community will not disagree on interpretation. And indeed, if the critic were so constrained by his community that he were unable to have any latitude in interpretation, then all with similar cultures and backgrounds would agree. But as we know they do not.

Fish might respond to this by saying that yes there is some freedom to have differing interpretations, but it is freedom sanctioned or doled out by the institution, thus removing himself from criticism once again, proving himself to be the slippery fellow that he is. Wittgenstein would not agree that two differing communities are separated from communication. As we saw earlier the scientist and the religious adherent are not unable to communicate, they can communicate but the "proofs" for each discipline are inappropriate to the other.

This is the point of claiming that language games have family resemblance's as it makes communication possible. Furthermore, his example of why we call something a "number" reminds us that it has a relationship to other things that have been called number and he draws the analogy of a spinning thread in which fibre is twisted upon fibre. We can use this idea to criticize Fish's radical separateness of interpretive communities: just as communities use words and concepts which overlap, so one community can "understand" another by the relatedness of their concepts bearing "family resemblance's" and the similarities of their form of life.

In the real world cultures overlap and few are completely isolated from every other. Even historically speaking our culture is not isolated from the past as our word usage, forms of life, and language games are dependant on those of our ancestors so that there is an overlap between cultures historically. Thus our culture is not completely different from that of Shakespeare, Dante, or even the apostle John.

And Fish has not explained how it is that one interpretive community could stop and another begin with complete disjuncture. One of the difficulties with the notion of interpretive community is its ill-defined nature. Fish has not attempted, to my knowledge, to clearly define what such a community is. If meaning is, as Fish maintains in words reminiscent of Wittgenstein, "something acquired in the context of an activity," then why can one not familiarize herself with the context or form of life in order to approximate meaning? Wittgenstein's idea that language games are founded on forms of life has several implications for Fish's theory.

Wittgenstein says, "The common behavior of mankind is the system of reference by means of which we interpret an unknown language." So that another language is only understood insofar as another form of life bears commonality with our own. Wittgenstein maintains, as we have seen, that language games are not totally independent, contra Fish. Even a language that had been isolated for centuries could be interpreted or "understood" because there is commonality in forms of life. Wittgenstein implies here that there is something essential about forms of life at the very least, which implies a kind of pragmatic essentialism in humanity. If there were nothing that one culture held in common with another culture or time period, translation, let alone communication, would not be possible. It is for this reason that Wittgenstein says, "If a lion could talk, we could not understand him." We could not understand him because he does not share our form of life, because its activities are so radically different from ours.

Fish maintains contra Wittgenstein that other cultures bear nothing in common with our own, especially those long dead. They are to us as lions. But fortunately distant cultures and time periods are not as radically different as Fish's theory assumes. Wittgenstein is correct in that there is a "common behavior of mankind."

Fish's thinking about interpretive communities leans toward a strong determinism. Fish as we saw earlier maintained that readers do not have their own strategies, rather they flow from the interpretive community and "at once enable and limit the operations of his consciousness."

The question naturally arises then, "How do you know?" Fish's determinism is self-stultifying. If readers are determined by their cultural contexts to read with certain pre-defined conceptual grids and are unable to scrutinize their own beliefs, how would Fish ever know this? Gerald Graff makes this very point in response to Fish, he "does not see that his present position would leave him without a vantage point for coherently stating that view." In order to perceive that communities are historically conditioned one must have an objective, encompassing perspective—which is exactly what Fish claims we do not and can not have. This view of the interpretive community is a much too monolithic, reductionist view which does not square with what we know by experience. Members of the same "interpretive community" approach a text with "an indefinite number of incompatible, mutually exclusive, conflicting, or different ways of talking that are consistent with our peculiar background assumptions or with the theoretical and practical constraints on our practice," as Battersby has put it.

REFERENCES

1. Brice R. Wachterhauser, *Hermeneutics and Modern Philosophy* (New York: Staty University of New York Press, 1991), 31.

2. Fish, "Interpreting the *Variorium,*" in *Reader-Response Criticism*, 183.
3. Gadamer, *Truth and Method*, 350.
4. Graff, "Response to Stanley Fish".
5. Hans-Georg Gadamer, *Truth and Method*, 2d ed. (New York: Crossroad Publishing, 1989), 185.
6. Hans-Georg Gadamer, *Truth and Method*, trans. Garrett Broden and John Cumming, 2d ed., (New York: Crossroad, 1982),
7. Jane P. Tompkins, *Reader Response Criticism* (Baltimore: Hohns Hopkins University Press, 1980), 223.
8. K.M. Newton, "Hermeneutics and Modern Literary Criticism," *British Journal of Aesthetics* 29, (Spring 1989): 117.
9. Kierkegaard, *Fear and Trembling*, p. 42.
10. Martin Heidegger, *Being and Time* (Oxford: Blackwell, 1962), quoted in Anthony Thiselton, *Two Horizons* (Grand Rapids: Eerdmans, 1980), 26.
11. Rollo May, Abraham Maslow, et al., *Existential Psychology*, Random House, New York, 1961, p. 16.
12. Shiv Kumar, "Toward a Theory of Romanticism," *British Romantic Poets*, New York: New York University Press, 1966.
13. Stanley Fish, "Literature in the Reader," in *Reader-Response Criticism*, 82.
14. Terry Eagleton, *Literary Theory: An Introduction* (Minneapolis: University of Minnesota Press, 1983), 55.
15. Vanhoozer, "Aesthetic Theology," 37.
16. Veith, *Postmodern Times*, p. 38.
17. W. K. Wimsatt and Monroe Beardsley, The Intentional Fallacy," chap. in *The Verbal Icon: Studies in the Meaning of Poetry* (Lexington: University of Kentucky Press, 1954), 194.
18. Wittgenstein, *Philosophical Investigations*, sec. 206.
19. Wofgang Iser, "The Reading Proscess: A Phenomenological Approach," in *Reader Response Criticism*, ed. Jane P. Tompkins (Baltimore: Johns Hopkins University Press, 1980), 50.

2

Major Schools of Criticism

"Men become bad and guilty because they speak and act without foreseeing the results of their words and deeds."

—*Franz Kafka*

With the passage of time many schools of literary criticism and theory emerged. Here in this chapter we will introduce you to some major schools. Some of these are given elaborate treatment separately in next chapters.

1. GENRE CRITICISM

From Aristotle on, many scholars have emphasized the readers' expectations about what such-and-such type of literature should be and do. (Thus Aristotle thought that a good tragedy has a noble hero with a tragic flaw, creates some emotional catharsis in the audience, etc.) And so the genre critic considers the conventions that make up a particular literary type (e.g., the gothic romance, the pastoral poem), often analyzing how a particular example of that genre follows—or flaunts—those conventions, and to what effect. (Thus this approach can best be deemed a type of formalist criticism with rhetorical/reader-response considerations factored in.) The most famous "genre" school of the 20th century is the neo-Aristotelian Chicago School, of R.S. Crane, Wayne Booth, etc. However, Mikhail Bakhtin's

DIALOGIC theory—with its emphasis on the novel genre and its sociological implications—has been more influential recently, in part because such notions as *polyphony* and *heteroglossia* allow for a quite politically "against-the-grain" reading of the text.

2. DECONSTRUCTION

Deconstruction involves the close reading of texts in order to demonstrate that any given text has irreconcilably contradictory meanings, rather than being a unified, logical whole. As J. Hillis Miller, the preeminent American deconstructor, has explained in an essay entitled "Stevens' Rock and Criticism as Cure" (1976), "Deconstruction is not a dismantling of the structure of a text, but a demonstration that it has already dismantled itself. Its apparently solid ground is no rock but thin air."

Deconstruction was both created and has been profoundly influenced by the French philosopher on language Jacques Derrida. Derrida, who coined the term deconstruction, argues that in Western culture, people tend to think and express their thoughts in terms of binary oppositions. Something is white but not black, masculine and therefore not feminine, a cause rather than an effect. Other common and mutually exclusive pairs include beginning/end, conscious/unconscious, presence/absence, and speech/writing.

Derrida suggests these oppositions are hierarchies in miniature, containing one term that Western culture views as positive or superior and another considered negative or inferior, even if only slightly so. Through deconstruction, Derrida aims to erase the boundary between binary oppositions—and to do so in such a way that the hierarchy implied by the oppositions is thrown into question. Although its ultimate aim may be to criticize Western logic, deconstruction arose as a response to structuralism and formalism. Structuralists believed that all elements of human culture, including literature, may be understood as parts of a system of signs.

Derrida did not believe that structuralists could explain the laws governing human signification and thus provide the key to understanding the form and meaning of everything from an African village to Greek myth to a literary text. He also rejected the structuralist belief that texts have identifiable "centers" of meaning—a belief structuralists shared with formalists. Formalist critics, such as the New Critics, assume that a work of literature is a freestanding, self-contained object whose meaning can be found in the complex network of relations between its parts (allusions, images, rhythms, sounds, etc.).

Deconstructors, by contrast, see works in terms of their undecidability. They reject the formalist view that a work of literary art is demonstrably unified from beginning to end, in one certain way, or that it is organized around a single center that ultimately can be identified. As a result, deconstructors see texts as more radically heterogeneous than do formalists. Formalists ultimately make sense of the ambiguities they find in a given text, arguing that every ambiguity serves a definite, meaningful, and demonstrable literary function.

Undecidability, by contrast, is never reduced, let alone mastered. Though a deconstructive reading can reveal the incompatible possibilities generated by the text, it is impossible for the reader to decide among them.

[Adapted from The Bedford Glossary of Critical and Literary Terms by Ross Murfin and Supriya M. Ray. Copyright 1998 by Bedford Books.]

3. THE NEW HISTORICISM

The new historicism developed during the 1980s, largely in reaction to the text-only approach pursued by formalist New Critics and the critics who challenged the New Criticism in the 1970s. New historicists, like formalists and their critics, acknowledge the importance of the literary text, but they also analyze the text with an eye to history. In this respect, the new historicism is not "new"; the majority of critics between 1920 and 1950 focused on a work's historical content and based their interpretations on the interplay between the text and historical contexts (such as the author's life or intentions in writing the work).

In other respects, however, the new historicism differs from the historical criticism of the 1930s and 1940s. It is informed by the poststructuralist and reader-response theory of the 1970s, as well as by the thinking of feminist, cultural, and Marxist critics whose work was also "new" in the 1980s. They are less fact- and event-oriented than historical critics used to be, perhaps because they have come to wonder whether the truth about what really happened can ever be purely or objectively known. They are less likely to see history as linear and progressive, as something developing toward the present, and they are also less likely to think of it in terms of specific eras, each with a definite, persistent, and consistent zeitgeist (spirit of the times). Hence they are unlikely to suggest that a literary text has a single or easily identifiable historical context.

New historicist critics also tend to define the discipline of history more broadly than did their predecessors. They view history as a social science like anthropology and sociology, whereas older historicists tended to view history as literature's "background" and the social sciences as being properly historical. They have erased the line dividing historical and literary materials, showing not only that the production of one of William Shakespeare's historical plays was both a political act and a historical event, but also that the coronation of Elizabeth I was carried out with the same care for staging and symbol lavished on works of dramatic art.

New historicists remind us that it is treacherous to reconstruct the past as it really was—rather than as we have been conditioned by our own place and time to believe that it was. And they know that the job is impossible for those who are unaware of that difficulty, insensitive to the bent or bias of their own historical vantage point. Thus, when new historicist critics describe a historical change, they are highly conscious of (and even likely to discuss) the theory of historical change that informs their account.

Many new historicists have acknowledged a profound indebtedness to the writings of Michel Foucault. A French philosophical historian, Foucault brought together incidents and phenomena from areas normally seen as unconnected, encouraging new historicists and new cultural historicists to redefine the boundaries of historical inquiry. Like the philosopher Friedrich Nietzsche, Foucault refused to see history as an evolutionary process, a continuous development from cause to effect, from past to present toward THE END, a moment of definite closure, a Day of Judgment. No historical event, according to Foucault, has a single cause; rather, each event is tied into a vast web of economic, social, and political factors. Like Karl Marx, Foucault saw history in terms of power, but unlike Marx, he viewed power not simply as a repressive force or a tool of conspiracy but rather as a complex of forces that produces what happens. Not even a tyrannical aristocrat simply wields power, for the aristocrat is himself empowered by discourses and practices that constitute power.

Not all new historicist critics owe their greatest debt to Foucault. Some, like Stephen Greenblatt, have been most nearly influenced by the British cultural critic Raymond Williams, and others, like Brook Thomas, have been more influenced by German Marxist critic Walter Benjamin. Still others—Jerome McGann, for example—have followed the lead of Soviet critic Mikhail Bakhtin, who viewed literary works in terms of polyphonic discourses and dialogues between the official, legitimate voices of society and other, more challenging or critical voices echoing popular culture.

[Adapted from *The Bedford Glossary of Critical and Literary Terms* by Ross Murfin and Supriya M. Ray. Copyright 1998 by Bedford Books.]

4. READER-RESPONSE CRITICISM

Reader-response criticism encompasses various approaches to literature that explore and seek to explain the diversity (and often divergence) of readers' responses to literary works.Louise Rosenblatt is often credited with pioneering the approaches in *Literature as Exploration* (1938). In her 1969 essay "Towards a Transactional Theory of Reading," she summed up her position as follows: "A poem is what the reader lives through under the guidance of the text and experiences as relevant to the text." Recognizing that many critics would reject this definition, Rosenblatt wrote, "The idea that a *poem* presupposes a *reader* actively involved with a *text* is particularly shocking to those seeking to emphasize the objectivity of their interpretations." Rosenblatt implicitly and generally refers to formalists (the most influential of whom are the New Critics) when she speaks of supposedly objective interpreters shocked by the notion that a "poem" is cooperatively produced by a "reader" and a "text." Formalists spoke of "the poem itself," the "concrete work of art," the "real poem." They had no interest in what a work of literature makes a reader "live through." In fact, in *The Verbal Icon* (1954), William K. Wimsatt and Monroe C. Beardsley used the term *affective fallacy* to define as erroneous the very idea that a reader's response is relevant to the meaning of a literary work.

Stanley Fish, whose early work is seen by some as marking the true beginning of contemporary reader-response criticism, also took issue with the tenets of formalism. In "Literature in the Reader: Affective Stylistics" (1970), he argued that any school of criticism that sees a literary work as an object, claiming to describe what it is and never what it does, misconstrues the very essence of literature and reading. Literature exists and signifies when it is read, Fish suggests, and its force is an affective one. Furthermore, reading is a temporal process, not a spatial one as formalists assume when they step back and survey the literary work as if it were an object spread out before them.

The German critic Wolfgang Iser has described that process in *The Implied Reader: Patterns of Communication in Prose Fiction from Bunyan to Beckett* (1974) and *The Act of Reading: A Theory of Aesthetic Response* (1976). Iser argues that texts contain gaps (or blanks) that powerfully affect the reader, who must explain them, connect what they separate, and create in his or her mind aspects of a work that aren't *in* the text but are incited by the text.

With the redefinition of literature as something that only exists meaningfully in the mind of the reader, and with the redefinition of the literary work as a catalyst of mental events, comes a redefinition of the reader. No longer is the reader the passive recipient of those ideas that an author has planted in a text. "The reader is *active,*" Rosenblatt had insisted. Fish makes the same point in "Literature in the Reader": "Reading is . . . something you *do.*" Iser, in focusing critical interest on the gaps in texts, on the blanks that readers have to fill in, similarly redefines the reader as an active maker of meaning. Other reader-response critics define the reader differently. Wayne Booth uses the phrase *the implied reader* to mean the reader "created by the work." Iser also uses the term *the implied reader* but substitutes *the educated reader* for what Fish calls *the intended reader.*

Since the mid-1970s, reader-response criticism has evolved into a variety of new forms. Subjectivists like David Bleich, Norman Holland, and Robert Crosman have viewed the reader's response not as one "guided" by the text but rather as one motivated by deep-seated, personal, psychological needs. Holland has suggested that, when we read, we find our own "identity theme" in the text by using "the literary work to symbolize and finally replicate ourselves. We work out through the text our own characteristic patterns of desire." Even Fish has moved away from reader-response criticism as he had initially helped define it, focusing on "interpretive strategies" held in common by "interpretive communities"—such as the one comprised by American college students reading a novel as a class assignment.

Fish's shift in focus is in many ways typical of changes that have taken place within the field of reader-response criticism—a field that, because of those changes, is increasingly being referred to as *reader-oriented criticism.* Recent reader-oriented critics, responding to Fish's emphasis on interpretive communities and also to the historically oriented perception theory of Hans Robert Jauss, have studied the way a given reading public's "horizons of expectations" change over time. Many of these contemporary critics view themselves as reader-oriented critics and as practitioners of some other critical approach as well. Certain feminist and gender critics with an interest in reader response have asked whether there is such a thing as "reading like a woman." Reading-oriented new historicists have looked at the way in which racism affects and is affected by reading and, more generally, at the way in which politics can affect reading practices and outcomes. Gay and lesbian critics, such as Wayne Koestenbaum, have argued that sexualities have been similarly constructed within and by social discourses and that there may even be a homosexual way of reading.

[Adapted from *The Bedford Glossary of Critical and Literary Terms* by Ross Murfin and Supriya M. Ray. Copyright 1998 by Bedford Books.]

5. PSYCHOANALYTIC CRITICSM

Psychoanalytic criticism originated in the work of Austrian psychoanalyst Sigmund Freud, who pioneered the technique of psychoanalysis. Freud developed a language that described, a model that explained, and a theory that encompassed human psychology. His theories are directly and indirectly concerned with the nature of the unconscious mind.

The psychoanalytic approach to literature not only rests on the theories of Freud; it may even be said to have begun with Freud, who wrote literary criticism as well as psychoanalytic theory. Probably because of Freud's characterization of the artist's mind as "one urged on by instincts that are too clamorous," psychoanalytic criticism written before 1950 tended to psychoanalyze the individual author.

Literary works were read—sometimes unconvincingly—as fantasies that allowed authors to indulge repressed wishes, to protect themselves from deep-seated anxieties, or both. After 1950, psychoanalytic critics began to emphasize the ways in which authors create works that appeal to readers' repressed wishes and fantasies. Consequently, they shifted their focus away from the author's psyche toward the psychology of the reader and the text. Norman Holland's theories, concerned more with the reader than with the text, helped to establish reader-response criticism.

Critics influenced by D.W. Winnicott, an object-relations theorist, have questioned the tendency to see the reader/text as an either/or construct; instead, they have seen reader and text (or audience and play) in terms of a relationship taking place in what Winnicott calls a "transitional" or "potential space"—space in which binary oppositions like real/illusory and objective/subjective have little or no meaning. Jacques Lacan, another post-Freudian psychoanalytic theorist, focused on language and language-related issues. Lacan treats the unconscious as a language; consequently, he views the dream not as Freud did (that is, as a form and symptom of repression) but rather as a form of discourse. Thus we may study dreams psychoanalytically in order to learn about literature, even as we may study literature in order to learn more about the unconscious.

Lacan also revised Freud's concept of the Oedipus complex—the childhood wish to displace the parent of one's own sex and take his or her place in the affections of the parent of the opposite sex—by relating it to the issue of language. He argues that the pre-oedipal stage is also a preverbal or "mirror stage," a stage he associates with the imaginary order. He associates the subsequent oedipal stage—which roughly coincides with the child's entry into language—with what he calls the symbolic order, in which words are not the things they stand for but substitutes for those things. The imaginary order and the symbolic order are two of Lacan's three orders of subjectivity, the third being the real, which involves intractable and substantial things or states that cannot be imagined, symbolized, or known directly (such as death).

[Adapted from *The Bedford Glossary of Critical and Literary Terms* by Ross Murfin and Supriya M. Ray. Copyright 1998 by Bedford Books.]

6. MARXIST CRITICISM

Marxist criticism is a type of criticism in which literary works are viewed as the product of work and whose practitioners emphasize the role of class and ideology as they reflect, propagate, and even challenge the prevailing social order. Rather than viewing texts as repositories for hidden meanings, Marxist critics view texts as material products to be understood in broadly historical terms. In short, literary works are viewed as a product of work (and hence of the realm of production and consumption we call economics).

Marxism began with Karl Marx, the nineteenth-century German philosopher best known for Das Kapital (1867; Capital), the seminal work of the communist movement. Marx was also the first Marxist literary critic, writing critical essays in the 1830s on such writers as Johann Wolfgang von Goethe and William Shakespeare. Even after Marx met Friedrich Engels in 1843 and began collaborating on overtly political works such as The German Ideology (1846) and The Communist Manifesto (1848), he maintained a keen interest in literature. In The German Ideology, Marx and Engels discuss the relationship between the arts, politics, and basic economic reality in terms of a general social theory. Economics, they argue, provides the base, or infrastructure, of society, from which a superstructure consisting of law, politics, philosophy, religion, and art emerges.

The revolution anticipated by Marx and Engels did not occur in their century, let alone in their lifetime. When it did occur, in 1917, it did so in a place unimagined by either theorist: Russia, a country long ruled by despotic czars but also enlightened by the works of powerful novelists and playwrights including Anton Chekhov, Alexander Pushkin, Leo Tolstoy, and Fyodor Dostoyevsky. Russia produced revolutionaries like Vladimir Lenin, who shared not only Marx's interest in literature but also his belief in its ultimate importance. Leon Trotsky, Lenin's comrade in revolution, took a strong interest in literary matters as well, publishing Literature and Revolution (1924), which is still viewed as a classic of Marxist literary criticism.

Of those critics active in the Soviet Union after the expulsion of Trotsky and the triumph of Stalin, two stand out: Mikhail Bakhtin and Georg Lukács. Bakhtin viewed language—especially literary texts—in terms of discourses and dialogues. A novel written in a society in flux, for instance, might include an official, legitimate discourse, as well as one infiltrated by challenging comments. Lukács, a Hungarian who converted to Marxism in 1919, appreciated pre revolutionary realistic novels that broadly reflected cultural "totalities" and were populated with characters representing human "types" of the author's place and time.

Perhaps because Lukács was the best of the Soviet communists writing Marxist criticism in the 1930s and 1940s, non-Soviet Marxists tended to develop their ideas by publicly opposing his. In Germany, dramatist and critic Bertolt Brecht criticized Lukács for his attempt to enshrine realism at the expense not only of the other "isms" but also of poetry and drama, which Lukács had largely ignored. Walter Benjamin praised new art forms ushered in by the age of mechanical reproduction, and Theodor Adorno attacked Lukács for his dogmatic rejection of nonrealist modern literature and for his elevation of content over form.

In addition to opposing Lukács and his overly constrictive canon, non-Soviet Marxists took advantage of insights generated by non-Marxist critical theories being developed in post—World War II Europe. Lucien Goldmann, a Romanian critic living in Paris, combined structuralist principles with Marx's base superstructure model in order to show how economics determines the mental structures of social groups, which are reflected in literary texts. Goldmann rejected the idea of individual human genius, choosing instead to see works as the "collective" products of "trans-individual" mental structures. French Marxist Louis Althusser drew on the ideas of psychoanalytic theorist Jacques Lacan and the Italian communist Antonio Gramsci, who discussed the relationship between ideology and hegemony, the pervasive system of assumptions and values that shapes the perception of reality for people in a given culture. Althusser's followers included Pierre Macherey, who in A Theory of Literary Production (1966) developed Althusser's concept of the relationship between literature and ideology; Terry Eagleton, who proposes an elaborate theory about how history enters texts, which in turn may alter history; and Frederic Jameson, who has argued that form is "but the working out" of content "in the realm of the superstructure."

[Adapted from *The Bedford Glossary of Critical and Literary Terms* by Ross Murfin and Supriya M. Ray. Copyright 1998 by Bedford

7. STRUCTURALISM

Structuralism is a theory of humankind in which all elements of human culture, including literature, are thought to be parts of a system of signs. Critic Robert Scholes has described structuralism as a reaction to "'modernist' alienation and despair."

European structuralists such as Roman Jakobson, Claude Lévi-Strauss, and Roland Barthes (before his shift toward poststructuralism) attempted to develop a semiology, or semiotics (science of signs). Barthes, among others, sought to recover literature and even language from the isolation in which they had been studied and to show that the laws that govern them govern all signs, from road signs to articles of clothing.

Structuralism was heavily influenced by linguistics, especially by the pioneering work of Ferdinand de Saussure. Particularly useful to structuralists was Saussure's concept of the phoneme (the smallest basic speech sound or unit of pronunciation) and his idea that phonemes exist in two kinds of relationships: diachronic and synchronic. A phoneme has a diachronic, or "horizontal," relationship with those other phonemes that precede and follow it (as the words appear, left to right, on this page) in a particular usage, utterance, or narrative—what Saussure, a linguist, called parole (French for "word"). A phoneme has a synchronic, or "vertical," relationship with the entire system of language within which individual usages, utterances, or narratives have meaning—what Saussure called langue (French for "tongue," as in "native tongue," meaning language). An means what it means in English because those of us who speak the language are plugged into the same system (think of it as a computer network where different individuals can access the same information in the same way at a given time).

Following Saussure, Lévi-Strauss, an anthropologist, studied hundreds of myths, breaking them into their smallest meaningful units, which he called "mythemes." Removing each from its diachronic relations with other mythemes in a single myth (such as the myth of Oedipus and his mother), he vertically aligned those mythemes that he found to be homologous (structurally correspondent). He then studied the relationships within as well as between vertically aligned columns, in an attempt to understand scientifically, through ratios and proportions, those thoughts and processes that humankind has shared, both at one particular time and across time. Whether Lévi-Strauss was studying the structure of myths or the structure of villages, he looked for recurring, common elements that transcended the differences within and among cultures.

Structuralists followed Saussure in preferring to think about the overriding langue, or language of myth, in which each mytheme and mytheme-constituted myth fits meaningfully, rather than about isolated individual paroles, or narratives. Structuralists also followed Saussure's lead in believing that sign systems must be understood in terms of binary oppositions (a proposition later disputed by poststructuralist Jacques Derrida). In analyzing myths and texts to find basic structures, structuralists found that opposite terms modulate until they are finally resolved or reconciled by some intermediary third term. Thus a structuralist reading of Milton's Paradise Lost (1667) might show that the war between God and the rebellious angels becomes a rift between God and sinful, fallen man, a rift that is healed by the Son of God, the mediating third term.

Although structuralism was largely a European phenomenon in its origin and development, it was influenced by American thinkers as well. Noam Chomsky, for instance, who powerfully influenced structuralism through works such as Reflections on Language (1975), identified and distinguished between "surface structures" and "deep structures" in language and linguistic literatures, including texts.

[Adapted from *The Bedford Glossary of Critical and Literary Terms* by Ross Murfin and Supriya M. Ray. Copyright 1998 by Bedford Books.]

8. POSTCOLONIAL CRITICISM

A type of cultural criticism, postcolonial criticism usually involves the analysis of literary texts produced in countries and cultures that have come under the control of European colonial powers at some point in their history. Alternatively, it can refer to the analysis of texts written about colonized places by writers hailing from the colonizing culture. In Orientalism (1978), Edward Said, a pioneer of postcolonial criticism and studies, focused on the way in which the colonizing First World has invented false images and myths of the Third (postcolonial) World—stereotypical images and myths that have conveniently justified Western exploitation and domination of Eastern and Middle Eastern cultures and peoples. In the essay "Postcolonial Criticism" (1992), Homi K. Bhabha has shown how certain cultures (mis)represent other cultures, thereby extending their political and social domination in the modern world order.

Postcolonial studies, a type of cultural studies, refers more broadly to the study of cultural groups, practices, and discourses—including but not limited to literary discourses—in the colonized world. The term postcolonial is usually used broadly to refer to the study of works written at any point after colonization first occurred in a given country, although it is sometimes used more specifically to refer to the analysis of texts and other cultural discourses that emerged after the end of the colonial period (after the success of the liberation and independence movements). Among feminist critics, the postcolonial perspective has inspired an attempt to recover whole cultures of women heretofore ignored or marginalized—women who speak not only from colonized places but also from the colonizing places to which many of them fled.

Postcolonial criticism has been influenced by Marxist thought, by the work of Michel Foucault (whose theories about the power of discourses have influenced the new historicism), and by deconstruction, which has challenged not only hierarchical, binary oppositions such as West/East and North/South but also the notions of superiority associated with the first term of each opposition.

[Adapted from *The Bedford Glossary of Critical and Literary Terms* by Ross Murfin and Supriya M. Ray. Copyright 1998 by Bedford Books.]

9. RHETORICAL CRITICISM

Usually with deep roots in Aristotle and other Classical rhetorical scholarship, this catch-all category includes various takes on how the audience is "manipulated" via rhetorical devices, poetical tropes, etc. (When said devices are genre-specific, we're approaching GENRE criticism, as in the neo-Aristotelian Chicago School.) Important 20th-century contributions in this line include those of Kenneth Burke, Wayne Booth, and the SPEECH-ACT THEORY of J.L. Austin & John Searle, an influential analysis of the rhetorical intent(s) of oral communication, applicable (or not?!) to literary texts.

10. IMPRESSIONIST(IC) CRITICISM

"Gut-level" response to a literary work; immediate & intuitive judgment of its worth, determined to a great extent by the reader's personality type and past experiences (including his/her past experiences with other works of literature). Also: the literary "critiques" of many pre-20th-century (especially 19th-century Romantic) critics, whose criticism was as much self-expression as anything else. "Few" links here, since it's a rather disparaging label, connotative of the affective fallacy, that no one would subscribe to in this day and age. Read De Quincey's "On the Knocking on the Gate in Macbeth" for a good example of responding to literature quite subjectively, often in quite serendipitous or idiosyncratic fashion; or recall your own (or your students') freewriting/gut-feeling responses to assigned texts. See also Anatole France's "The Adventures of the Soul" for an eloquent defense of such personalistic criticism. Valuable—and perhaps inevitable—starting-point to any response of literature, but dangerously subjective ("oh, no!"), and best combined with one or more of the following, more "intellectually reputable," types of literary criticism.

11. PHENOMENOLOGICAL/HERMENEUTIC/ READER-RESPONSE CRITICISM

General comments: Phenomenology (Husserl), Hermeneutics (Gadamer and Ricoeur), and Reader-Response criticism are closely related labels, all of which attempt a psycho-philosophical analysis of how a reader encounters & interprets a text. Some of the more radical permutations lead to an almost complete reader subjectivism (the text is what the individual reader *thinks* it means, however absurd), while other versions analyze the means by which various readers arrive at a consensus regarding the "meaning"—which can then be assumed to be a pretty much "correct" interpretation by the "ideal reader" (cf. Iser's "implied reader"). Specific schools and figures include the GENEVA SCHOOL (Ingarden and Poulet), the CONSTANCE SCHOOL (Jauss and Iser's RECEPTION THEORY), and more recent scholars such as J. Hillis Miller and Stanley Fish. And while the general philosophical origins of this approach are mainly Continental, British critics such as William Empson and I.A. Richards were doing a form of "reader-response" criticism before the label itself became common. Note that the now over-used term "reader-response" is hardly synonymous with impressionistic criticism (above), though the former label is sometimes loosely employed to mean the latter.

12. EXPRESSIVE CRITICISM

M.H. Abrams' term for the Romantics' privileging of the "poet's mind," or creative genius. Like "impressionist" criticism, not a label that many in the 20th century have adopted, although various "critics" from a creative-writing background and/or an introverted intuitive philosophy have no doubt given a more appreciative glance at the inner workings of "Genius" and "Imagination" than others. (It's probably also very true that people of true "genius & imagination," if there be such a thing, have, in general, "wasted" less time writing literary criticism?!)

13. BIOGRAPHICAL CRITICISM

A now *passé* approach both fascinating and dangerous in its attempt to apply details from an author's life to his/her works—and then drawing conclusions, perhaps, about the author's "inner mental workings." (Poor Shakespeare: the "literary bios" I've read about him!) In any case, the author's personal biography becomes the focus. For instance, this method might lead to a discussion of the fantastic images in "Kubla Khan" as by-products of Coleridge's addiction to laudanum: momentarily enlightening, perhaps, but ultimately misleading (and blatantly reductive) in its emphasis. Significantly, the "Artist/Author" aspect of Abrams' quaternity isn't even included in recent lit-crit focuses on "text," "reader," and "world," for this very reason: discussing a text based on your notions of the author's psyche and intent is usually deemed a heinous crime nowadays. (And yet some version of "biographical criticism" has snuck in through the back door in much recent "political" criticism, in which speaking of an author's [or other critic's] intent, in the guise of "ideology," seems perfectly okay. For instance, queer theorists' assumption that Shakespeare was gay remains problematic, IMHO.) Bio-literary studies by Caroline Spurgeon and Van Wyck Brooks in the first half of the 20th century are a few of the more well-known examples of this approach. (Finally, my general critique above is less directed at works whose main intent is that of literary biography, as in Ellmann's study of James Joyce).

14. HUMANIST/MORAL CRITICISM

Here, the critic brings the cultural/religious assumptions of his or her own time to bear upon a literary work, judging the text according to how well it fits the critic's own ethical values system. At its best, this approach heaps praise on works of literature for their superlative expression of humankind's highest ideals & aspirations. (Thus are the writings of Homer, Shakespeare, and Goethe often lauded.) However, the critic's subjective bias often leads to abuse: thus adherents of existentialism may regard King Lear *only* as a great "early" expression of existential rebellion and malaise, while some Christian critics might consider Milton's Paradise Lost a great epic solely on its merits of religious orthodoxy(?!). As for specific schools, the early

20th-century New Humanism of Irving Babbitt and P.E. More was a "neo-Classical" reaction of sorts that condemned Romanticism for a "hazy & lazy" spirituality that wasn't in accord with their own (more "subdued" & rationalist) ethical viewpoint. Obviously, abuse of this method can easily evolve into dogmatic condemnation and censorship, and indeed, many works otherwise deemed as "aesthetically" great have been blacklisted, banned, or burned throughout the history of humankind by well-meaning "moral" critics. (Indeed, even Plato wanted to keep poets out of his utopian Republic because their inspiration bordered on insanity and were thus a danger to the general morality.)

15. RUSSIAN FORMALISM

Instead of the New Critics' emphasis on irony, the Russian Formalists were most famous for the concept of *defamiliarization,* by which a text "announces," as it were, via formal *devices,* its status as a special use of language—its *literariness,* in short. Also, Propp's formalist analysis of fairy tales was instrumental in the development of Narratology.

16. FORMALISM

For the formalist, the careful-thoughtful-and-well-informed reader judges the merits of the work as a finely-crafted aesthetic whole—considering, for instance, in a work of fiction, its use of plot, style, characterization, etc.; in a work of poetry, matters of prosody, diction, figurative language, et al. At last, attentiveness to the purely formal aspects of literature is an antidote to the reader's propensity for straying too far from the text. Indeed, formalist criticism is supposedly unique among critical methods in being completely "intrinsic," dealing only with aesthetic techniques evident within the work per se.

All other critical approaches are extrinsic, bringing to bear considerations outside the text. For the formalist, such intrinsic analyses should at least be an integral part of any well-rounded critical discussion of literature, and the psychologically or politically based critic (for example) runs the danger of a distorted interpretation if formalistic matters are not also taken into consideration. The paragraph above presents formalism in its best light. On the negative side, in dealing with specific literary "devices" in isolation (irony, point of view, etc.), this approach may actually tend to destroy a work's "organic unity": as Wordsworth says, "We murder to dissect." Also, the claim to non-political "objectivity" has been severely called into question by politically-oriented critics, for whom all critical statements are ideological, even—and especially—those that claim not to be so. In sum, a "retreat" to formalism might well be said to be an implicit support of the political status quo.

17. ARCHETYPAL (OR JUNGIAN) (OR MYTHIC) CRITICISM

Another "both fascinating and dangerous" approach that assumes that all of humankind's creative works—including literature, myths, and religious rituals & symbols, and indeed, our very dreams—emanate from the same inner psychic source, the *collective unconscious,* as formulated by Carl Jung.

Therefore one may find in many works of literature archetypal (universal-to-our-species) symbols that represent the various emotions and aspirations of humankind's ancestral psychological heritage. And so the author may (unconsciously) invoke the images of night and sunrise, and the reader may unexplainably respond with great emotion: well, there resides within the collective unconscious (common to both writer and reader) a myriad of ancestral memories that associate night with fear and death and the unknown, and sunrise with relief, and joy, and "life" and "rebirth" and—? (for finally, Jung agrees with the German Romantics [and Coleridge] that a true symbol is inexhaustible in its associations).

And at last, all archetypal symbols are ultimately *intrapsychic* (in Jung's original theory, anyway), representing figures or processes *within* the psyche: "night," then, may connote the strange "otherness" of the unconscious "within" our own psyches, which our conscious egohood fears with all its might, because the unconscious is by definition unknown. "Sunrise" may carry connotations of the "dawn" of ego consciousness, or its "rebirth," depending upon the context of the poem or myth—or dream. (This approach's common reliance on the oppositions of night & day, summer & winter, etc., reveals it to be a kind of psychological structuralism.) The archetypal method is also commonly called MYTH or MYTHIC criticism because archetypal figures & processes—such as the shadow, the anima/animus, the wise old man, the god-image (or "Self"), the journey, the "divine marriage," and rebirth—are profusely evident in humankind's myths and rituals. The drawbacks of archetypal criticism are two-fold: 1) the Jungian critic is sometimes guilty of finding an "archetype" in every image, character, and twist of plot, thus weakening the impact of the critic's discoveries of the truly(?!) archetypal; 2) this approach is not able to judge the greatness of an artistic work solely on the presence of archetypal symbols, for, although Macbeth is replete with archetypal symbolism, so, too, is the graffiti on the bathroom walls in the bar downtown (but, of course, this latter limitation is really true of all "extrinsic" criticism); and 3) Jung's archetypes, as he presents them, are very much culturally and racially specific: e.g., to claim that dreaming of a "black man" is archetypally symbolic of the "shadow figure" applies, at best, to a quite white, Eurocentric psyche.

18. SOCIO-POLITICAL CRITICISM

Another catch-all-general category that (traditionally) borders on historical criticism, if the critic limits his/her task to a non-judgmental(?!) study of an author's sociological milieu. More characteristically today, however, it refers to any critical angle with a conscious political ax to grind. Indeed, this general orientation—including all the remaining approaches—brings to the fore a political awareness relatively new to literary study, in explicit opposition to the "text-only" emphasis of the formalists, making laudable contributions to our attitudes towards literature through an often impassioned concern for the social oppressed and downtrodden.

However, like moral criticism, this method may become proscriptive and condemnatory. For instance, the socio-political critic with a Marxist bent might reject as worthless any literary classic—Homer's Iliad, for example—that implicitly accepts the framework of a class-based society—even though Homer was unable to be instructed in the wonders of Marxist dialectic before he wrote his 9th c. B.C. feudal-warrior epic. Similarly, the feminist critic might question the merits of any literary work with an implicitly sexist view—in other words, most literature written before this century. Certainly no one in this day & age supports men-beat-women-rich-cudgel-poor social systems—well, most of us don't [*pace,* Mr. Limbaugh]—but to condemn out of hand an aesthetically fine(?!) literary classic for "bad politics" is perhaps too harsh. Again, and ultimately, such critics' efforts to approach literature via a specific political "angle" is one of the most significant events of recent literary scholarship.

19. HISTORICAL CRITICISM

Next to formalist criticism, traditionally considered the most "objective" critical approach. The historical critic may be concerned with 1) the historical context per se, and thus be concerned about the effects of the writer's historical milieu (race, place, & time [cf. Taine]) upon the literary work at hand—e.g., the effects of the Industrial Revolution on the work of a particular English Romantic poet; or 2) the cultural/philosophical—"HISTORY OF IDEAS"—background of the writer's milieu—e.g., the impact of Einstein's theory of relativity on, say, the novels of James Joyce—or 3) the effects of previous works of literature (literary history) on the writer & his/her work—e.g., the influence of Whitman's free verse and mystical worldview on American Beat poetry of the 1950's & 60's.

20. FEMINIST CRITICISM

Feminist criticism (very simply put) champions the downtrodden of the "war of the sexes," critiquing *patriarchal* (or *phallocentric)* texts and championing neglected (and recent) "pro-woman" literary works. Like Marxism, feminism quite often teams up with poststructuralism in its critique of the dominant male "hegemony." One might conveniently divide feminism into two "camps": 1) those who posit an innate (and culturally repressed) "female" way of writing, reading, even thinking (essentialist); and 2) those who see sex or gender as socially conditioned and linguistically constructed (constructivist). Either way, patriarchal dominance/oppression has been—and continues to be, to a great extent (as I see on MTV!)—the order of the day.

Other convenient sub-categories: the "French feminists" (Kristeva, Cixous, Irigaray); feminist + race/minority angle (e.g., bell hooks, P.G. Allen, Trinh Minh-ha); feminist +

queer-theory angle (e.g., J. Butler); and feminist + ecology angle (ecofeminists: e.g., A. Kolodny, Merchant).

21. NEW HISTORICISM (CULTURAL POETICS)

In the 1980's, Anglo-American critics read the French philosopher FOUCAULT and developed a "New Historicism" that differed from traditional historical criticism in several important ways. For one thing, they usually read a period's "texts"—characteristically, those of the Renaissance & Romantic eras—as contestatory, reflective of the time's socio-political forces of *power / coercion / containment* vs. *rebellion / subversion.* (But while they often at least implicitly viewed the latter more favorably, the two contestatory forces seem to be usually presented in a state of unresolvable tension—geez, much like the Reagan era in which they wrote!) Secondly, the New Historicists saw everything as a "text" (a precedent established by French structuralism) and went "outside the canon" of traditional literary studies, examining, for instance, private letters, obscure public documents, and forgotten/"minor" literary texts—and even, and almost especially, public spectacles and displays—in their analyses of the workings of social power.

22. ECOCRITICISM

The most recent "school" to arrive on the scene (1990's, mostly), ecocriticism examines the relationship of literature and nature, often from a quite political (environmentalist or animal rights) point of view. Not surprisingly, (creative) "nature writers" such as Thoreau, Annie Dillard, and Edward Abbey are commonly championed by such critics. Ecocritic William Howarth has defined the "ecocritic," in a rather tongue-in-cheek fashion, as follows: "a person who judges the merits and faults of writings that depict the effects of culture upon nature, with a view towards celebrating nature, berating its despoilers, and reversing the harm through political action." Ecocriticism asks such questions as—"Does the 'nature' in this novel do more than just serve as a clichéd setting, acting instead as a major 'character' therein?" (And, either way, "Is that 'nature' a healthy ecosystem, or a [female] 'body' to be raped and ruined by the human characters who inhabit it?"); "What if I read this book from the point of view of one the animals in it, rather than just the human characters?"; "Are the birds in Wordsworth acknowledged as authentic, unique beings for-themselves, or are they simply used, 'othered,' as surrogate-object, substitutional metaphors for Wordsworth's longing for his mother (as in 'mother nature')?" (Ooh, a little bit of psychoanalytical criticism has crept in. Also, as evident in some of the questions above, feminism and ecocriticism are frequently combined; thus the term, *Ecofeminism.).*

23. CULTURAL STUDIES

Beginning with the *Birmingham School* (of British Cultural Studies), this movement brings critical theory concertedly to bear upon pop culture, and might best be deemed a new academic discipline or "subject matter"—at last, a radical extension of the "literary" canon—rather than a specific approach. Indeed, in crucial ways, it is an extension of structuralism and New Historicism in its propensity to "read" all cultural artifacts as "codes" and "text," from Hollywood movies to matchbook covers—which are inevitably indicative of the contestatory ideologies at work in the culture at hand (i.e., our culture). Not surprisingly, given their origins, cultural critics often employ the "tools" of (neo-)Marxism—especially the Frankfurt School—against, for instance, the onslaught of global capitalism upon the consumer masses.

24. RACE/MINORITY STUDIES/CRITICISM

With class and gender, race may be said to complete the main triumvirate of oppressed social groups "writing back" against dominant Western culture. But with such demeaning labels as "African-American Studies" and "Native American Studies," much of the scholarship here may also be said to be truly on the "outside lookin' in." And yet the criticism of Henry Louis Gates, Jr., Houston Baker, Jr., and bell hooks makes African-American lit. ctir. one of the more fascinating and powerful branches of literary scholarship today. Likewise—and given my own "native" heritage—Vine Deloria, Jr., N. Scott Momaday, Paula Gunn Allen, and the poststructuralist "postindian" musings of Gerald Vizenor point towards a renaissance in "Native American lit. crit.," too.

25. QUEER THEORY

Queer theory—to repeat my by-now-generic-and-oversimplified formula—champions the downtrodden of sexual persuasion, critiquing homophobic texts, and championing neglected (and/or recent) gay and lesbian authors & literary works. Via poststructuralism and, often, psychoanalysis, the writings of Eve SEDGWICK, for instance, also point out how much the dominant male heterosexual worldview includes a homoerotic (or *"homosocial")* element. Queer theory, like feminism, is often quite constructivist, and the battle is waged in the sphere of discourse; witness, then, these scholars' move to resignify the traditionally negative label "queer" as a positive term, and Judith BUTLER's (and others', of course) argument that gender identity itself is ultimately discursive.

3

Gender Criticism

> "The superior man is firm in the right way and not merely firm."
>
> —*Confucius*

Gender criticism is much debated school of literary thought. In this chapter we have presented this school elaborately. The chapter is based on the write-up of noted scholar Eve Kosofsky Sedgnick.

First it is significant to mention that "Gender criticism" sounds like a euphemism for something. In practice it is a euphemism for several things, and more than that. One of its subtexts is gay and lesbian criticism. There can be no mystery about why that highly stigmatic label, though increasingly common, should be self-applied with care—however proudly—by those of us who do this scholarship.

For instance, I almost never put "gay and lesbian" in the title of undergraduate gay and lesbian studies courses, though I always use the words in the catalog copy. To ask students to mark their transcripts permanently with so much as the name of this subject of study would have unpredictably disabling consequences for them in the future: the military, most churches, the CIA, and much of the psychoanalytic establishment, to mention only a few plausible professions, are still unblinking about wanting to exclude suspected lesbians and gay men, while in only a handful of places in the U.S. does anyone have even nominal legal protection against the routine denial of employment, housing, insurance, custody, or other rights on the basis of her or his perceived or supposed sexual orientation.

Within and around academic institutions, as well, there can be similarly persuasive reasons for soft-selling the challenge to an oppression whose legal, institutional, and extrajudicial sanctions extend, uniquely, quite uninterruptedly up to the present.

Besides code-naming a range of gay and lesbian-centered theoretical inquiries, "gender studies" also stands in a usably unmarked relation to another rubric, "feminist studies." Feminist studies might be defined as the study of the dynamics of gender definition, inequality, oppression, and change in human societies. To the extent that gender is thus at the definitional center of feminist studies, "gender studies" can sometimes be used as an alternative name for feminist studies, euphemistic only in not specifying, as the "feminist" label more than implicitly does, how far inequality, oppression, and struggle between genders may be seen as differentially constituting gender itself. *Women's* studies today is commonly defined, at least in practice, by the gender of its object of study by contrast to women's studies, feminist studies, whose name specifies the angle of an inquiry rather than the sex of either its subject or its object, can make (and indeed has needed to make) the claim of having as privileged a view of male as of female cultural production. What, then, can or does distinguish the project of gender studies from that of feminist studies? In some cases, as I have suggested, "gender studies" is another, equally appropriate way of designating "feminist studies"—

the reasons for offering the emollient name no more than tactical. In other cases, however, "gender studies" can mean "feminist studies" *minus feminism*; or, in another version of the same deadening equation, "women's studies" (in the most positivist meaning of the term) *plus sonme compensatory entity called "men's studies."* Although they offer an illusion of enhanced inclusiveness, these are the arithmetics that can give "gender studies" a sinister sound to the very scholars most involved in active gender critique. The assumptions behind these usages are intellectually as well as politically stultifying.

To assume that the study of gender can be definitionally detached from the analysis and critique of gender inequality, oppression, and struggle (that is, from some form of feminism) ignores, among other things, the telling fact that gender analysis *per se* became possible only under the pressure of the most pointed and political feminist demand. It ignores, that is to say, the degree to which the otherwise available analytic tools of Western culture had already been structured by precisely the need to naturalize or to deny, and hence to allow the continuance of, a gender inequality already assumed. To figure gender studies as a mere sum of women's studies plus something called "men's studies," on the other hand, reduces both women's studies and the supposedly symmetrical men's studies to static denominations of subject matter, and reduces any understanding of relations between genders to something equally static and additive. That genders are constituted as such, not only in dialectical relation to one another, but in relation to the oppression historically exercised by one over the other, is a knowledge repressed by this impulse toward the separate-but-equal. Things get even worse when the rationale for an additive gender-studies agenda involves, not a nominally depoliticized and positivist study of women-as-women and men-as-men, but rather the conscious promotion of masculist viewpoints (under the men's-studies rubric) as a remedial "balance" against feminist ones. One can only summon up the foundational feminist assertion that colleges don't need something called "men's studies" because so much of the rest of the curriculum already fulfills that function: the function, that is, not only of studying the cultural production of men, but of furthering the interest many of them have in rationalizing, maintaining, or increasing their gender privilege over women.

It seems, then, that insofar as "gender studies" actually is the study of gender, its most substantive and intellectually respectable meanings make it coextensive with "feminist studies," and gender criticism coextensive with feminist criticism. Where, in that case, to look for the distinctive projects of gender criticism beyond its overlap with feminist criticism? In the context of this volume, where feminist criticism has its own topical assignment, distinct from this chapter as it is from that devoted to women's literature, it seems particularly possible to insist on the question. And where, for that matter, to look for the already fecund connection of gender criticism with the agendas of gay and lesbian-centered critique to which I began by alluding? *Homosexual* is not, after all, today understood as the name of a gender, though it alludes to gender and is defined by reference to it. Nor has the feminist analysis of mutually-constitutive relations and oppressions *between* genders proven to have an adequate purchase on how relations, identities, and oppressions are constituted, as in the exemplary gay instance, *within* them. Yet so far the greatest success—institutionally as well as intellectually—of gender criticism *per se* has been specifically in gay and lesbian criticism.

Let me suggest that the most distinctive task of gender

criticism-not-coextensive-with-feminist criticism may be, not to do gender analysis, but to explore what resists it: to ask, with respect to certain categories that can't be *a priori* disentangled from gender, nonetheless *what isn't gender*. "Gender criticism" might here be taken to mean, then, not criticism *through* the categories of gender analysis, but criticism *of* them, mapping of the fractal borderlines between gender and its others. And if gay and lesbian criticism is so far the typifying site of such interrogations of gender analysis, then the first other of gender would seem to be, in this defining instance, sexuality.

Sex and Gender

Sex, gender, sexuality: three terms whose usage relations and analytical relations are almost irremediably slippery. The charting of a space between something called "sex" and something called "gender" has been one of the most influential and successful undertakings of feminist thought. For the purposes of that undertaking, "sex" has had the meaning of a certain group of irreducible, biological differentiations between members of the species *homo sapiens* who have XX and those who have XY chromosomes. These include (or are ordinarily thought to include) more or less marked dimorphisms of genital formation, hair growth (in populations that have body hair), fat distribution, hormonal function, and reproductive capacity. "Sex" in this sense—what I'll demarcate as "chromosomal sex"—is seen as the relatively minimal raw material on which is then based the social construction of *gender*. Gender, then, is the far more elaborated, more fully and rigidly dichotomized social production and reproduction of male and female identities and behaviors—of male and female *persons*—in a cultural system for which "male/female" functions as a primary and perhaps model binarism affecting the structure and meaning of many, many other binarisms whose apparent connection to chromosomal sex will often be exiguous or nonexistent. Compared to chromosomal sex which is seen (by these definitions) as tending to be immutable, immanent in the individual, and biologically based, the meaning of gender is seen as culturally mutable and variable, highly relational (in the sense that each of the binarized genders is defined primarily by its relation to the other), and inextricable from a history of power differentials between genders. This feminist charting of what Gayle Rubin refers to as a "sex/gender system" ("Traffic," 159), the system by which chromosomal sex is turned into, and processed as, cultural gender, has tended to minimize the attribution of people's various behaviors and identities to chromosomal sex, and to maximize their attribution to socialized gender constructs. The purpose of that strategy has been to gain analytic and critical leverage on the female-disadvantaging social arrangements that prevail at a given time in a given society, by throwing into question their legitimative ideological grounding in biologically-based narratives of the "natural."

"Sex" is, however, a term that extends indefinitely beyond chromosomal sex. That its history of usage often overlaps with what might, now, more properly be called "gender" is only one problem. ("I can only love someone of my own sex." Should "sex" be "gender" in such a sentence? "M. saw that the person who approached was of the opposite sex." Genders—insofar as there are two and they are defined in contradistinction to one another—may be said to be opposite; but in what sense is XX the opposite of XY?) Beyond chromosomes, however, the association of "sex," precisely through the physical body, with reproduction and with genital activity and sensation keeps offering new challenges to the conceptual clarity or even possibility of sex/gender differentiation. There is a powerful argument to be made that a primary (or *the* primary) issue in gender differentiation and gender struggle is the question of who is to have control of women's (biologically) distinctive reproductive capability. Indeed, the intimacy of the association between several of the most signal forms of gender oppression and "the facts" of women's bodies and women's reproductive activity has led some radical feminists to question, more or less explicitly, the usefulness of insisting on a sex/gender distinction.

For these reasons, even usages involving the "sex/gender system" within feminist theory are able to use "sex/gender" only to delineate a problematical *space*, rather than a crisp distinction. My loose usage here will be to denominate that problematized space of the sex/gender system, the whole package of physical and cultural distinctions between women and men, more simply under the rubric "gender." I do this in order to reduce the likelihood of confusion between "sex" in the sense of "the space of differences between male and female" and "sex" in the sense of sexuality.

For meanwhile the whole realm of what modern culture refers to as "sexuality" and *also* calls "sex"— the array of acts, expectations, narratives, pleasures, identity-formations, and knowledges, in both women and men, that tends to cluster most densely around certain genital sensations but is not adequately defined by them—that realm is virtually impossible to situate on a map delimited by the feminist-defined sex/gender distinction.

To the degree that it has a center or starting-point in certain physical sites, acts, and rhythms associated (however contingently) with procreation or the potential for it, *sexuality* in this sense may seem to be of a piece with *chromosomal sex*: biologically necessary to species survival, tending toward the individually immanent, the socially immutable, the given. But to the extent that, as Freud argued and Foucault assumed, the distinctively sexual nature of human sexuality has to do precisely with its excess over or potential difference from the bare choreographies of procreation, "sexuality" might be the very opposite of what we originally referred to as (chromosomal-based) sex: it could occupy, instead, even more than "gender" the polar position of the relational, the social/symbolic, the constructed, the variable, the representational.

In "Thinking Sex," an influential essay published in 1984, Gayle Rubin hypothesizes that the question of gender and the question of sexuality, inextricable from one another though they are in that each can be expressed only in the terms of the other, are nonetheless not the same question, that in twentieth-century western culture gender and sexuality represent two analytic axes that may productively be imagined as being as distinct from one another as, say, gender and class, or class and race. Distinct, that is to say, no more than minimally, but none the less usefully.

Under this hypothesis, just as one has learned to assume that no issue of racial meaning fails to be embodied through the specificity of a particular class position—and no issue of class, for instance, through the specificity of a particular gender position—so no issue of gender would fail to be embodied through the specificity of a particular sexuality, and vice versa; but nonetheless, there could be use in keeping the analytic axes distinct.

An objection to this analogy might be that gender is *definitionally* built into determinations of sexuality, in a way that neither of them is definitionally intertwined with, for instance, determinations of class or race. It is certainly true that without a concept of gender there could be, quite simply, no concept of homo- or heterosexuality. But many other dimensions of sexual choice (auto- or alloerotic, within or between generations, species, etc.) have no such distinctive, explicit definitional connection with gender; indeed some dimensions of sexuality might be tied, *instead* of gender, to differences or similarities of race or class. The definitional narrowing-down in this century of sexuality as a whole to a binarized calculus of *homo*- or *hetero*sexuality is a weighty fact but an entirely historical one. To use that *fait accompli* as a reason for analytically conflating sexuality per se with gender would obscure the degree to which the fact itself requires explanation. It would also, I think, risk obscuring yet again the extreme intimacy with which all these available analytic axes do after all mutually constitute one another: to assume the distinctiveness of the *intimacy* between sexuality and gender might well risk assuming too much about the definitional *separability* of either of them from determinations of, say, class or race.

It may be, as well, that—as Judith Butler argues in *Gender Trouble*—a damaging bias toward heterosocial or heterosexist assumptions inheres unavoidably in the very concept of gender. This bias would be built into any gender-based analytic perspective to the extent that gender definition and gender identity are necessarily relational between genders—to the extent, that is, that in any gender system, female identity or definition is constructed by analogy, supplementarity, or contrast to male, or vice versa. Although many gender-based forms of analysis do involve accounts, sometimes fairly rich ones, of intra-gender behaviors and relations, the ultimate definitional appeal in any gender-based analysis must necessarily be to the diacritical frontier between different genders.

This gives heterosocial and heterosexual relations a conceptual privilege of incalculable consequence. Undeniably, residues, markers, tracks, signs referring to that diacritical frontier between genders are everywhere, as well, internal to and determinative of the experience of each gender and its intra-gender relations; gender-based analysis can never be dispensed with in even the most purely intra-gender context. Nevertheless it seems predictable that the analytic bite of a purely gender-based account will grow less incisive and direct as the distance of its subject from a social interface between different genders increases. It is unrealistic to expect a close, textured analysis of same-sex relations through an optic calibrated in the first place to the coarser stigmata of gender difference. The development of an alternative analytic axis—call it sexuality—must be, therefore, if anything a peculiarly central project to gay/lesbian and antihomophobic inquiry.

The gravity of gender division and gender oppression does have, however, the consequence that it can never be taken for granted how much women's same-sex relations will have analytically or experientially in common with men's; so the sense of talking about "gay/lesbian" critique at all is itself always, and with good reason, contested. Nevertheless, it does seem that the interpretive frameworks within which lesbian writers, readers, and interlocutors are likely to process male-centered reflections on homo/heterosexual issues, and vice versa, are currently in a phase of destabilizing flux and promise.

The lesbian interpretive framework most readily available until recently to critics and theorists was the separatist-feminist one that emerged from the 1970s. According to that framework, there were essentially no valid grounds of commonality between gay male and lesbian experience and identity; to the contrary, women-loving women and men-loving men must be at precisely opposite ends of the gender spectrum. The assumptions at work here were indeed radical ones: most importantly, the stunningly efficacious re-visioning, in female terms, of same-sex desire as being at the very definitional center of each gender, rather than as occupying a cross-gender or liminal position between them. Thus, women who loved women were seen as *more* female, men who loved men as quite possibly more male, than those whose desire crossed boundaries of gender; the self-identification of the virilized woman gave way, at least for many, to that of the "woman-identified woman." The axis of sexuality, in this view, was not only exactly coextensive with the axis of gender, but expressive of its most heightened essence: "Feminism is the theory, lesbianism is the practice." By analogy, male homosexuality could be, and often was, seen as the practice for which male supremacy was the theory. A particular reading of modern gender history was, of course, implicit in and in turn propelled by this gender-separatist framework. In accord with, for instance, Adrienne Rich's understanding of many aspects of women's bonds as constituting a "lesbian continuum" (*"Compulsory Heterosexuality"* 79) this history, found in its purest form in the work of Lilian Faderman, de-emphasized the definitional discontinuities and perturbations between more and less sexualized, more and less prohibited, and more and less gender-identity-bound, forms of female same-sex bonding. Insofar as lesbian object-choice was viewed as epitomizing a specificity of female experience and resistance, insofar as a symmetrically opposite understanding of gay male object-choice also obtained, and insofar also as feminism necessarily posited male and female experiences and interests as different and opposed, the implication was that an understanding of male homo/

heterosexual definition could offer little or no affordance or interest for any lesbian theoretical project. Indeed, the powerful impetus of a gender-polarized feminist ethical schema made it possible for a profoundly anti-homophobic reading of lesbian desire (as a quintessence of the female) to fuel a correspondingly homophobic reading of gay male desire (as a quintessence of the male).

Since the late 70s, however, there has emerged a variety of challenges to this understanding of how lesbian and gay male desires and identities might be mapped against each other. Each challenge has led many to a refreshed sense that lesbians and gay men may share important though contested aspects of one another's histories, cultures, identities, politics, and destinies. These challenges have emerged from the "sex wars" within feminism over pornography and s/m, which seemed to many pro-sex feminists to expose a devastating continuity between a certain, theretofore privileged feminist understanding of a resistant female identity, on the one hand, and on the other, repressive nineteenth-century bourgeois constructions of a sphere of pure femininity. Such challenges emerged as well from the reclamation and relegitimation of a courageous history of lesbian trans-gender role-playing and identification. Along with this new historical making-visible of self-defined mannish lesbians came a new salience of the many ways in which male and female homosexual identities had in fact been constructed through and in relation to each other over the last century—by the variously homophobic discourses of professional expertise, but also and just as actively by many lesbians and gay men. The irrepressible, relatively class-nonspecific popular culture in which James Dean has been as numinous an icon for lesbians as Garbo or Dietrich has for gay men seems resistant to a purely feminist theorization. It is in these contexts that calls for a theorized axis of sexuality as distinct from gender have developed. And after the anti-s/m, anti-pornography liberal-feminist move toward labelling and stigmatizing particular sexualities joined its energies with those of the much longer-established conservative sanctions against all forms of sexual "deviance," it remained only for the terrible accident of the HIV epidemic, and the terrifying societal threats constructed around it, to reconstruct a category of the pervert capacious enough to admit homosexuals of any gender. The newly virulent homophobia of the 1980s, directed alike against women and men even though its medical pretext ought, if anything, logically to give a relative exemptive privilege to lesbians, reminds un-gently that it is more to our friends than to our enemies that sexually nonconforming women and men are perceptible as distinct groups. At the same time, however, the internal perspective of the gay movements shows women and men increasingly, though far from uncontestingly and far from equally, working together on mutually antihomophobic agendas. The contributions brought by lesbians to current gay and AIDS activism are weighty, not despite, but because of the intervening lessons of feminism. Feminist perspectives on medicine and health-care issues, on civil disobedience, and on the politics of class and race as well as of sexuality, for instance, have been centrally enabling for the recent waves of AIDS activism; while the extensive repertoire of intellectual strategies amassed and tested by feminism has been of incalculable benefit to emergent gay as well as lesbian theory. What these developments return to the lesbians involved in them may include a more richly pluralized range of imaginings of lines of gender and sexual identification.

Historicizing Sexuality

It is indicative of the disjunctive positioning of "sexuality" in gender criticism that the book that made "sexuality" a usable critical term—the book whose English publication (1978) thus probably offers the best date for the inception of gender criticism in the present sense—should have been itself virtually uninterested in gender; so that the task of fitting analyses of gender and of sexuality to one another has remained a conceptually intractable, hence a vibrant one. That book, Foucault's *History of Sexuality, Volume I: An Introduction*, enabled a newly productive discourse of sexuality by making clear how fully modern sexuality is already produced through and indeed *as* discourse. Foucault first shows how heavily prior understandings of sexuality (including the psychoanalytic and Marxist) have depended on what he calls the "repressive hypothesis," the understanding of sexuality as a quantitative absolute of a distinctive kind of energy, immanent in the individual, whose silencing and regulation is the supposed task of political and cultural power. Foucault, on the other hand, though he is far from claiming "that sex has not been prohibited or barred or masked or misapprehended since the classical age", is more struck by the proliferation of modern discourses of sexuality than by their suppression. Or rather, he perceives that there may really be no "rupture" between "repression and the critical analysis of repression"; responding to the paradox of a society "which speaks verbosely of its own silence, [and] takes great pains to relate in detail the things it does not say", he sees the modern period as defined, to the contrary, by "the multiplication of discourses concerning sex in the field of exercise of power itself: an institutional incitement to speak about it, and to do so more and more; a determination on the part of agencies of power to hear it spoken about, and to cause *it* to speak through explicit articulation and endlessly accumulated detail". Thus, the would-be-liberatory repressive hypothesis itself comes to be seen as a kind of ruse for mandating ever more of the verbal proliferation that had also gone on before and around it.

Rather than envisioning "power" as something exercised prohibitively from the top of society downward, against a sexuality envisioned as forcing its way upward from the level of the individual, Foucault thus describes both sexuality and power as relations that are incessantly and locally produced and productive at every level of modern culture, through "the task of passing everything having to do with sex through the endless mill of speech". He locates the imperative to utterance in the premodern institutional discourses of law and especially religion (both founded on protocols of confession), but most symptomatically in the newly prestigious ones of psychiatry, psychoanalysis, demography, medicine, and education.

By refusing to distinguish between sexuality "itself" and the discourses that structure, delimit, and (he argues) produce and reproduce it, Foucault undoes the positivist assumption that to write historically about sexuality involves increasingly direct, immediate knowledge or "understanding" of some unchanging sexual essence. To the contrary, he argues that modern sexuality itself is so intimately entangled with the historically distinctive contexts and structures that now count as *knowledge*, that such "knowledge" can scarcely be a transparent window onto a separate realm of sexuality: rather, it constitutes that sexuality.

Indeed, he goes beyond this. His ultimate argument is that sexuality per se comes into existence, not with the first sexual acts or even sexual prohibitions, but during the long process, culminating in the nineteenth century, by which, as sex learned an infinity of new paths into discourse, the value of Truth itself—in particular the Truth of individual identity—came to be lodged in the uncovery or expression of the Truth of sexuality.

That is, what distinguishes modern sexuality from premodern sex is the extreme, indeed unlimited epistemological pressure everywhere placed on it, and the epistemological centrality in turn accorded it in the wider field of all knowledges and institutions.

No doubt it will be clear why the analysis offered in Foucault's book has proven problematical in relation to other forms of politically-oriented analysis. As in most of Foucault's writing, the accounts of agency, or for that matter of causality or change, are elusive at best. His dissolutory insistence on the most local or molecular vantage makes class identity, interest, or struggle, or gender identity, interest, or struggle extraordinarily difficult to keep in focus. His renunciation of any economic metaphor based on scarcity or deprivation would seem to silence most forms of materialism. His refusal to distinguish between the realms of power and of eroticism is only one example of the resistance his work mounts to moralistic—indeed, to any ethicizing—appropriation; and while fugitive utopian or elegaic moments certainly animate his writing, what is more solidly founded there is an analysis of the utopian impulse as yet another alibi of the repressive hypothesis.

No doubt it will also be clear, however, why this volume was to prove so catalytic for literary study. Coarsely put: it justifies a view of writing as a form of sex, indeed as its most direct form; at the same time it justifies a view of sexuality as the central repository of the truth-values of modernity. How could these not be deeply energizing assertions for writers and scholars—at least if Foucault is right in his estimate of the prestige, the promise of epistemological force, the "sex appeal," of sexuality in our century? This is also to say, of course, that, far from offering resistance to the modern "scheme for transforming sex into discourse" and "interplay of truth and sex", processes that Foucault treats as historically unidirectional and inescapable, the effect of his book has instead been to accelerate that trajectory and load it with ever greater explanatory force. Rather than attempt vainly to impede it, he has, if successful, merely *displaced* and re-propelled it unpredictably by making less tenable the "repressive hypothesis" by which its subjects have concealed its itineraries from themselves. "Merely" displaced and re-propelled: but that is a more direct path of rhetorical efficacy—of historical intervention, which is to say, in Foucault, of seduction—than most critical works admit to undertaking. Thus, again excitingly for any writer, this work has seemed to offer new accesses to the performative force of writing. In the unmentioned, only slightly displaced continuity between what the book *says* and what it seems to *make happen*, readers can register the gap of unrationalized rhetorical force that the author has already thematized in the distance between what the "repressive hypothesis" says (sex is forbidden) and the almost hilarious proliferation of sexualized discourse that it in fact effects.

Specifying Sexuality

So far we have discussed a fairly unified, though vast, field of phenomena around "sexuality" that Foucault's volume at once describes and enacts. But the fact is that its incitements have not issued in a new movement of "sexuality criticism." Rather, its strongest effects have been radically partial—partial enough, perhaps, even to call into question the mapping of that neatly unified "sexual" field. That is to say, the discursive progeny of *The History of Sexuality, Vol. 1: An Introduction* has been, not the mythic "sexuality criticism," but a renewed, ambitious, assertive, splendidly explicit, and unprecedentedly insitutionalized movement of gay/lesbian criticism. The metonym for "sexuality" that is effectually installed by *The History of Sexuality, Vol. 1* is homosexuality.

Yet the least clear thing about this book is in what sense it can be said to be a gay book. The author is not explicit about his own sexuality between its covers; and discussions of the history of homosexuality per se are few and brief (the index lists three references), and embedded in discussions of other sexualities or of sexuality more broadly. Take, for instance, the book's most famous and agenda-setting formulation about the history of homosexuality, under the heading of the "*incorporation of perversions* and a new *specification of individuals*":

> As defined by the ancient civil or canonical codes, sodomy was a category of forbidden acts; their perpetrator was nothing more than the juridical subject of them. The nineteenth-century homosexual became a personage, a past, a case history, and a childhood . . . . [His sexuality] was everywhere present in him: at the root of all his actions because it was their insidious and indefinitely active principle; written immodestly on his face and body because it was a secret that always gave itself away. . . . [T]he psychological, psychiatric, medical category of homosexuality was constituted from the moment it was characterized—Westphal's famous article of 1870 on "contrary sexual sensations" can stand as its date of birth—less by a type of sexual relations that by a certain quality of sexual sensibility. . . . The sodomite had been a temporary aberration; the homosexual was now a species.

Foucault's discussion here of the invention of "the

homosexual" is presented as an exemplifying instance of a process of specification, of the emergence of *identities* where previously there had been *acts*, that also included "all those minor perverts whom nineteenth-century psychiatrists entomologized by giving them strange baptismal names: there were Krafft-Ebing's zoophiles and zooerasts, Rohleder's auto-monosexualists; and later, mixoscopophiles, gynecomasts, presbyophiles, sexoesthetic inverts, and dyspareunist women" , and those other "figures" and "privileged objects of knowledge," the hysterical woman and the masturbating child. The newly reified homosexuality, in short, is but one, representative example of "*these thousand aberrant sexualities*" that came, in their plurality, to define sexuality itself.

Yet the discursive context in which Foucault's book does its performative work is not, as it happens, one that prominently features the classification of "these thousand aberrant sexualities." The rhetorical strategy of the book is to allow a reader to imagine, as it were by default, that the 19th-century social formations that emerge from its narrative are in essence those of the present day: "We `Other Victorians,'" the first chapter is entitled. But in the late-twentieth-century scene of the book's actual address, after the lapse of the century elided in "We `Other Victorians,'" to specify someone's sexuality is not to locate her or him on a map teeming with zoophiles, gynecomasts, sexoesthetic inverts . . . . Hysterical women are no longer taxonomized; and to imagine, as nineteenth-century psychiatry did, "the masturbator" as a particular *kind of person* distinct from other kinds of people would seem laughable. This change does not reflect any lightening of the burden of meaning placed on issues of sexual definition since the period described by Foucault. Rather, it reflects an astonishing simplification of the fraught identity-categories through which sexuality is conceived. In the late twentieth century, if I ask you what your sexual orientation or sexual preference is, you will understand me to be asking precisely one thing: whether you are homosexual or heterosexual. And whether or not you find these terms inadequate or even irrelevant to your particular desires and velleities, you will be confident in interpreting "sexual orientation" as a reference to that differential and only that.

This startlingly coarse dichotomy-effect operates, unremarked, in and on the reading gestalt of Foucault's study. It operates all the more decisively for its silence, however, and in ways that inevitably drive wedges in at the joints between the book's constative and its performative projects. The first dichotomy-effect on the book is to install homosexuality in a more than just metonymically representational relation to sexuality as a whole. That the other "species"-identities attached to nonconforming sexual desires in the nineteenth century have only lost taxonomic power since then, while homosexual identity has so decisively gained it, implicitly installs homo/heterosexual definition as *the* (unasked) question of Foucauldian sexuality; but beyond that, as we must discuss further, Foucault seems to exclude even the hetero- side of any homo/hetero dichotomy from the purlieus of sexuality, insofar as "sexuality" itself is said to comprise more and more simply "a world of perversion".

It happens repeatedly that dynamics and meanings attributed to "sexuality" in Foucault act and mean differently when they are read in the light of the homosexual metonym. There are many places where Foucault's generalizations about "sexuality" seem acutely truer when applied to homosexuality—but truer because different, and again, different because truer. He says, for instance, "What is peculiar to modern societies . . . is not that they consigned sex to a shadow existence, but that they dedicated themselves to speaking of it *ad infinitum*, while exploiting it as *the* secret". But what could be less secret than the, as it were, surplus *the*-ness of one particular secret within the open secret of sex, the one named by Christianity and multiple reinscriptions of Western law as the Unspeakable itself, *nefandam libidinem*, "that sin which should be neither named nor committed," the crime "of so black a hue, of so abominable a nature, that we cannot pretend to give any report of it," "so detestable and repugnant to the common feeling of our nature that by no word can it be described without committing an outrage against decency"—*videlicet*, "the love that dare not speak its name." The particular case of homosexuality here marks an intensification of, but by the same token a certain discontinuity from, the knowing reification "sex."

Similarly, if the regime of sexuality "in general" is seen by Foucault as instituting knowledge-relations that are ultimately productive of that obscure object of desire, *the unconscious*, how much the truer must this be of the particular knowledge-relations around the secret, relentlessly spectacularized, and therefore utterly social space of tacit homo/heterosexual definition: the closet? The complex communities of blackmail, complicity, condescension, glamorization, and every sort of cognitive leveraging that are incessantly generated around any closet or the mere space of the possibility of one, enabled in the past century by the newly reduced homo/hetero meaning of "sexual preference," render potent and priceless on many different markets the commodity of ignorance, especially self-ignorance.

Thus sex gradually became an object of great suspicion . . . the fragment of darkness that we each carry within us:

a general signification, a universal secret, an omnipresent cause, a fear that never ends. . . . We tell it its truth by deciphering what it tells us about that truth; it tells us our own by delivering up that part of it that escaped us. From this interplay there has evolved, over several centuries, a knowledge of the subject; a knowledge not so much of his form, but of that which divides him, determines him perhaps, but above all causes him to be ignorant of himself. . . . Causality in the subject, the unconscious of the subject, the truth of the subject in the other who knows, the knowledge he holds unbeknown to him, all this found an opportunity to deploy itself in the discourse of sex.

Here again, however, in narrating what appears to be the demystifyingly historicized story of sexuality per se and its centrality to a Western commonsense described in the tropes of Lacanian psychoanalysis, Foucault chooses not to make explicit the privileged referent of his "universal" noun phrases in the locus of a particular homo/heterosexual question. His refusal constitutes the closet of homo/heterosexual definition *as* "the unconscious" of this text: not in the sense that a certain homo/heterosexual specificity is cognitively unavailable to the author, but in the sense that the text's refusal to verbalize it forces its articulation or denial rather on the reader, whom it thus interpellates as "the other who knows [] the knowledge [the text] holds unbeknown to [itself]"; it founds the reader as the knowing Other of "that which divides [the text], determines [it] perhaps, but above all causes [it] to be ignorant of [it]self."

Foucault's analysis of the confessional tradition makes clear, if nothing else did, both how strongly and how resistantly this book is marked by its positioning at the end of the century that stretched between Karl-Heinrich Ulrichs (arguably the first European man to come out as a homosexual) and the gay liberation movement of the late 1960s. Even given the French context of its writing, more urbane and less hygienically dichotomized than the American context of its reading whose effects I here describe, Foucault's account of the confessional owes as much to the sacralized new ritual of coming out as to the psychoanalytic ritual that appears to be its first referent: "a ritual of discourse in which the speaking subject is also the subject of the statement; . . . a ritual that unfolds within a power relationship . . . ; a ritual in which the truth is corroborated by the obstacles and resistances it has had to surmount in order to be formulated; and finally, a ritual in which the expression alone, independently of its external consequences, produces intrinsic modifications in the person who articulates it". For Foucault to posit a historical continuity between religious confession and coming out is also, however, to unfold the reasons for his scepticism about the latter act.

> From the Christian penance to the present day, sex was a privileged theme of confession. A thing that was hidden, we are told. But what if, on the contrary, it was what, in a quite particular way, one confessed? Suppose the obligation to conceal it was but another aspect of the duty to admit to it (concealing it all the more and with greater care as the confession of it was more important, requiring a stricter ritual and promising more decisive effects)?

Characteristically, Foucault dislocates a conventional understanding of the individual will involved in political action; the conditions that make sense of the speech-act of coming out, he suggests, actually constitute it as a nominal defiance that marks the place of a more disabling acquiescence: acquiescence in the lie of the repressive hypothesis, that speech and silence are, in the discourses of sexuality, each other's polar opposites. The dignified and, in his terms, more profoundly resistant strategy of this book is to refuse either to conceal or to reveal the "sexuality" (i.e., either the homo- or the heterosexuality) of its speaker; and concomitantly to articulate the reader, rather than the text itself, as the agent of the implied *dis*articulation of the supposedly unified field of "sexuality."

Performing Foucault

Post-Foucauldian work in gender theory has both profited and suffered from the ruptures of this founding text. In *Forget Foucault*, Baudrillard remarks that Foucault's followers have tended to ignore how actively his discourse, "a mirror of the powers it describes," proffers disillusion about "the effect of truth it produces"; historians, as he points out, have instead used it to refine and perpetuate a positivist order of "the truth, nothing but the truth". In its own terms, this historical work has been extremely valuable, taking up Foucault's challenge to denaturalize by narrativizing present understandings of what sexuality is and entails. Yet the violently contradictory and volatile energies that every morning's newspaper proves to us are circulating even at this moment, in our society, around the issues of homo/heterosexual definition, show over and over again how preposterous must be anybody's urbane pretense at having a clear, simple story to tell about the outlines and meanings of what and who is homosexual and heterosexual. Jeffrey Weeks points out the thoroughgoing, coercive incoherence of the homophobic etiological models that prevail in our culture, according to which homosexuality is classified at the same time as "sin" *and* as "disease," "so that you can be born with [it], seduced into [it] and catch [it], all at the same time." Anti-homophobic analysis has the same divided conceptual heritage: the most current theoretical form in which this conflict is visible is in the debate in gay/lesbian studies between "social constructionist" and "essentialist" understandings of homo/heterosexual identity. The conflict, within both homophobic and anti-homophobic ideologies, has a long history; it is the most recent link in a more enduring chain of conceptual impasses, a deadlock between what might be called more generally *universalizing* and *minoritizing* accounts of the relation of homosexual desires or persons to the wider field of all desires or persons. Universalizing discourses are those that suggest that every person has the potential for same-sex, as for other-sex, desire or activity; minoritizing ones are those that attribute each of these desires to a fixed, unchangeable segment of the population. Each kind of account can underpin both virulently homophobic and supportively anti-homophobic ideological formations. As we have seen, historical narratives following Foucault have seemed to show universalizing paradigms, such as the terribly influential Judaeo-Christian proscription of particular *acts* called "sodomy" (acts that might be performed by anybody), as being displaced after the late nineteenth century by the definition of particular kinds of *persons*, specifically "homosexuals." A Classically-based but enduring honorific sub-tradition of durable and significant pedagogic/pederastic *bonds* between men of different ages was also seen as having been displaced by the new, minoritizing view of homosexual identity. It may, however, as we have seen in *reading* Foucault, be more descriptive to say that since the late nineteenth century the different understandings, contradictory though they are, have coexisted, creating in the space of their contradiction enormous potentials of discursive power.

Other, more theoretically or rhetorically adventurous work "after" Foucault has opened new disciplinary territory by embodying or enacting its contradictions less numbly.

This has been especially necessary, and especially powerful, in the critical analysis of what Foucault made it possible to think of as "the discourse of" AIDS. His conceptual centrality to activist understandings of the disease that silenced him is only one of the nightmarish overdeterminations typical of AIDS. Of those overdeterminations, the sickening rhyme between the disease's patterns of depredation and the lines of proscription already drawn by a homophobic and racist culture is the obvious and almost overwhelming one. To dismantle the murderous monolith that AIDS has kept threatening to forge out of the accidents of a virus; out of the established homophobic moralisms of state and church; out of the insatiable modern momentum toward increased surveillance; out of a centuries-old intertextual narrative linkage between fatality and male-male desire; out of the institutional consolidations of advanced medical research, and its ideology-drenched forms of figuration; out of an invidious capitalist health-care delivery system; out of the incoherences of modern discourses of addiction and the "foreign substance"; out of imperialist needs to constitute the third world as at once the incubator of western illness and the laboratory of western medicine; out of the vengeful iconographic traditions of both expert technical imaging and popular media—that pressing need has consolidated, under an academic banner of "cultural studies" but by no means confined to academia, a new axis of inquiry involving literary and communications theorists, film theorists, art historians, historians of medicine, artists, film and video makers, feminist community and cultural activists, and AIDS activist groups like ACT UP.

The generative energy that Foucauldian analysis has made available for this form of intellectual/political activism is still, however, intimately inscribed with the contradictory imperatives (of truth, of performance; of proliferation, of specification) transmitted by his work. For example, like thousands of other gay men lost to AIDS, Foucault acquired a sexuality visible to a broad public only when journalism (belatedly) specified his cause of death. It was AIDS that engraved the impoverishing homo/hetero dichotomy most indelibly on the retrospect of his work; slowly but unrelentingly, the obituary process revoked his potent refusal of (what he had figured as) confession. The epistemological stress that Foucault showed to be lodged in modern sexuality has not been dislodged by the crisis of AIDS, but rather yoked violently to an epistemological stress now also attached to death. In the decade of AIDS, the hidden sex of the obituary has been framed as a question of authority: in *New York Times* usage throughout the first decade of the epidemic, for example, cause of death was customarily given as an unattributed fact—that is to say, as one transparently known to *The Times*; in obituaries of unmarried, non-clergy men under 60 who didn't die in accidents, on the other hand, "a hospital spokesman" or a sibling or partner of the dead person was always specified as the source of information, whether or not AIDS-related illness was given as the cause of death, and presumably whether or not it actually was. Precisely by proffering a named authority—by making the authority-process, atypically, visible—*The Times* in these cases solicits and tendentiously points the skepticism of obituary readers: a skepticism normal obituary practice repels. It has been characteristic of the discourse around AIDS to be so tied to a truth-imperative whose form is intransitive but whose angle is killingly partial. Last year a friend of mine, being treated for a skin rash, came under pressure from his doctors to agree to an HIV-antibody test he had decided he did not want to take. The male doctor sent the female doctor out of the room, the better to set the stage for man-to-man epistemological heroics: "Don't you," the doctor, scalpel-eyed, at last bore down, "want *to know*?" "No, I don't," my friend bravely replied. "I think you're the one who wants *to know*."

Activist analysis can do everything but except itself from these dynamics, a truth dramatized in a pivotal text, *AIDS: Cultural Analysis, Cultural Activism*, edited by Douglas Crimp. This exemplary presentation of AIDS-related cultural radicalism deconstructs and critiques the scientific and media iconography of the disease, and suggests strategies of ideological and cultural resistance; authors of the essays include women and men, lawyers, gay theorists, a sex worker activist, named and unnamed people living with AIDS within and outside of academia, and scholars and artists in the cultural studies fields. The strategic enablements of Foucault's constructivist archaeology are everywhere visible in the volume, beginning with Crimp's introductory manifesto, "AIDS does not exist apart from the practices that conceptualize it, represent it, and respond to it."

The anti-idealist motive of Foucault's historicizing work is immensely productive here (in, to choose only one example, Simon Watney's useful formulation, "AIDS is increasingly being used to underwrite a widespread public ambition to erase the distinction between `the public' and `the private,' and to establish in their place a monolithic and legally binding category—`the family'—understood as the central term through which the world and the self are henceforth to be rendered intelligible". And it seems to mobilize by some relatively unproblematized mechanism a confident sense of political agency (Crimp: "We don't need to transcend the epidemic; we need to end it"; an assertive ideology of rights (titles include "A Patient's Bill of Rights" and "Further Violations of Our Rights"; and a protean and utopian sex-

affirmativeness (the volume ends with Crimp's words, "we are now reclaiming our subjectivities, our communities, our culture . . . and our promiscuous love of sex".

The dissonant note in the volume, but its most ambitious theoretical moment and in many ways its effectual centerpiece, is an essay by Leo Bersani with the characteristically confrontational title, "Is the Rectum a Grave?" Bersani's essay performs skeptical operations on what the volume otherwise presents as uninterrupted continuities between analysis and politics. Bersani deprecates as "pastoral" any gay-affirmative polemics, implicitly including virtually all the others in the volume, that are based on an ideology of sexual "pluralism," the rhetoric of sexual liberation in the '60s and '70s, a rhetoric that received its most prestigious intellectual justification from Foucault's call—especially in the first volume of his *History of Sexuality*—for a reinventing of the body as a surface of multiple sources of pleasure.

Such calls, for all their redemptive appeal, are, however, unnecessarily and even dangerously tame. The argument for diversity has the strategic advantage of making gays seem like passionate defenders of one of the primary values of mainstream liberal culture, but to make that argument is, it seems to me, to be disingenuous about the relation between homosexual behavior and the revulsion it inspires. The revulsion, it turns out, is all a big mistake: what we're really up to is pluralism and diversity, and getting buggered is just one moment in the practice of those laudable humanistic virtues.

Foucault could be especially perverse about all this: challenging, provoking, and yet, in spite of his radical intentions, somewhat appeasing in his emphases. Bersani, to the contrary, is impatient with any assumption that sex in general "has anything to do with community or love", or that the desires or habits of gay men are likely to be especially infused with political or protopolitical subversions of a status quo. A politically redemptive pluralism has, in his view, nothing to do with the real force of sex. Stubbornly locating both the cause of homophobic revulsion and the recalcitrant, invaluably resistant center of male homosexual desire in a single practice, a single organ, a single role, the receptive position of one man in anal intercourse with another, "a self-shattering solipsistic *jouissance* that drives them apart", Bersani celebrates "the inestimable value of sex as—at least in certain of its ineradicable aspects—*anti*communal, *anti*egalitarian, *anti*nurturing, *anti*loving" . "If, as [Jeffrey] Weeks puts it, gay men `gnaw at the roots of a male heterosexual identity,' it is not because of the parodistic distance that they take from that identity, but rather because, from within their nearly mad identification with it, *they never cease to feel the appeal of its being violated*".

Bersani frames his essay as an anti-Foucauldian intervention, by way of Freud, on a scene where Foucault's own analyses are viewed—by Bersani, by the other authors—as seamlessly continuous with an ideological praxis also identified with Foucault: the supposed "call for" a redemptive rediscovery of the pluralized body. Some features of Bersani's account, notably its refusal of diachronic historical narrative, do distinguish it sharply from any Foucauldian project. But I am much more impressed by the ways his essay performs, in relation to the volume as a whole, the propulsive rhetorical work of political refusal or blockage whose terms were also set by the same text of Foucault's.

In Bersani's treatment of sexual pluralism, as in

Foucault's treatment of the repressive hypothesis, the exposure of a culture-wide lie supposed to inhere in liberal sexual politics is the most relished trope: "In short," as Bersani says at one climactic moment, "to put the matter polemically and even rather brutally, we have been telling a few lies". But these emphatic gestures of disabuse must also entail, by reaction, an equally marked truth-effect; and for each theorist, the very strength of the truth-effect constitutes an argumentative obliquity. Bersani, after all, is asking readers to imagine a sexuality whose [redemptive] essence ("our primary hygienic practice of nonviolence" is that, given the irreducible opacity of its relation to the unconscious, it cannot be recuperated for redemptive projects. Meanwhile Foucault suggests a sexuality whose [true] essence is that it has no non-contingent connection to Truth. And Bersani's relation to the repressive hypothesis is in turn as double as Foucault's.

His essay begins with the announcement, "There is a big secret about sex: most people don't like it". Like Foucault, he disavows any connection between the secret *he* has to reveal about sex, on the one hand, and on the other the conventional exposure of how repressed and repressive are many people's relation to the "smoldering volcanoes" of sexual desire. Noting that the aversion to sex he wants to discuss, the one that is not the same as repression, has "both benign and malignant forms", Bersani first specifies that its malignant forms include the homophobic and AIDS-phobic manifestations also documented and decried elsewhere in the volume. The essay then moves to its withering appraisal of the redemptive gay-liberationist rhetoric of sexual pluralism, and from there to its own proposal of the "arduous representational discipline" by which gay male desire, at least the specific one in which Bersani is interested, can be accorded its proper value on the basis of its dangerous truth "as a mode of ascesis".

Interestingly, however, Bersani never explicitly identifies the "benign" form of the aversion to sex. Is that more properly represented by the gay liberationist position he sees as a pious, perhaps necessary lie, or by Bersani's own position, which celebrates sex precisely and exclusively for the way it creates, in its participants, aversion—the passionate turning away, the "anticommunal" and "antiloving," the *jouissance* that "drives" men "apart"? The introductory gesture of the essay seems to join speaker and reader in an enunciatory compact of people who "like" sex against some distinguishable majority of those who "don't." But what's "like" got to do with it? and what reader, on Bersani's rebarbative showing, could fully identify with her assigned, confidently sex-affirmative place in this schema? It seems as though, to the degree that the essay is structured by the revelation of the "secret" that sex is commonly aversive, it both makes a polemical point (the rather vulgar one that the repressive hypothesis so regularly enables: one's opponents can't say the truth because they are not truly sexual) and makes at the same time a theoretical point that quite undoes the presumptive community of its address. It positions a reader, if compellingly, incoherently. By the same token, although Bersani insists that the meaning of a particular sexual *act* is of far more consequence than gay life-style or *identity*, concepts with which he is especially impatient, the rhetoric by which he sets out to unmask that normalizing minority identity depends, as it happens, on constant appeals to a conventional, identity-based semiotic presumed to be internal to each of his readers. Note, for instance, his use of the second person (flattering? threatening? —full, in any event, of unspoken identity-presumption) in describing "the classic put-down: the butch number swaggering into a bar in a leather get-up opens his mouth and sounds like a pansy, takes you home, where the first thing you notice is the complete works of Jane Austen, gets you into bed, and—well, you know the rest".

"And this brings us back to the question not of the reflection or expression of politics in sex, but rather of the extremely obscure process by which sexual pleasure *generates* politics". To trace these multi-directional dynamics discredits Bersani's essay no more than it does Foucault's book. To the contrary, what would most discredit the argument of either would be the very possibility of a self-transparent, performatively inert relation among the politics of sexuality, the truth-claiming language in which sexual epistemologies may be explored, and the experiential material that gets called sexuality itself. What rather I hope I have assembled some terms to account for is a more unexpected effect: that, far from discrediting either its own argument or (more predictably) the impugned politics of the rest of the collection in which it appears, Bersani's essay, bursting as it is with transverse aggessions, seems to have served for many demanding readers to *legitimate* the project of gay-liberation-based AIDS cultural criticism represented by this important volume. If that is so, it is not, I think, because it offers the generalized spectacle of what Trollope would call "moderate schism." The validation that Bersani offers is far more substantial than a mere staging of internal controversy to confirm the elasticity and differentiability of a fairly new political movement. He makes one assertion to whose truth the very frustrations of the felt pressure toward programmatic clarity all minister: each eclipse, collapse, or collision of authorial or readerly positionings makes more serious and present to the reader that extreme obscurity, noted by Bersani, in "the process by which sexual pleasure *generates* politics." "While it is indisputably true that sexuality is always being politicized, the ways in which *having sex* politicizes are highly problematical". It seems that to thematize, and at the same time but unrationalizably to dramatize, the deep epistemological fractures that necessarily gape under the pressure of a new political need and possibility, may actually render that possibility more intimately recognizable. It may do so especially to an audience whose present need for both sexual theory and sexual activism is tied so closely to our repeated, publicly specularized, politically motivating, shared, but at some level immiscibly private and implacably privative experiences of loss, mourning, and dread.

Professional Boundaries, Political Connections, Erogenous Zones

The difficult politics and erotics of representation, as all of us know, hardly stop short inside the threshold of the text. Although the present account of gender citicism has not focused, as it might have, on direct applications to readings of literary texts, I have meant it to suggest several distinctive ways in which gay/lesbian inquiry has raised specifically representational issues that traverse, exceed, and alter the definitional boundaries of our discipline. Let me say something, finally, about the representational issues raised by its presence, along with that of other explicitly political projects, within the university.

It is very hard to come up with useful images for the synecdochic relation of academic institutions to the larger world of productive institutions in our culture. One important thing about academia is how drastically it tends to *condense*. The very name of the *univers*ity conveys that its ambition is to represent something huge in a disproportionately tiny space—a space that thereby tends to be rendered, of course, unreal or hyperreal, so that the desublimation of its *un*transformed relations across the local "real"—for instance, its infrastructural labor relations, its health-care provisions, its effects on real estate values and municipal tax bases, its symbiosis with various industries and communities—requires repeated wrenching acts of re-recognition. Moreover, the condensation that the university effects on its universe is not only uneven but tendentious, partial, and intermittent in its coverage: increasingly important segments of the society can seem to escape its purview entirely.

Beyond being condensed, and thus tending toward the unreal or the hyperreal, in its synecdochic relation to the universe it claims to represent, the university is also in an anachronistic relation to it. People may choose an academic vocation, not in the first place because of their cognitive talents or because they have particular political values or identifications, but because academic labor, at least at its most privileged and visible levels, is still in many ways so amazingly unrationalized. Compared to industrial or to other service labor—even compared to the other professions—our fealty to the stop-clock and to time discipline, to the bottom line of profitable or even of quantifiable results, to the public/private stresses of office or factory interaction, to the suppression or denial of affective charge, and in particular to the forcible alienation of our labor in the service of projects conceived by and for someone else, is still, for some, almost miraculously attenuated. Projects conceived in relation to identity politics, such as feminist or gay/lesbian inquiry, are continually testing and redefining the limits of such a professional exemption. Delusive as some of these freedoms may be, the space of work for at least some in this industry can seem strikingly close to an idealized preindustrial workspace of task orientation, work continuity, and the relatively meaningful choice of tasks based on perceptible need and aptitude.

The complex temporality of our representational space has a variety of consequences. First and most obviously, it means that academia and academics are always almost definitionally in danger of embodying various simply nostalgic or reactionary politics. Second, it means that the many, very distinctly rationalized and alienating aspects of academic labor, which form all or most of the conditions of work for so very many academics, always risk being occluded or mystified by this more elegiac ideal. Third, it of course marks the vulnerability of this space to the scouring triumphalism of capitalist rationalization; while the relatively decentered structure and diffuse status-economy of U.S. higher education pose some resistance to our instant, wholesale Thatcherization, this state's hypersensitivity to interventions into the discourses of gender and of homo/heterosexuality, in particular, may represent the threshold of an extreme risk.

Fourth and more encouragingly, our anomalous temporality is one of the things that allows academia to function as a kind of cognitive gene-pool of precisely anachronistic ideas, impulses, or information that, unusable under one set of political circumstances, might be preserved in this relatively unrationalized space to emerge with a potentially priceless relevance under changed ones. And fifth, I think many of us are very responsive to the utopian potential of this vision of a form of relatively unalienated, sometimes collaborative labor. No less dangerously grounded in the retrospect than any other utopian formation, it can nevertheless afford energies and leverages for change both within and around the institution.

In an influential recent essay, "Theory, Pragmatisms, and Politics," Cornel West has written that "to be an engaged progressive intellectual is to be a critical organic catalyst whose vocation is to fuse the best of the life of the mind from within the academy with the best of the organized forces for greater democracy and freedom from outside the academy". One image that keeps recurring to me, as a way of recording both the extreme condensation and the extreme temporal discontinuities by which our profession represents the world around it, is that of the progressive academy as one of several erogenous zones for our culture.

This image seems thematically available to me, no doubt, as it might not to some "otherwise-engaged" intellectuals, because the path of my own engagement travels so much through the politics of gender and sexuality. Even for other political projects, however, the erogenous-zone metaphor may usefully record some of the representational circumferences across which we struggle to orient ourselves. For example, Naomi Schor has identified the clitoris as the appropriate figure, in rhetorical theory, for the trope of synecdoche itself, a trope that she argues may be retrieved from the gender-binarized structuralist and poststructuralist conflation of all figures into (an often phallicly-figured) metaphor and (an often vaginally-figured) metonyny. The clitoris also makes literal, as for that matter may mouth, anus, and some other zones chargeable as erotic, the space of an irreducible difference from procreation that homosexuality may be in the best position to represent, as well, for other sexualities—perhaps even, if it can stand for a displacing resistance to the untransformed reproduction of labor, for other institutions.

This can hardly be to say that our theory or politics can be read in any transparent way off of anything so static or given as to be called *identity*. If gay and lesbian theory demonstrates any one thing, it demonstrates—more radically even than can the theory of gender or race—how difficult, distortive, and incoherent, though at the same time how profoundly consequential, are such processes as the self-assignment or allo-assignment of a definitional identity within a hierarchized system of specification.

Our paths to them are very particular paths, and often—perhaps always—oblique; if cognitive work can expand or transform them, the process is a slow one that goes finger's breadth by finger's breadth. It is a rare figure (one thinks, perhaps, of an Audre Lorde) who has managed to feel and think a way through to an experiential understanding that makes more than one politics, one's own politics.

The process cannot be an *a priori* one for the approach to any new or other politics. Whereas one consequence of this condensation and embeddedness is the extreme difficulty, not at all to say impossibility, of doing or thinking coalition politics at more than a superficial level. A second consequence, one that has been severely underestimated by the current academy, is simply the recalcitrance of the barrier that a relative privilege in our mode of labor is inevitably going to oppose to most of our investment of real creativity, courage, and steadfastness in a class-based political analysis.

But another consequence is the very possibility of any political commitment that can be responsive to a strong theoretical moment, but whose energies, needs, and desires (and for this we are very fortunate) can also, in altered forms, outlast it.

[*Courtesy:* Eve Kosofsky Sedgnick.]

4

Reader-Response Criticism

> Reader-response criticism DOES NOT mean or imply some personal "reaction" (e.g. "this text was boring because..."). In writing this type of criticism, concentrate on the effect of texts or the reactions of GROUPS of readers, or what Fish calls "interpretive communities," which may or may not be historically "real."

Reader-response criticism encompasses various approaches to literature that explore and seek to explain the diversity (and often divergence) of readers' responses to literary works.

Louise Rosenblatt is often credited with pioneering the approaches in Literature as Exploration (1938). In her 1969 essay "Towards a Transactional Theory of Reading," she summed up her position as follows: "A poem is what the reader lives through under the guidance of the text and experiences as relevant to the text." Recognizing that many critics would reject this definition, Rosenblatt wrote, "The idea that a poem presupposes a reader actively involved with a text is particularly shocking to those seeking to emphasize the objectivity of their interpretations." Rosenblatt implicitly and generally refers to formalists (the most influential of whom are the New Critics) when she speaks of supposedly objective interpreters shocked by the notion that a "poem" is cooperatively produced by a "reader" and a "text." Formalists spoke of "the poem itself," the "concrete work of art," the "real poem." They had no interest in what a work of literature makes a reader "live through." In fact, in The Verbal Icon (1954), William K. Wimsatt and Monroe C. Beardsley used the term affective fallacy to define as erroneous the very idea that a reader's response is relevant to the meaning of a literary work.

Stanley Fish, whose early work is seen by some as marking the true beginning of contemporary reader-response criticism, also took issue with the tenets of formalism. In "Literature in the Reader: Affective Stylistics" (1970), he argued that any school of criticism that sees a literary work as an object, claiming to describe what it is and never what it does, misconstrues the very essence of literature and reading. Literature exists and signifies when it is read, Fish suggests, and its force is an affective one. Furthermore, reading is a temporal process, not a spatial one as formalists assume when they step back and survey the literary work as if it were an object spread out before them.

The German critic Wolfgang Iser has described that process in *The Implied Reader: Patterns of Communication in Prose Fiction from Bunyan to Beckett* (1974) and The Act of Reading: A Theory of Aesthetic Response (1976). Iser argues that texts contain gaps (or blanks) that powerfully affect the reader, who must explain them, connect what they separate, and create in his or her mind aspects of a work that aren't in the text but are incited by the text.

With the redefinition of literature as something that only exists meaningfully in the mind of the reader, and with the redefinition of the literary work as a catalyst of mental events, comes a redefinition of the reader. No longer is the reader the passive recipient of those ideas that an author has planted in a text. "The reader is active," Rosenblatt had insisted. Fish makes the same point in "Literature in the Reader": "Reading is . . . something you do." Iser, in focusing critical interest on the gaps in texts, on the blanks that readers have to fill in, similarly redefines the reader as an active maker of meaning. Other reader-response critics define the reader differently. Wayne Booth uses the phrase the implied reader to mean the reader "created by the work." Iser also uses the term the implied reader but substitutes the educated reader for what Fish calls the intended reader.

Since the mid-1970s, reader-response criticism has evolved into a variety of new forms. Subjectivists like David Bleich, Norman Holland, and Robert Crosman have viewed the reader's response not as one "guided" by the text but rather as one motivated by deep-seated, personal, psychological needs.

Holland has suggested that, when we read, we find our own "identity theme" in the text by using "the literary work to symbolize and finally replicate ourselves. We work out through the text our own characteristic patterns of desire." Even Fish has moved away from reader-response criticism as he had initially helped define it, focusing on "interpretive strategies" held in common by "interpretive communities"—such as the one comprised by American college students reading a novel as a class assignment.

Fish's shift in focus is in many ways typical of changes that have taken place within the field of reader-response criticism—a field that, because of those changes, is increasingly being referred to as reader-oriented criticism. Recent reader-oriented critics, responding to Fish's emphasis on interpretive communities and also to the historically oriented perception theory of Hans Robert Jauss, have studied the way a given reading public's "horizons of expectations" change over time. Many of these contemporary critics view themselves as reader-oriented critics and as practitioners of some other critical approach as well. Certain feminist and gender critics with an interest in reader response have asked whether there is such a thing as "reading like a woman." Reading-oriented new historicists have looked at the way in which racism affects and is affected by reading and, more generally, at the way in which politics can affect reading practices and outcomes. Gay and lesbian critics, such as Wayne Koestenbaum, have argued that sexualities have been similarly constructed within and by social discourses and that there may even be a homosexual way of reading

[Adapted from *The Bedford Glossary of Critical and Literary Terms* by Ross Murfin and Supriya M. Ray. Copyright 1998 by Bedford Books.]

Here it is remarkable to note that 'Reader-Response criticism is really a collective term used to describe a number of critical theories that have emerged since the 1960's, all of which focus on the response of the reader to the text rather than the text itself as the source of meaning in a literary work. In Reader-Response criticism a text is viewed as a process that goes on in the mind of the reader rather than as a stable entity with a single "correct meaning". In this sense the reader actually participates in creating the text.

Regardless of their particular perspectives, all reader-response critics agree that since, in varying degrees, the individual reader creates the meanings of a text, there is no one correct meaning for a text. However, these critics offer differing opinions regarding how readers do in fact "read". Questions prominent to the studies of reader-response theorists are: What are the specific factors that influence the readers response? What meaning, if any, is inherent in the text? What power does the author or the text have in shaping the responses of the reader.

In fact, following scholars are considered the pioneers of this movement:

(a) Wolfgang Iser

(b) Norman Holland

(c) Jonathan Culler

(d) Harold Bloom

It is pertinent to note that if we keep in mind the New Critics' aversion to types of criticism which take precisely the reader's "affective" or emotional response into account (codified by Wimsatt and Beardsley's book *The Verbal Icon* as "the affective fallacy").

Stanley Fish's term "affective stylistics" (first described quite cautiously in the Appendix to Fish's early book on Milton) can be seen as a direct address—if not challenge—to the reign of New Critical terror.

Reminding us that the complexities of meaning the New Critics liked to derive from texts are hardly organic but rather after-the-fact and not-very-accurate RECONSTRUCTIONS of what literature is, Fish wrote criticism that followed the reader's path—working from left to right, and top to bottom.

Working in these lines, it became quickly obvious that at no point in the experience of reading is the "whole" work available to us, and thus we became free once again to work with longer texts (non-poems, for example) which had proved too unwieldy for New Criticism's need to "unify" the complex relations of the text. Of course, paying attention to "the reader" opens up a new Pandora's box. What "reader" are we referring to? The reader who read, say, a 19th - century novel when it first appeared, or a reader reading that same text today? Would two "critiques" of this same novel as it was read by various readers refer to the same text?

As we move our attention away from "the text itself" to what texts DO to certain readers at certain times, the text (literature) seems to have been demoted to some secondary consideration. Following the logic of the philosopher's question, "if the tree falls in the woods with no one around to hear it, does it make a sound?" reader-response critics by-pass the problem of "demoting" literature to second position by pointing out pragmatically that every text is read in some context, and to the degree that one's context (one's social, political, gendered pointed of view, as well as one's history or experience of the themes, forms, issues in the text in question or very generally, "literature" of any kind) informs what one understands from a text, a text's "meaning"—or even its existence—may vary with every reading. The question becomes not "what does the text mean?" but "what does it mean to whom, when, why, and to some extent "how?"

Thus, reader-response criticism can be written to answer any number of questions: HOW have different audiences interpreted this same text? WHAT does that tell us about those readers? about the text? Considering the text very minutely (not that the previous questions cannot be considered at the level of individual words or lines), HOW do the text's formal elements (see handout for New Criticism) work ONE by ONE, in ORDER, to create specific meanings for readers? Will every reader experience the same formal progression? Which relations will most readers miss without your scholarly help?

It is true, much good reader-response criticism has been done in what is known as "cultural studies," where the object of study is not only literature but "culture" as a whole, identifying through readers' responses to literature general cultural traits or "horizons of expectations" which reveal intellectual and/or ideological historical trends. Still, reader-response has been incorporated valuably into other critical methods, from the deconstruction of the 70s and 80s to the so-called "multi-cultural criticism" of the 1990s.

Rather than denoting a specific method or critical practice, reader-response criticism is a general term that refers to a number of different approaches of modern criticism and literary theory that focus on the responses of readers—either individual readers or readers belonging to specific categories, such as class, gender, ethnicity, etc.—to literary works, rather than on the works themselves considered as self-contained entities. It is not a single agreed theory so much as a shared concern with a set of problems involving the extent and nature of readers' contribution to the meanings of literary works, approached from various positions including those of structuralism and psychoanalysis, phenomenology, and hermeneutics.

The common factor is a shift from the description of texts in terms of their inherent properties to a discussion of the production of meanings within the reading process. In this regard, one might very roughly periodize the history of modern literary theory in three stages: a preoccupation with the author (Romanticism and the nineteenth century); and exclusive concern with the text (New Criticism); and a marked shift of attention to the reader over recent years. The reader has always been the most underprivileged of this trio—strangely, since without him or her there would be no literary texts at all.

Literary texts do not exist on bookshelves: they are processes of signification materialized only in the practice of reading. For literature to happen, the reader is quite as vital as the writer of the text. Where Formalism sought to sequester the text, purging all extraneous elements that might interfere with a pure perception of the words on the page, in recent decades a growing number of theoreticians now assert that there is no such thing as a pure, or neutral, encounter with a text. Every work is read—or "constructed"—differently.

Reader-Response criticism's emphasis on the construction of a text originates in the branch of philosophy called Phenomenology. Phenomenology deals with the "understanding of how things appear." The phenomenological idea of knowledge is that reality is to be found not in the external world itself, but rather in the mental *perception* of externals.

That is, all that we human beings can know—actual *knowledge*—is our collective and personal understanding of the world and our conclusions about it. As a consequence of the phenomenological concept, Reader-Response theory holds that the reader is a necessary third party in the author-text-reader relationship that constitutes the literary work. The work, in other words, is not fully crated until readers make a *transaction* with it by assimilating and *actualizing* it in the light of their own knowledge and experience. The representative questions of the theory are these: What does this work mean to me, in my present intellectual and moral makeup? What particular aspects of my life may help me understand and appreciate the work? How can the work improve my understanding and widen my insights? How can my increasing understanding help me understand the work more deeply? To what extent does a text circumscribes or directs a particular response? Which aspects of a text may be considered inherent and objective? And which are reader-constructed and thus subjective?

Also important to reader-response critics is an identification and description of the fundamental elements that inform a reader's response to a text The theory is that the free interchange or transaction that such questions bring about leads toward interest and growth so that readers may assimilate literary works and accept them as part of their lives.

In fact, Reader-Response theory recognizes the engagement of the reader within several contexts. Primarily, there is the immediate context of "concretization"—the sentence-by-sentence creation of text. By privileging the reader and focusing on the process of reading as, at least partially, a construction of the text, Reader-Response criticism has significantly contributed to discussions of issues such as the indeterminacy of meaning. Important contributions to this debate include Wolfgang Iser's *The Art of Reading* (1978), which sees readers as "actualizing" texts by filling in their "gaps" (logical and sequential holes that we must fill in) or "indeterminacies" (uncertainties) of meaning, and also Stanley Fish's *Is There a Text in this Class?* (1980), which gives the reader an even more active role as the text's true producer.

All of these approaches recognize that when we read a work, especially for the first time, we do not simply move our eyes back and forth and wait for images and concepts to announce themselves. We exert great energy, making surmises, arranging details into pictures, venturing and revising predictions. We stitch the clues together, closing up "gaps" and contending with "indeterminacies". We follow the text as if it were a shooting script for a film, trying to represent the action for ourselves on our mental screens. The larger context of Reader-Response criticism recognizes that readings of any given work are likely to differ from reader to reader, sometimes to an extraordinary extent. The reception is necessarily affected by the reader's age, gender, cultural background, personal life-experience, beliefs, and historical vantage.

A high school student reading a story about adulterous passion will have one set of reactions, a middle-aged man who has divorced over accusations of infidelity will have quite another. To see these two contexts at work, consider the opening sentences of Joyce Carol Oates's "The Lady with the Pet Dog":

> Strangers parted as if to make room for him.
>
> There he stood. He was there in the aisle, a few yards away, watching her.
>
> She leaned forward at once in her seat, her hand jerked up to her face as if to ward off a blow—but then the crowd in the aisle hid him, he was gone. She pressed both hands against her cheeks. He was not there, she had imagined him.

Obviously, if we have not read the story before, then we begin in complete ignorance (though a reader who knows Anton Chekhov's story of a similar title may find certain *expectations* aroused). We must turn ourselves into detectives, readers of clues. We must simultaneously comb the sentences carefully for information *and* allow our imaginations free play in conjuring up possibilities. What do we learn? That there is a he and a she; that they are in a public place (a cinema, a train, at a baseball game?); that she reacts with surprise (or alarm, or shock) when she catches sight of him.

The suppositions we make depend in part upon logical deductions, and in part upon our own disposition as readers. One reader straightaway concludes that these are old lovers; another thinks that it might be an estranged father and daughter. Most readers will probably assume that these are young or middle-aged adults, but there is no reason they could not be old people. And on and on we go, noting clues, making guesses, modifying the scenario. Each new sentence curtails certain possibilities, and opens others. An ever more specific picture takes shape. But specificity notwithstanding, there will never be two readers who can be said to have had an identical literary experience. The human response mechanisms are too subtle and various.

The issues that arise are obvious. If readings of the same work vary according to the reader, on what grounds are interpretations to be judged? Can there be a "right" or "best" reading of the work? Or is it finally a matter of what you say versus what I say? And whom can we say is truly the "author" of the text? Indeed, since the 1960s the concept of the "death of the author" has been a popular refrain in Reader-Response criticism.

In fact, Reader-Response criticism, in its various forms, has gained a considerable foothold in American and European literary criticism. Nevertheless, as may be expected, the literary community is hardly unanimous on the intent, practice, and utility of the methodology. On one end of the spectrum is the position taken by E. D. Hirsch in his book

Validity in Interpretation. Hirsch affirms that while we cannot know for certain what an author intended in the creation of a work, we are nonetheless constrained by our estimate of the probable intent. In other words, the reader who would argue that *Moby-Dick* is first and foremost a work of sexual symbolism would have to contend with the legacy of evidence (assembled by critics, biographers, and historians) that suggests that Melville's motives had more to do with religious allegory and with philosophical considerations of good and evil. Critics such as Stanley Fish, in his book *Is There a Text in This Class?*, offers the challenge of complete relativism. There is, Fish believes, no central or authorized reading of a text; there are only readings. The idea of constraining interpretation through an appeal to authorial intention is a chimera.

The only way that anything approaches consensus can be reached is through the application of common "interpretive strategies," such as are likely to be found in academic communities where readers agree to certain premises and procedures. A somewhat distinct line of Reader-Response theory which emphasizes historical investigation is represented by the Reception Theory of Hans Robert Jauss.

Stanley Fish, a prominent, contemporary literary theorist, is best known for his theory of reader-response criticism. Fish believed that the way in which a person will interpret a piece of literature is based on the reader's own personal experience with a text. With this type of criticism, literature can be seen as an art form in which the reader generates their own "performance" within the words. Fish decided that we will determine the meaning of a particular text based upon our own "interpretive communities." He asserts that Interpretive communities are made up of those who share interpretive strategies not for reading [in the conventional sense] but for writing texts, for constituting their properties and assigning their intentions (Lodge 304).

It is impossible to know our own interpretive community because even inquiring about it at all would be, as Fish says, an act of interpretation. Fish has been criticized for giving the reader too much control over a text. But he argues that

> They are ignored because the text is taken to be self-sufficient-everything is in it-and they are devalued because when they are not thought of at all, they are thought of as the disposable machinery of extraction (Lodge 296).

The control and meaning is always in the hands of the reader. In fact, a meaning will not even exist until the reader creates one. An example of this is baseball umpire, Bill Klem, who once waited a long time to call a particular pitch. The player asked him, impatiently, "Well, is it a ball or strike?" Klem's reply: "Sonny, it ain't nothing 'til I call it." What Fish is saying is, balls and strikes are not undeniable truths; rather, they "come into being only on the call of an umpire" (Stanley Fish).

If we attempt to apply Fish's theory of reader-response criticism to a piece of literature, it will be easier to understand how the theory actually works. In Raymond Carver's short story, Cathedral, the narrator appears to have it all- a lovely, sympathetic wife, enough food on the table to keep them happy, and the often underestimated gift of sight. But behind this satisfied exterior seems to lie a wealth of blindness, ignorance, jealousy, and a substance abuse problem that the narrator uses to escape the rigors of his reality. This is only one interpretation of the narrator. I view the narrator in this way based on my own personal experiences and what I have learned and extracted from reading the text. My interpretive community is "no more stable than texts because interpretive strategies are not natural or universal, but learned" (Lodge 304). On the other hand, I would say that the pitied blind man is really the one who should be envied. He appears to have a more accurate view of the world than most individuals with two healthy eyes. In addition, he has a closer relationship with the narrator's wife than the narrator does himself. The blind man's high came from his relationship with his own wife, and not mind-altering substances. But to the narrator's surprise, as the story progresses the narrator's eyes are opened to the blind man's world. This seems to be implied by the author, and yet another person may create a completely different interpretation than the one I have laid out here. The way in which I happen to interpret is not perfect, but also not wrong: The ability to interpret is not acquired; it is constitutive of being human. What is acquired are the ways of interpreting and those same ways can also be forgotten or supplanted, or complicated or dropped from favour ['no one reads that way anymore'] (Lodge 305).

On the outside, it would appear as if the narrator could see and the blind man was the one without sight. But on the contrary, the narrator was blinded by his own ignorance. Although he knew little about the blind visitor, the narrator passed judgment on him before even meeting him. "And his being blind bothered me. My idea of blindness came from the movies. In the movies, the blind moved slowly and never laughed" (Carver 186). Clearly it shows he had little knowledge about the blind when he says, "I'd always thought dark glasses were a must for the blind" or "I remembered reading somewhere that the blind didn't smoke" (190-191). This shows that we all have different perspectives based on our own experiences. The blind man and the narrator, if given the same exact text, would undoubtedly have a different experience with it because of their unique personalities. Unlike the narrator, the blind man keeps an open mind to new experiences and states that he is always learning something because learning never ends, thus demonstrating his lack of ignorance.

Later in the story, the blind man asks the narrator to describe the cathedrals for him. At this point he is introduced into the blind man's world and begins to see what it is like for him to have no sight. This allows the narrator to step outside of his own boundaries and free himself of the ignorant world in which he has been living. In the last few lines of the story, he realises for himself that he is free. "My eyes were still closed. I was in my house. I knew that. But I didn't feel like I was inside anything" (196). The idea that both of the main characters, the narrator and the blind man, see the world from different perspectives is much like Fish's theory. The narrator makes up one interpretive community while the blind man constitutes another. They interpret the "literary text" (in this case, the world with or without having sight) differently and are unable to see outside of their own interpretive community.

The binaries working within this story seem to point out that after taking a second glance, the blind man may be better off than was once thought. Robert possesses the physical blindness over seeing, but he has the gift of knowing and understanding people over the narrator's ignorance. He sees through the ignorance of the narrator and looks beyond it to help the young man understand the blind man's own world. In addition, Robert is more compassionate to the wife's feelings and uses people to enrich his life, compared to the narrator's unawareness of his wife's feelings and his hopeless escape into a lifestyle of drug use. Despite their world of differences, both the young man and the old man are able to see each other's point of view. The blind man is able to feel what a cathedral is like in the eyes of the narrator, and the narrator feels the struggle of trying to understand what other people can see. The blindness that separates the narrator from Robert in the beginning of the story brings them together in the end. But if one looks at it from a different angle, the story could simply be recalling a miniscule event in time with no "lesson to be learned." Not every story needs a lesson and the reader is the only one to determine whether one can be found from this or if it is simply just an entertaining recollection of a blind man's visit.

From this we can safely assume that the reader will see what he or she wants to see. Or maybe more accurately, he or she will see what we have been taught to see. Keeping this in mind, it is important, especially for a teacher, to be careful about preconceived notions in any given work. Someone teaching a piece of literature mustn't just assume that a student understands the same things the teacher does. It will mean much more to a person if they are given the opportunity to tackle the literature themselves and extract the meaning that they find rather than the meaning they were told to find. In Fish's own words,

The meaning they have is a consequence of their not being empty; for they include the making and revising of assumptions, the rendering and regretting of judgments, the coming to and abandoning of conclusions, the giving and withdrawing of approval, the specifying of causes, the asking of questions, the supplying of answers, the solving of puzzles" (Lodge 296).

So whether one believes my own interpretation of Carver's Cathedral, or something completely different, it all comes down to the reader. In other words, the actual act of reading is when the text obtains its meaning. Every question and every thought a reader has while reading a piece of literature is all connected to the meaning of the literature.

5

School of New Criticism

It is significant to mention first that the term "New Criticism" defines the critical theory that has dominated Anglo-American literary criticism for the past six-seven decades. Its method of close reading and emphasis on the text provided a corrective to fuzzy biographical criticism and subjective enthusiasm, but for many teachers in North America and Britain, it became not a method of criticism, but criticism itself. Alternatives to its interpretive strategies have until recently been regarded with deep suspicion.

It is important to understand the precepts of the New Criticism as critical positions and not as the truth about literature before looking at other strategies. The New Criticism is a type of formalist literary criticism that reached its height during the 1940s and 1950s and that received its name from John Crowe Ransom's 1941 book *The New Criticism.*

New Critics treat a work of literature as if it were a self-contained, self-referential object. Rather than basing their interpretations of a text on the reader's response, the author's stated intentions, or parallels between the text and historical contexts (such as author's life), New Critics perform a close reading, concentrating on the relationships within the text that give it its own distinctive character or form. New Critics emphasize that the structure of a work should not be divorced from meaning, viewing the two as constituting a quasi-organic unity. Special attention is paid to repetition, particularly of images or symbols, but also of sound effects and rhythms in poetry. New Critics especially appreciate the use of literary devices, such as irony, to achieve a balance or reconciliation between dissimilar, even conflicting, elements in a text.

Because it stresses close textual analysis and viewing the text as a carefully crafted, orderly object containing formal, observable patterns, the New Criticism has sometimes been called an "objective" approach to literature. New Critics are more likely than certain other critics to believe and say that the meaning of a text can be known objectively. For instance, reader-response critics see meaning as a function either of each reader's experience or of the norms that govern a particular interpretive community, and deconstructors argue that texts mean opposite things at the same time.

In fact, the foundations of the New Criticism were laid in books and essays written during the 1920s and 1930s by I. A. Richards (*Practical Criticism* [1929]), William Empson (*Seven Types of Ambiguity* [1930]), and T. S. Eliot ("The Function of Criticism" [1933]). The approach was significantly developed later, however, by a group of American poets and critics, including R. P. Blackmur, Cleanth Brooks, John Crowe Ransom, Allen Tate, Robert Penn Warren, and William K. Wimsatt. Although we associate the New Criticism with certain principles and terms—such as *affective fallacy* (the notion that the reader's response is relevant to the meaning of a work) and *intentional fallacy* (the notion that the author's intention determines the work's meaning)—

the New Critics were trying to make a cultural statement rather than to establish a critical dogma. Generally southern, religious, and culturally conservative, they advocated the inherent value of literary works (particularly of literary works regarded as beautiful art objects) because they were sick of the growing ugliness of modern life and contemporary events. Some recent theorists even link the rising popularity after World War II of the New Criticism (and other types of formalist literary criticism such as the Chicago School) to American isolationism. These critics tend to view the formalist tendency to isolate literature from biography and history as symptomatic of American fatigue with wider involvements.

Whatever the source of the New Criticism's popularity (or the reason for its eventual decline), its practitioners and the textbooks they wrote were so influential in American academia that the approach became standard in college and even high school curricula through the 1960s and well into the 1970s.

[Adapted from *The Bedford Glossary of Critical and Literary Terms* by Ross Murfin and Supriya M. Ray. Copyright 1998 by Bedford Books.]

Remarkably, the New Criticism posits that every text is *autonomous*. History, biography, sociology, psychology, author's intention and reader's private experience are all irrelevant. Any attempt to look at the author's relationship to a work is called "*the intentional fallacy*." Any attempt to look at the reader's individual response is called "*the affective fallacy*." Primarily 'New Criticism' is an approach to literature which was developed by a group of American critics, most of whom taught at southern universities during the years following the World War I.

The New Critics wanted to avoid impressionistic criticism , which risked being shallow and arbitrary, and social/

historical approaches which might easily be subsumed by other disciplines. Thus, they attempted to systematize the study of literature, to develop an approach which was centered on the rigorous study of the text itself. They were given their name by John Crowe Ransom, who describes the new American formalists in his *The New Criticism* (1941).

New Critical Formalism

New Criticism is distinctly formalist in character . It stresses close attention to the internal characteristics of the text itself, and it discourages the use of external evidence to explain the work. The method of New Criticism is foremost a close reading, concentrating on such formal aspects as rhythm, meter, theme, imagery, metaphor, etc. The interpretation of a text shows that these aspects serve to support the structure of meaning within the text.

The aesthetic qualities praised by the New Critics were largely inherited from the critical writings of Samuel Taylor Coleridge. Coleridge was the first to elaborate on a concept of the poem as a unified, organic whole which reconciled its internal conflicts and achieved some final balance or harmony.

In his magnum opus *The Well-Wrought Urn* (1947), Cleanth Brooks integrates these considerations into the New Critical approach. In interpreting canonical works of poetry, Brooks constantly analyzes the devices with which they set up opposing these and then resolve them. Through the use of "ironic contrast" and "ambivalence" , the poet is able to create internal paradoxes which are always resolved. Under close New Critical analysis, the poem is shown to be a hierarchical structure of meaning, of which one correct reading can be given. Although the New Critics do not assert that the meaning of a poem is inconsequential, they reject approaches which view the poem as an attempt at representing the "real world."

They justify the avoidance of discussion of a poem's content through the doctrine of the "Heresy of Paraphrase," which is also described in *The Well-Wrought Urn*. Brooks asserts that the meaning of a poem is complex and precise, and that any attempt to paraphrase it inevitably distorts or reduces it. Thus, any attempt to say what a poem means is heretical, because it is an insult to the integrity of the complex structure of meaning within the work.

In *The Verbal Icon* (1954), William Wimsatt and Monroe Beardsley describe two other fallacies which are encountered in the study of literature. The "Intentional Fallacy" is the mistake of attempting to understand the author's intentions when interpreting a literary work. Such an approach is fallacious because the meaning of a work should be contained solely within the work itself, and attempts to understand the author's intention violate the autonomy of the work.

The "Affective Fallacy" is the mistake of equating a work with its emotional effects upon an audience. The new critics believed that a text should not have to be understood relative to the responses of its readers; its merit (and meaning) must be inherent.

As such the New Critics privileged poetry over other forms of literary expression because the saw the poem as the purest exemplification of the literary values which they upheld. However, the techniques of close reading and structural analysis of texts have also been applied to fiction, drama, and other literary forms. These techniques remain the dominant critical approach in many modern literature courses. Since New Criticism is such a rigid and structured program for the study of literature, it is open to criticism on many fronts. First, in its insistence on excluding external evidence, New Criticism disqualifies many possibly fruitful perspectives for understanding texts, such as historicism, psychoanalysis, and Marxism. Since New Criticism aims at finding one "correct" reading, it also ignores the ambiguity of language and the active nature of the perception of meaning described by poststructuralists.

Finally, it can even be perceived as elitist, because it excludes those readers who lack the background for arriving at the "correct" interpretation. However, defenders of New Criticism might remind us that this approach is meant to deal with the poem on its own terms. While New Criticism may not offer us a wide range of perspectives on texts, it does attempt to deal with the text as a work of literary art and nothing else.

New Criticism argues that each text has a *central unity*. The responsibility of the reader is to discover this *unity*. The reader's job is to *interpret* the text, telling in what ways each of its parts contributes to the *central unity*. The primary interest is in *themes*. A text is spoken by a *persona* (narrator or speaker) who expresses an *attitude* which must be defined and who speaks in a *tone* which helps define the attitude: *ironic*, *straightforward* or *ambiguous*. Judgements of the value of a text must be based on the *richness of the attitude* and the *complexity* and the *balance* of the text. The key phrases are *ambivalence, ambiguity, tension, irony and paradox.*

The reader's analysis of these elements lead him to an examination of the *themes.* A work is good or bad depending on whether the *themes* are *complex* and whether or not they contribute to the *central, unifying theme*. The more *complex* the themes are and the more closely they contribute to a central theme *(unity)* the better the work.

Usually, the New Critics define their themes as *oppositions*: Life and death, good and evil, love and hate, harmony and strife, order and disorder, eternity and time, reality and appearance, truth and falsehood, emotion and reason, simplicity and complexity, nature and art. The analysis of a text is an exercise in showing how all of its parts contribute to a *complex* but single (*unified*) statement about human problems.

The method the reader must use is "*close analysis*." The reader must look at the words, the syntax, the images, the structure (usually, "*the argument*"). The words must be understood to be *ambiguous*. (The more possible meanings a word has, the richer the *ambiguity*. The reader should search out *irony* (*ambiguous* meaning) and *paradox* (contradictory meaning, hence also *ambiguity*). The reader must discover *tensions* in the work. These will be the results of *thematic oppositions,* though they may also occur as *oppositions* in imagery: light versus dark, beautiful versus ugly, graceful versus clumsy. The *oppositions* may also be in the words chosen: concrete versus abstract, energetic versus placid.

The reader must guard against two evils, *stock responses* (autumn should not make the reader sad unless the poem directs sadness at the thought of autumn) and *idiosyncratic* (affective) responses. (Lush grass should not make the reader think of cows however often he or she has seen cows in lush grass unless the poem clearly directs the reader to associate cows and lush grass).

Main Characteristics

New Criticism Occurred Partially in Response to:

(a) Biographical Criticism that understood art primarily as a reflection of the author's life (sometimes to the point that the texts themselves weren't even read!).

(b) Competition for dollars and students from sciences in academia.

(c) New forms of mass literature and literacy, an increasingly consumerist society and the increasingly visible role of commerce, mass media, and advertising in people's lives.

New Criticism Tends to Emphasize:

(a) The text as an autotelic artifact, something complete with in itself, written for its own sake, unified in its form and not dependent on its relation to the author's life or intent, history, or anything else.

(b) The formal and technical properties of work of art.

Assumptions:

(a) The critic's job is to help us appreciate the technique and form of art and the mastery of the artist.

(b) That the "Western tradition" is an unbroken, internally consistent set of artistic conventions and traditions going back to ancient Greece and continuing up to this day, and that good art participates in and extends these traditions. Similarly, criticism's job is to uphold these traditions and protect them from encroachments from commercialism, political posturing, and vulgarity.

(c) That there are a finite number of good texts (a notion now often tied to "the canon" of texts traditionally taught). The closer that a text comes to achieving an ideal unity, where each element contributes to an overall effect, the more worthy it is of discussion.

(d) Studying literature is an intrinsically edifying process. It hones the sensibilities and discrimination of students and sets them apart from the unreflective masses.

(e) That "cream rises," and works of genius will eventually be "vindicated by posterity."

(f) That there is a firm and fast distinction between "high" art and popular art.

(g) That good art reflects unchanging, universal human issues, experiences, and values.

(h) Technical definitions and analyses are vital to understanding literature. The text's relationship to a world that extends beyond it is of little interest.

Criticisms Sometimes Made of New Criticism:

(a) That it's emphases on technique, unity of effect, and the autotelic status of art works best on the lyric poem, but has problems with larger, more historically recent forms like the novel.

(b) That it makes the Western tradition out to be more unified than it is by ignoring diversity and contradictory forces within it, and more monadic than it is by ignoring the exchange between non-western and western cultures (Aristotle, for instance, central to new critical concepts, was introduced to medieval Europe via the Islamic world).

(c) That artistic standards of value are variable and posterity is fickle. Particular pieces of art are viewed as important because they do important cultural work, represent values that segments of the culture (say editors and English professors) believe are of vital import, or help us understand our history.

(d) That the values New Critics celebrated were neither unchanging nor universal, but instead reflected their own, historically and experientially specific concerns, values and ambitions.

(e) That context is just as important as form to understanding a work of art.

Main Concepts

The notion of ambiguity is an important concept within New Criticism; several prominent New Critics have been enamored above all else with the way that a "text" can display multiple simultaneous meanings. In the 1930s, I.A. Richards borrowed Sigmund Freud's term "overdetermination" (which Louis Althusser would later revive in Marxist political theory) to refer to the multiple meanings which he believed were always simultaneously present in language. To Richards, claiming that a work has "One And Only One True Meaning" is an act of superstition (The Philosophy of Rhetoric, 39).

In 1954, William K. Wimsatt and Monroe Beardsley published an essay entitled "The intentional fallacy", in which they argued strongly against any discussion of an author's intention, or "intended meaning."

For Wimsatt and Beardsley, the words on the page were all that mattered; importation of meanings from outside the text was quite irrelevant, and potentially distracting. This became a central tenet of New Criticism. As New Critics admit no information other than that contained in the "text" which they study, no proper New Critical investigation should include biographical information on the author. Furthermore, studying a passage of prose or poetry in New Critical style requires careful, exacting scrutiny of the passage itself, since after all no other information source is permissable - a rigid attitude for which the New Critics were often scolded in later times: their immanent readings may also be taken as a conservative attempt to isolate the text as a solid, immutable entity, shielded from any external influences. Nevertheless, immanent reading or close reading is now a fundamental tool of literary criticism. Such a reading places great emphasis on the particular over the general, paying close attention to individual words, syntax, and the order in which sentences and ideas unfold as they are read. They look at, for example, theme, imagery, metaphor, rhythm, meter, etc.

Apart from the names mentioned above, other prominent New Critical figures include the following:

- T.S. Eliot
- F.R. Leavis
- William Empson
- Robert Penn Warren
- John Crowe Ransom
- Cleanth Brooks

Not all the thoughts and works stemming from these individuals fall within the New Critical camp. For example, Eliot's relationship with New Criticism was rather complicated. In 1956, he claimed that he failed "to see any school of criticism which can be said to derive from myself," referring to the New Criticism as "the lemon-squeezer school of criticism." He never understood the ways that the New Critics had come to interpret *The Waste Land*, noting in "Thoughts after Lambeth" (1931) that "when I wrote a poem called *The Waste Land* some of the more approving critics said that I had expressed the 'disillusionment of a generation,' which is nonsense. I may have expressed for them their own illusion of being disillusioned, but that did not form part of my intention." A New Critic might respond that paying Eliot any mind would fall into the "intentional fallacy".

Empson, too, attempted to distance himself from the New Criticism, and was particularly critical of Wimsatt. His last book, *Using Biography*, was largely an attempt to refute the doctrine of the "intentional fallacy."

Satire

The New Criticism is one of the concepts satirized in Isaac Asimov's short story "The Immortal Bard" (1954), in which a physics professor learns the secret of time travel and tries bringing prominent individuals from the past into the present. After failing with notable scientists like Archimedes and Galileo, who are not adaptable enough to cope with 20th-century society, he tries retrieving William Shakespeare, who he hopes can understand human beings of any time.

Shakespeare becomes ravenous to learn what posterity made of his work, so the professor enrolls him in a colleague's evening-extension class on Shakespeare, with less than stellar results. "God ha' mercy!" cries Asimov's Shakespeare. "What cannot be racked from words in five centuries? One could wring, methinks, a flood from a damp clout!" No exaggeration, *New Criticism* was an influential 'school' of southern-based Formal Criticism that reigned over American Poetry Criticism (APC) from the mid 1930s until about 1970.

It was highly political in nature, even as it ever claimed to disdain politics in favor of 'true' or 'high' art- of which poetry was the 'highest'- a rare truth the NCs* were to feast on. Some of its adherents were: John Crowe Ransom, Allen Tate, R.P. Blackmur, Robert Penn Warren, I.A. Richards, William Empsom, Cleanth Brooks, William Wimsatt, and Monroe Beardsley.

Of import to note is that all but RPW were literary mediocrities whose own works, in essence, necessitated their place as critics- or lovers of literature- rather than producers of it. Some key works associated with NC were CB's & RPW's *Understanding Poetry*, WE's *Seven Types of Ambiguity*, IAR's *Practical Criticism*, and CB's *The Well Wrought Urn* (the most well-known and respected of the tomes). They were given their collective sobriquet, however, by JCR in his own *The New Criticism* (1941).

The NCs claimed to want to avoid *Impressionistic Criticism*, which they saw as vapid, *Social & Historical Criticism*, which they saw as formless. But, in large measure, politically, it was their immanent Conservatism that responded most violently to *Biographical Criticism*: the theory that art is primarily a reflection of the writer's life, and the only way to even begin to come to grips with art is to study intimately, and in detail, the artist's life. NCs failed to see that a good critic should incorporate all these critical aspects to form a good critical base, and then pick & choose which approach (or approaches) to apply to any given work. Alas, like those before and after, they did not, and eventually their own limited purview proved after their critical undoing.

Let us briefly peep at some NC peeves and desires: NC sees the text as an *autotelic* (a word that was a NC fave) artifact; it is something autonomous, written for its own

---

* Abbreviations are given at the end of the chapter.

sake, unified (an aspect never fully fleshed out in any logical or coherent way by the NCs) in form, and independent of the writer's life, intent, etc. In fact three, of the major tenets of NC were:

Self-sufficiency: the poem should be independent of biography, historical content or effect on the reader– which were called the *Intentional*, *Historical* & *Affective* fallacies.

Unity: the poem should be a coherent whole- a very traditional view, albeit limited.

Complexity: though to be the central element of poetry.

NC believed it was the *reader's duty* to seek this out in the art. Violations of these tenets were examples of the *Intentional Fallacy*- that the artist's intent is the primary value of the art. The NC damning of this canard is perhaps the lone good idea to survive from NC. Its almost forgotten corollary was the *Affective Fallacy* — or how an individual reader reacts to a work of art is the primary thing. That no two people will react in similar ways (a good thing) is impossible- well.... Another ax of the NCs was the *Heresy of Paraphrase*, which CB railed against in *The Well-Wrought Urn*. He states that the meaning of a poem is complex and precise, and any attempt to paraphrase it inevitably distorts and/or reduces it: i.e.- any attempt to say what a poem *means* is heretical, because it insults the complexity and integrity of the work. Lost to him was that the HOP irreducibly obviates the very act of criticism! Wherefore, then, the critic?

NC assumed the critic's job is to help appreciate technique and form in art- not state what the art means or is. This is another example of NC common sense. But, then they veered wrongly in their extensions from this plinth. It also viewed Western Tradition as an unbroken, internally consistent set of artistic formulae dating from Classical Greece and continuing into futurity. The NCs defined the themes inherent in all good or great art as eternal oppositions: life/death, good/evil, love/hate, truth/lie, emotion/reason, etc. Ambiguity, therefore, is thus held out as a paragon: the more meanings a word has, the richer the ambiguity- and the meaning. The reader's job is to search out irony (ambiguous meaning) and paradox (contradictory meaning).

This gives a work its dramatic tension, which causes an art appreciator to want to delve even more deeply. Two other things NCs railed against were *stock responses* (i.e.- someone's departure should not make the reader sad unless the poem elicits sadness at the departure- this is so flimsy and personalized a rationale that to debunk it would waste both our times), and *idiosyncratic (or* affective*) responses* (i.e.- milk should not make the reader think of cows no matter how direct the connection is- the poem should be the vehicle for the connection. No doubt, an early hero of the NCs was poet Samuel Taylor Coleridge and his criticism, which was among the 1st set of dicta to elaborate on the poem as being a unified, organic whole, and whose purpose was forging some internal harmony- in the poem, itself. A more coeval hero was T.S. Eliot and his mounds of self-centered gibberish.

Foremost in the gibber his *Objective Correlative* (OC) — a term to identify an image, action, or situation in a literary text in which the reader's response is suddenly focused, and from which the rest of the art either will fail or succeed depending on its fidelity to that focused thing. Basically TSE held that an artwork failed if it did not meet certain 'objective' standards. The OC failed, basically, as a critical tool because TSE saw himself as the sole arbiter of 'objectivity'- got that nice piece of intellectual contortion?

In a famously idiotic case in point, TSE declared *Hamlet* a failure because Hamlet's character development did not seem to usher forth from the specific dramatic situations of the play. This theory was of bizarre interest to NCs, for they believed an OC provided that focal point of the 'organic unity' for the text. Got it [trey]? These were all principles believed to have descended from Hellenistic times. They formed a (or rather, *The*) *Western Tradition*. The NC stated that good art participates in and extends this tradition. Also, the critic's job is to uphold that tradition and save it from life's abasements and vulgarisms whatsoever..

To a NC the closer a text comes to achieving 'unity', where each element contributes to the overall art, the more worthy it is of *being* art. High art is the province of NC- not pop art; for high art reflects unchanging, universally human issues, ethics, and experiences passed down through the ages. In short, the best art is a totality unto itself. This myopic insularity has since been twisted and led to the wild PC Elitism which inversely declares that art is not art *unless* it engages politics at every turn, and avoids hermetic insularity. Both extremes are laughable, and easily seen as such to the sane reader and art afficionado.

No doubt, NC's ills were plentiful. Its emphasis on technique, unity of effect, and that damnable autotelic status works best only in evaluating the simpler structures of lyric poetry. More complex poetry- say of a Hart Crane, or W.B. Yeats, or poetry that does depend (to a degree) on a historic, personal, or something-specific aspect, or most prose, is largely immune to such simplistic evaluations. Another valid point against NC is that it makes the *Western Canon* seem far more unified than it is by ignoring diversity & contradictions as well as isolating the Canon from the rest of the art of humanity. The changing taste of societies is also posited as a flaw in NC. Recall the damnations heaped upon Walt Whitman & Charles Baudelaire, in the 1850s, for perversion & evil. Yet, now we recognize them as the American & European pillars to poetic modernity (not Modernism).

Despite these often manifest failings NC has its defenders to this day. In a famed retort called *The Attack on Literature* Rene Wellek charged that the major accusations leveled at the NC are false. RW answered the four major retorts against the NCs:

1. NCs were formalists with no interest in the humanity of literature.
2. NCs ignore the historical context of literature.
3. NCs bastardize literature to a science.
4. the NCs 'close reading' & 'unity' are pedagogical devices.

RW asserts NC has not been vilified because it is wrong (although the bulk of it is) but for its correctness. RW believed that NCs were seen as bastions of Old Boy Elitism- and they were. Had they not been the reaction against their ideas may have modulated into a sane critical middle, rather than the hysterical PC Elitism which suffocates most contemporary criticism.

1. The basic thrust of this tenet is that the artwork is an inviolate thing unto itself. There are plenty of times that that is manifestly and undeniably true but only to an extent limitation. Here is where we encounter one of NC's greatest ills: absolutism; the same malady that has afflicted the NCs latter-day counterparts- the PC Elitists. Logically and obviously since words connote and denote things other than

the written word, there is no way a poem could ever be 100% self-sustaining. But, it can come close to this on occasions. Whether this is desirable, or indicates any greater success rate in art, is a tangential question. Is the art all to itself? Does a poem fail merely because it is not self-sustaining?

2. *Meaning & structure are one* . That's what the 2nd NC tenet boils down to. Also, a good critic must be able to notice & explicate this basic organic unity, or synthesis of meaning & structure. Well, we do want critics to act as intermediaries & break down some things within a work of art. It's the essence of a critics job- that, & to state whether the poem does or does not succeed in doing so.

3. The next bit of mumbo-jumbo from the NCs is that images & lingual elements contribute to the organic unity of the text. Well, yes & no. Yes- in the *Duh!* aspect that, of course, poems contain images and lingual devices- it's literature, after all! But the answer is also no, in that the NCs meant that these things are fundamental to the poem's unity- or, ala tenet one, they help hermetically seal the poem off from the rest of the cosmos.

4. T.S. Eliot's *Objective Correlative* nonsense, which posits singular responses to singular stimuli, is not really a NC posit- it actually predates NC- yet the NCs clung to it as if it were- in spirit, if not word. Things must logically outflow from something else, this is the basic dictum. This provides 'thematic unity'- another highfalutin', yet ultimately intellectually sterile phrase. But how often does life (& especially our personal emotional dramas) veer from logic? The OC was also, basically, TSE's biases

writ large, & self-justified. The whole thing was totally & utterly dependent upon some objective source clairvoyantly knowing a character's or artist's intent. See? It is this kind of pretzel logic that hallmarks NC. OC is, fundamentally, antithetical to the dictum & values the NCs championed- most specifically the *Intentional Fallacy*.

5. Every part of the text contributes to the meaning of the text. I.e.- everything in a poem matters- *Duh! [Deux!]* What the NCs meant was that they wanted a justification for every iota in a poem. While not a bad suggestion, off the top, there is 1 serious drawback that any great artist will recognize: it kills the element of 'magic'- for lack of a better word. There is that alchemical reaction that all great art produces, a synergy beyond description, that one just has to accept, lest fall into a delirium of explicative froth that says nothing & lasts little longer than the second it takes to read it. One can decode all the sources & meanings, but- ultimately- there will be that bit of ineffable oomph that separates the technically excellent from the flat-out great.

The basic problem with NC was that NC was so vague in its conjectures that it really had no validity. Then, again, any notion/theory of art that is so ironclad (& is not any theory for art such?) is bound to suffocate the art it purports to value. This schism between what they declared they valued & what they produced (especially, since the NCs, as poets, were notoriously mediocre-bad) provided ample fodder to damn them well. But it also provided the loam for the dastardly PC Elitists to take root, with their equally dull & simpleminded tautologies in the opposite direction. As with the NCs, PCEs are equally simple-minded in their declarations that all art MUST serve the betterment of Mankind (or, as they prefer- Humanity) politically. That the act of art, of any sort (& if of quality), by its nature seems to better its observer, seems to have slipped by PCEs' grasp.

But their silly dicta got its start totally in the NC's prior contra-assertions. Yet, these 2 thought systems not only followed each other in time, & are opposing, but NC- in a way- actually melded in to PCE, even as it spawned it. It is not such a great journey, after all, between absolutisms- how often has the addict become the born-again religiot? Another aspect about NC should be evident from this essay's approach vis-à-vis other essays you might read about NC. I've paraphrased & condensed most of the NC ideas, rather than drone on & on, quoting bloated passages filled with attempts at critical sleight-of-hand which says nothing. Most of NC writing was so dull & turgid that most essays about it simply rehash the top 8-10 quotable excerpts. While that shortens the time required to produce an essay it also shortchanges a discerning reader- thus my paraphrasings.

The major point to be reckoned is this: NC had some definite virtues- its assorted *Fallacies*- & some ludicrous demerits- the *Heresy of Paraphrase*- but it was the inability to provide depth & flexibility to their viewpoints, either way, that fossilized the cult, & proved their undoing. A demise that is proof that good & bad tend to get their respective dues over time- at least 99% of the time. Yes, some of their posits were common sensical, but all too often they did not adhere to their own strictures- either in criticism or, more tellingly, in their prose & poetry. Why? Because it fundamentally makes no sense to so suffocate & delimit one's art. The NCs' writerly side rebelled against their critical cast- & rightly so! This, in itself, gives some pretty strong proof that the whole NC movement was politically, not artistically, based.

Further evidence can be mounted by showing the lack of poetic corpuses addressed by the NCs from black, female, & other minority poets of their day. NCs also refused to embrace their own aims, which we've noted was evidence of an internal schism- but also they never even attempted to push their aims to their logical ends, & raise the bar higher- none of the five poets whose poems grace this essay were ever remotely associated with NC, yet each poem could be admired & damned by NC standards. Ah, the dread complexity of being a good critic! It's so much easier when you have an –Ism to grind! Speaking of which- let's primp the bow that ties NC with its bastard spawn PCE. 1st off, let's posit why NC thrived 50 years ago but PCE thrives today. The 1st notable thing about the two systems (internally) is that, aside from their seeming 180° political sentiments, the 2 –isms are not that different: they share absolutist stances politically, a rigidity of artistic mindset, that will soon date PCE to the millennium as easily as NC dates to the mid-20th Century, and an overriding simplemindedness that refuses to acknowledge complexities beyond their limited fields. As for the external let me reiterate a point whose consequences have never been fully addressed in the Academic halls nor the 'Outsider' poetic worlds: 50 years ago, in a given year, there were perhaps about 50 outlets for a published poem to appear.

Nowadays there are 100-200 times that amount of venues. Rigidity ruled when there were fewer outlets. Laxity is king when outlets are plentiful. The net effect is that PCEs' stance is, to a large degree, a justification for the need to simply fill the space. NCs' stance was, in large measure, a justification for the need to screen out the riff-raff. However, by percentage, the rate of good poems/poets per 100 is about the same. The difference is purely access related.

Critics of the Old New Criticism

Amidst the pugnacious practitioners of academic literary studies, who agree among themselves on almost nothing, there is one consensus: the New Criticism that is, the *old* New Criticism associated with the stalwarts like T. S. Eliot, Allen Tate, John Crowe Ransom, Cleanth Brooks- *that* New Criticism is over, finished, defunct. What is more, this shift in critical fashion is widely perceived not merely as a routine scholarly development, but as a great liberation, the lifting of an onerous burden-as if literature professors had somehow been bearing the entire weight of *The World's Body* upon their shoulders, or as if textbooks like *Understanding Poetry* and *Sound and Sense* constituted a form of bondage or a grand imposition on the credulity of college English teachers. Never again, they seem to proclaim in the smug tone of someone conscious of having recovered righteousness, will we submit to that unhistorical formalism or subject our students to the cultural elitism of canonical works.

Everywhere the atmosphere of classrooms and library bookstack carrels thickens with an almost palpable fog of sanctimony. Now, considered objectively, this is a very strange state of affairs. The New Criticism flourished during the thirties, forties, and fifties and remained formidably influential even through the sixties when its dominance over literary study was everywhere challenged. This was the time when the study of literature in the modern vernacular languages was established once and for all in the curriculum of American universities; English and

American literature, in particular, assumed a central role in undergraduate education and became a major focus of graduate training and academic scholarship.

It is not too much to say that the activities of the New Critics and their followers staked out the literary field and defined the university environment in which the revisionists now operate. If the movement known as New Criticism had never occurred, it is improbable that the position and activities of literary scholars would be of much significance in the contemporary university. Whatever shortcomings may have emerged in the New Critical program, whatever defects or excesses of method or substance may have stood in need of correction, one would expect the beneficiaries of the achievements of the New Criticism to regard it with at least an affectionate tolerance.

Hence the current attitude among the denizens of English and foreign language departments, which ranges from severe disapproval to scathing repudiation, is more than a little surprising. It is still more surprising when one realizes that the condemnation of the New Criticism is founded on misconceptions, if not outright deceptions. In *The Attack on Literature* Rene Wellek has demonstrated conclusively that the major accusations leveled at the New Criticism are "baseless."

Wellek lists four common allegations against the New Critics: (1) that they are "formalists" with no interest in the human content of literature, (2) that they ignore the historical context of literature, (3) that they reduce literature to an abstract science, and (4) that the "close reading" practiced by the New Critics is a mere pedagogical device, an American version of *explication du texte*, fit only for undergraduates in provincial colleges. These allegations "can be so convincingly refuted by an appeal to the texts," says Wellek, "that I wonder whether current commentators have ever actually read the writings of the New Critics."

In fact, we may corroborate Wellek's suspicion: more of the "current commentators" have probably read deconstructionists like Frank Lentricchia or Jonathan Culler inveighing against the "formalism" of the New Critics than have actually read the New Critics themselves. The New Criticism has not been vilified because of its errors and vices, which doubtless afflict it as they do all things human, but has rather been scourged for its virtues. It is not too much to say that the New Critics have been the victims of what is called in counterespionage circles a campaign of disinformation.

The charge that comes up again and again in current discussions of the New Criticism is "formalism," "an opprobrious term," Wellek notes, "first used by Marxists against a group of Russian scholars in the twenties." Later the contemporary academic scene is steeped in Marxism (albeit often unconscious), and "formalism" is the inevitable dismissive term applied to the New Criticism, meant to suggest that the New Critics were concerned about literature only as an objectified verbal configuration, devoid of human significance and cut off from the realities of history.

If this were true, however, the New Criticism would be a threat to no one and would hardly provoke such hostility. The fact is that the New Criticism is condemned not because it treats the literary work as an empty form remote from history, but because it understands literary form and the relation between meaning and history in a way that undermines the Gnostic materialism characteristic of most contemporary ideologies.

At their best the New Critics stress not "mere form," but form as a structure of significance, an embodiment of human experience. By capturing human experience in words and isolating it from the flow of time-in other words, by creating aesthetic distance-the literary work of art furnishes unique and invaluable access to that experience. Thus, far from evincing a lack of interest in history, this view of literature strengthens the relation between the author and history by treating the literary work as a portal into the meaning of the ceaseless currents of the historical process.

Precisely insofar as it transcends the particular biases and individual purposes of its author, as well as the immediate expectations and assumptions of its readers along with the political and socioeconomic conditions of its era, the work of literature is a testimony to the inherent significance and purpose of human life. In proposing such an understanding of literature, the New Critics are not aping either the mathematical or the empirical modes of scientific knowledge; they are, rather, urging us to recognize alternative ways of knowing that comprehend a broader spectrum of reality. Finally, although it seems quixotic in this day and age to stigmatize as being a mere pedagogical device a critical method that teaches students to read and write, it is also true that the New Criticism-at least when it has not been abused-provides far more than a mere repertoire of verbal techniques.

In regarding the literary work of art as a subsistent structure of meaning-that is, in granting it, in some sense, an independent ontological status—the New Criticism establishes the study of literature as a principal means of handing on the culture of Western civilization. This is an educational undertaking of crucial importance. Now all of this is anathema to the dominant ideologies of the contemporary university. If the language and tone of the current academic setting are broadly Marxist, it is helpful to think about the radical predilection of the modern world in general in terms of the Gnostic paradigm formulated by Eric Voegelin in *The New Science of Politics*.

Gnostic dualism both despises the material creation and sees it as decisive in forming the character and conduct of human beings: the evil that men do is not attributable to the sinful will of the individual; it is rather an intrinsic and hence inevitable result of physical existence. At the same time, the Gnostics also believe that those who attain to a special knowledge, or gnosis, become part of an elite group who rise above the condition and destiny of ordinary mortals. Combine this with empirical science and technology, and the result looks very much like modern Marxism: the entirety of human reality, including the "superstructure" of culture and society, derives from the material forces and conditions of the economic "infrastructure."

Yet again, there is the elite, now comprising radical intellectuals and politicians, able somehow to escape the fateful determinism of material life and, in the wake of the industrial revolution, forge a utopia in which all aspirations are realized, all desires gratified. Obviously only a small minority of contemporary academics would expressly subscribe to an overt Marxism, and few (at least of my acquaintance) could even identify Gnosticism with any confidence; nevertheless, a set of analogous attitudes permeates a broad range of the academic community, and the influence of Marxism and associated ideologies has become especially notable on literature faculties in recent years. It is evident in a pervasive malaise in the academic world-a discontent with the limits embedded in the actual nature of human reality-and in the concomitant, if contradictory, preoccupation with the autonomy of the individual and the exaltation of his subjective longings. The literary critic in this frame of mind will be inclined to approach a story or a poem or a play less as an imaginative rendering or revelation of the structure of reality than as an open-ended vehicle for the free play of individual fantasies.

Now it is not hard to see why the New Criticism, with its insistence on the objective integrity of the literary work, would hold little appeal for the contemporary academic ideologue. At its inception the New Criticism was, among other things, a reaction against the impressionistic "appreciations" of literature by genteel dabblers, against the late Romantic worship of the author as prophet or genius, and against a school of literary history that buried individual works under a mass of trivial details about influences and fashions while altogether eschewing the serious task of critical judgment. The New Criticism was, above all, an assertion that a piece of fiction or poetry or drama could matter, could have significance in and of itself. Such a view of the literary work entails certain metaphysical and moral premises that are incompatible with the radicalism that now dominates academic and intellectual life.

First, the New Critics almost all insist that the proper end of literary study is the work itself conceived as an independent object, and that investigations of the author's biography, of the historical situation in which he wrote, of the work's "reception history" and relations to other works of literature-all of this is ancillary to the interpretation and evaluation of the work itself. These premises assume that a literary work exists independently of the interests and purposes (conscious or unconscious) of the author, or of the responses to or experience of the work on the part of any particular reader or collection of readers in any given time or place.

In fact, a work of literature, then, stands as a testimony to the independence of the human spirit from material necessity: a man who can in words create a structure of significance that transcends the constraints of physical causation, or who can respond to it with sympathy and understanding, is himself in that measure a transcendent being; that is, he is a free, rational agent. By the same token, the work of literature in some ways rehabilitates that very material universe: it is seen neither as the realm of sheer darkness and despair of the ancient Gnostics nor as the meaningless grinding process of their Marxist heirs, but rather as a purposive design in which mankind is, or ought to be, temporarily at home. Literature is precisely humanity's imaginative ordering of the experience of the world.

The moral implications of the New Criticism are equally repugnant to radical ideology: if a literary work is a sign of human freedom, it is also a reminder of the limits of that freedom. As a representation of reality, a literary work is a manifestation of the structure of reality that exists independently of, and sometimes in conflict with, individual expectation and desire.

As an embodiment of meaning apart from author and interpreter alike, the literary work is a reminder that human beings can discover significance, but not manufacture it. The New Criticism thus responds affirmatively to what we might call the moral realism of great literature. Consider, for example, how many tragedies manifest the dignity and grandeur of human beings as morally free agents who yet can degrade and destroy themselves through the proud abuse of freedom and the refusal to respect the limitations inherent in the nature of reality.

Similarly, the interpreter of the drama is free to explore the richness of the play and draw out as much as he can of its inexhaustible significance, but he must respect the integrity of the text and acknowledge its meaning as its own and not his. Now virtually every effort to discredit the New Criticism also involves an attack upon the objective integrity of the literary work of art, along with a concomitant exaltation of the reader or interpreter.

As Elaine Pagels says of the Gnostics' relation to Christ's message (in her work *The Gnostic Gospels*), what they sought-and seek-is not a true interpretation of the message, but a unique, wholly subjective self-realization. The authority of canonical scripture and apostolic tradition are set aside in favor of the individual's interior divinity. Gnosticism provides so useful a model because the ancient Gnostic, like the modern Marxist, is preoccupied with escaping or transforming an unsatisfactory reality in the interests of personal domination or self- satisfaction. Because of its fictionality, literature can be regarded as a useful vehicle for this, but only if it is severed from reality by the denial of its status as a representation and rendered entirely responsive to the will of the interpreter.

The various debates between the New Critics and traditional literary historians and between the New Critics and the Chicago Aristotelians, back in the forties and fifties, tended to be either personal or technical-matters of tone and temperament or emphasis and degree. In principle, they were nearly all resolvable.

Beginning late in the 1950s, however, with the "archetypal" criticism of Northrop Frye, the various attacks upon the New Criticism began to arise from a fundamentally incompatible understanding of the nature and purpose of literature. Frye would reduce all works of literature to a collection of variations on a few basic myths, universal in a vaguely Jungian sense, and he deprecates value judgments and hierarchical discriminations deriving from aesthetic considerations. After all, if what is distinctive about a work of literature is its embodiment of an archetypal myth, its unique features as a specific work will hardly be prized. From Frye's quasi-religious perspective, literature constitutes a "secular scripture," with its authority drawn not from its own inherent revelatory features, but rather conferred by the interpreter, for whom each work serves as a vehicle for his own mythic fantasies and wish-fulfillments.

This is even more the case with one of Frye's most notable successors, Harold Bloom, who began as a champion of the revolutionary Romantics, especially Blake and Shelley, in the face of their depreciation by Eliot and the New Critics. Bloom's animus against the New Criticism is expressly political and religious, and in recent years-in *Agon*, for example-he has identified himself as a "Jewish Gnostic." He adapts Freudian concepts to the service of a visionary radicalism in which the writing and reading of poetry are a displaced version of Oedipal repression. The literary work becomes a contested site in which the egos of the author, his literary predecessors, and his readers struggle for psychic dominance.

Other critics who have come under the spell of psychoanalysis, most notably Norman Holland and David Bleich, have simply denied any substance at all to the literary work, except as it exists in the mind of the reader. This theory would seem to be a dream come true for the duller sort of undergraduate who repeatedly demands recognition in aggrieved tones for "what the story means to me." Stanley Fish, who began his career as a proponent of the reader-response school under the rubric "affective stylistics," soon realized that such an approach does nothing to enhance the prestige of the scholarly community, since it provides no basis for preferring the reading of a full professor to that of the most callow freshman.

Fish has spent the last decade developing the concept of the "interpretive community": according to which the very existence of a work of literature lies in the meaning conferred upon it by the members of a group defined by their common adherence to a set of criteria for reading and judging and arguing. In practice it means that a work of literature is the creature of recognized, published scholars in academic institutions. The independent existence of the work of literature fares no better in the psychoanalytic criticism influenced by the French neo-Freudian, Jacques Lacan.

Lacan's disciples in the field of literary criticism are mainly academic feminists and their allies, bent upon discomfiting what they call "patriarchy" wherever it rears its ugly head. Since the vast majority of writers in the canon of Western literature have been men, and since they have most often been so foolish as to write with an object called a pen of a most suspicious shape, there is little surprise in the discovery that most literature is "phallocentric." In this mode of criticism, the ontological status of the literary work would seem to be largely determined by the gonads of author and reader. Two of the principal continental developments of the sixties similarly diminished the independent existence of the literary work.

The so-called "Geneva School," exemplified most notably

by Georges Poulet, is generally uninterested in the particular poem, play, or novel, which is exploited, along with diaries, letters, and obiter dicta, to reconstruct and empathize, or even identify, with the total consciousness of the author. Parisian structuralism, with its close attention to details of language and form, bears a superficial methodological similarity to the New Critical approach; however, it differs sharply in its pretense to a scientific, almost mathematical rigor, and in its treatment of literature as a system, which is in turn only part of a larger system of cultural signs. Hence the study of literature is part of linguistics, linguistics part of semiotics.

Although the methods of Geneva and Paris are opposed insofar as the one seems obsessed with authorial intentionality while the other utterly discounts it, they are alike in dismissing or denying the objective existence of the literary work itself. Both of these schools have in turn been furiously assailed by the "postmodernist" theorists who have come to dominate academic literary study during the past two decades. And these latter have, if that were possible, only further diminished the status of the literary work. Deconstruction, the brainchild of the French philosopher Jacques Derrida, asserts the failure of intentional presence both in the author's consciousness and in the text.

Like every other human utterance, a work of literature has neither substantial existence nor distinctive identity. In the New Historicism, of course, Marxist principles of materialist determinism become explicit: new historicist critics view a work of literature as in essence no different from any other document or text; all are products of the sociopolitical conditions attendant upon their composition. When the various attacks upon the New Criticism in the course of the last three decades are thus considered, it is evident that they are all essentially attacks upon the ontological integrity of the literary work as such.

Deconstruction and the New Historicism take the next step, making explicit that which is common to all of these theoretical perspectives, i.e., a denial of the concept of imaginative literature as a distinct category of writing. The New Criticism is the ideological enemy because imaginative literature itself-poetry, fiction, drama-is the ideological enemy. Rene Wellek, an eminent defender of the significance of the written text, quotes Roland Barthes, a fashionable deconstructor, asserting that "literature is constitutionally reactionary" and then, somewhat incredulously, proceeds to show that Barthes is mistaken, that literature and literary figures have in fact often been in the vanguard of social protest and revolution. One is reminded of E.D. Hirsch's frustrated astonishment in *Cultural Literacy* at radical demands for the dismantling of the teaching of traditional humanist disciplines. Surely everyone must recognize, Hirsch argues, that it is only by mastering the verbal skills and traditional knowledge required by cultivated literacy that one will be able to effect social change and do away with injustice.

The exasperation of Wellek and Hirsch and many others is understandable, but in large measure it assumes that today's academic radicals are interested in reforming Western society and its cultural institutions when, in fact, they are mainly interested in obliterating them. Wellek himself points out that a leveling nihilism is at the heart of the matter: "All these objections to the concept of literature," he says, "have one trait in common: they do not recognize quality as a criterion of literature; quality that may be either aesthetic or intellectual, but which in either case sets off a specific realm of verbal expression from daily transactions in language."

Given the radical perspective of the ideologues who currently dominate the literature departments of universities, literature *is* a conservative force because it implies a standard of discrimination and judgment. The old New Critics regarded the study of genuine works of imaginative literature as a powerful civilizing force because it is educative in the strict sense: it is a means of leading the student *out* of the narrow, self-interested realm of individual and peer group; it is a confrontation with landmarks of cultural tradition whose significance and authority persist from generation to generation and provide norms of thought, feeling, and behavior. In the New Critical scheme the work of critics and scholars is ancillary to the masterpieces that constitute this literary culture. Its task is to define and identify literary excellence and through interpretation to point out how literature represents and reveals the nature of reality.

Probably it is precisely for its insistence upon literary quality that the New Criticism is currently hated and feared. As Heather Dubrow and Richard Strier, editors of a recent collection of essays on *The Historical Renaissance*, aver, "New Criticism distinguished and privileged 'literary' language; the characteristic richness and ambiguity with which literature was associated was seen to render it a far fitter object of study than other types of texts, such as descriptions of cities or political tracts." Now, they continue, we know better: "Today scholars of the English Renaissance are intensely concerned with the connections between literary texts and social and historical phenomena-and, indeed, with collapsing the boundaries suggested by those very distinctions."

In other words, the distinction between works of

literature and what used to be called historical documents is wiped away; whatever is written is a "text," and all texts are equal. The same strictures apply to discriminations among different levels of fiction: no distinction is allowed between serious literature of aesthetic merit, or at least aspiration to such merit, and what once would have been called subliterature, pulp fiction, or *kitsch*. "Scholarship" dealing with "popular" literature is an academic growth industry.

For an academic, perhaps the best evidence of the power of this new industry is the number of his colleagues who seem to spend more time listening to hard rock and watching music videos than reading poetry. There are two main consequences of all this: the reduction of literature to so much grist for the ideological mill and the concomitant total empowerment of the interpreter.

In *Criticism and Social Change* Frank Lentricchia maintains that the effort to interpret a text objectively is merely a form of collaboration with the political status quo, since "Literature is inherently nothing; or it is a body of rhetorical stategies waiting to be seized." His Duke colleague Stanley Fish argues that when the interpreter approaches a literary text not with the aim of *demonstrating* its meaning and value, but rather of *persuading* his audience to accept it on his terms, then the interpreter supersedes the text: "But perhaps the greatest gain that falls to us under a persuasion model is a greatly enhanced sense of the importance of our activities. (In certain quarters, of course, where the critical ideal is one of self-effacement, this will be perceived to be the greatest danger.) No longer is the critic the humble servant of texts whose glories exist independently of anything he might do; it is what he does, within the constraints embedded in the literary institution, that brings texts into being and makes them available for analysis and appreciation. The practice of literary criticism is not something one must apologize for; it is absolutely essential not only to the maintenance of, but to the very production of, the objects of its attention."

Of course as Fish's language reveals, this interpretive license only operates "within the constraints embedded in the literary institution," or, as he has taken to calling it, the "interpretive community." It turns out that maximum freedom is maximum bondage, the critic being as much a product of his socioeconomic situation as a book. This state of affairs was anticipated by Cleanth Brooks some four decades ago. In the preface to *The Well Wrought Urn*, perhaps the single most important work of New Criticism, he observed, "The temper of our times is strongly relativistic," and in the face of this, he affirms the propriety, indeed the necessity, of seeing "what residuum, if any, is left after we have referred the poem to its cultural matrix." Brooks explicitly affirms the importance of literary history, and anyone familiar with his own critical practice will be aware of his profound knowledge of the historical context of the literary works he treats. "Yet," he continues, "if poetry exists as poetry in any meaningful sense, the attempt must be made. Otherwise the poetry of the past becomes significant merely as cultural anthropology, and the poetry of the present, merely as a political, or religious, or moral instrument."

The state of affairs about which Brooks offered this caution forty-odd years ago is now cheerfully flaunted as the New Historicism. The first chapter of *The Well Wrought Urn*, titled "The Language of Paradox," provides perhaps the most vivid clue to both the implications of the New Criticism and of ideological theories that have arisen to challenge it.

It is this chapter, for instance, that has been singled out for "deconstruction" by Jonathan Culler. In it Brooks sets out to show that the language of poetry is inherently paradoxical-a blend of "irony and wonder"; that is, what distinguishes a genuine poem is that its verbal pattern, especially its various figures of speech, cannot be reduced to any set of plain prose statements-or at least that any such paraphrase is not the same as, or interchangeable with, the poem. In the language of economics, poetry is not fungible. Precisely this irreducibility is what constitutes a poem's independent existence. The poem that Brooks cites to illustrate this view is "The Canonization" by John Donne, a brilliant, if extravagant and sometimes risque, deployment of religious language in defense of human sexual love. The poem is by turns outrageously and defiantly witty, tender, and impassioned.

What is more, there are numerous features of the poem that seem to reflect Donne's own life-he destroyed his hopes for preferment at Court and fell into disgrace and financial ruin by eloping with a very young woman staying in his employer's household. The poem, however, was not published until after the poet's death, and its actual relation to events in his life is finally a matter of speculation. Brooks' central thesis is that the seemingly contradictory tensions in "The Canonization"-the ironic, even bawdy, references to sexual intercourse jostling against the assertions of human love's transcendence-finally converge in a unified vision of our experience of love which cannot be expressed in our ordinary, commonsense statements about it. The vision that is verbally manifest in the poem may or may not have been inspired or provoked by this or that incident or preoccupation in the life of the man John Donne, but the poem itself is distinct from the aims and experiences of the poet, and accessible to the experience of readers in a way that the actual life experience of another is not. There are more puzzles and obscurities and complex tonal layers than we can begin to unravel here (that, after all, is the point), but I do wish to call attention to the closing couplet. Christ's Resurrection from death, one of the mysteries of the Christian faith, is evoked here at the same time *and in the same words* as a bawdy Renaissance pun on "dying" as the attainment of sexual climax. One could choose to regard this as mere blasphemy, but the tone of the poem as a whole seems to preclude such a simplification; yet the lines do gain much of their force from the *suggestion* of blasphemy. This passage, and finally the poem as a whole, sets out to acknowledge, and so far as possible embrace, our entire equivocal experience of human sexuality, which is funny, embarrassing, obscene, "dirty"; exciting and pleasurable and yet repugnant; tender, exalted, sacred. Marriage is, after all, regarded by some Christian communions as a sacrament and by all as a holy and honorable estate, and it is only consummated by sexual intercourse. Brooks' comment on the passage is instructive: "The lovers after the act are the same. Their love is not exhausted in mere lust. This is their title to canonization. Their love is like the phoenix. . . . Most important of all, the sexual submeaning of 'die' does not contradict the other meanings."

The enemies Brooks and his generation were accustomed to were likely to attack from the direction of positivism or a quasi-scientific rationalism: literature was dismissed as merely "emotive," inaccurate, not "empirically verifiable." Hence the New Critics were at pains to stress that the language of imaginative literature and of proper literary criticism was, in its own way, as precise as the language of science, that if the knowledge embodied in literature lacked the mathematical certitude of physics, it was nevertheless objective. From the deconstructivist perspective, however, no discourse can boast precision or objectivity; no signifier can make the signified fully present or available to the mind. Everything, then, is "literature," but this is not an honorific term. Scientific and philosophic discourse, legal documents, and pastoral elegies are all chains of signifiers that never terminate in the signified: textuality is our prison from which there is no escape.

The typical procedure of deconstruction is to grasp a loose thread in the textual weave of a discourse and to proceed with the unraveling. Jonathan Culler seizes upon Brooks' comment on the fourth stanza of "The Canonization," where the "sonnets" and "hymnes" celebrating the passion of the lovers are compared to a "well wrought urne." "The poem is an instance of the doctrine which it asserts," Brooks says; "it is both the assertion and the realization of the assertion. The poet has actually before our eyes built within the song the 'pretty room' with which he says the lovers can be content. The poem itself is the well-wrought urn which can hold the lovers' ashes and which will not suffer in comparison with the prince's 'halfe-acre tombe.'"

According to Culler, in *On Deconstruction*, Brooks is attributing to the poem a "self- reference"-a "self-reflexivity . . . seen as self-knowledge, self- possession, a self-understanding or presence of the poem to itself." But, he assures us, "Under exegetical pressure, self-reference demonstrates the impossibility of self-possession." Culler proceeds to insist that "The Canonization" is "not so much a self-contained urn as a chain of discourses and representations"; for "if the poem is the urn, then one of the principal features of the urn is that it portrays people responding to the urn."

It is pertinent to note here that to notice here.

First, "self- referentiality" is not Brooks' term, nor his concept; Culler imposes it with no justification. For a poem to be "both the assertion and the realization of the assertion" does not entail "self-reference" or "self- reflexivity." "The Canonization" refers not to itself, but to what it represents: the speech of a fictive character, whose attitudes and ideas doubtless had their origin in the consciousness of John Donne, but who is certainly not identical with that poet. (The "speaker" or "persona" is as "present" as he ever was; Donne is long since dead.) Second, when Brooks says, "The poem itself is the well wrought urn," this is a statement of a different order than, say, "The poem comprises forty-five lines." Brooks uses "well wrought urn" metaphorically, much as Donne does; and so the urn was "something other than an urn" long before Culler noticed. He might as well require Brooks to produce an enameled clay vessel decorated with "Countries, Townes, Courts"; or Keats to account for the deserted village on his "Grecian Urn."

The deconstructionists are quite the cleverest people around the English department these days, but occasionally they resemble the dullest undergraduates in their inability to distinguish between figurative and literal language-or between poetry and pottery. Definitely, a major goal of the deconstructive project is to put in question such binary oppositions as literal/figurative and literary/scientific; but as the example of Jonathan Culler suggests, we usually get question-begging rather than argument. His deconstruction of Brooks' reading of "The Canonization" begins by *assuming* that the notion of self-referentiality applies to a poem in the same fashion as it applies to, say, a legal document that defines itself. Likewise, he assumes that the nature of signification renders nugatory any real distinction between fact and fiction, between literal statement and metaphor.

Of course these are the very points that the deconstructionist is supposed to prove. But in fact deconstruction can, finally, prove nothing, for by denying the efficacy of discourse it undermines the significance of proof. Deconstruction is typical of contemporary literary theory in hating the word as an embodiment or manifestation of truth. Hence it attacks the integrity of the fictive world of imaginative literature precisely because literature defines itself in terms of the truth which it is not, but which it represents. A poem cannot exhaust reality, but it can arrest it: by manifesting a vision of experience available in no other way.

This is only possible because, like a physical urn, it is a distinct substantial object: only by its difference from human experience can a poem represent that experience, even as the urn can be a metaphor for a poem only if it is not itself a poem. The alternative to "crystalline closure" is not, then, an endless and chaotic "repetition and proliferation," but a structured relationship of significance.

[*Courtesy* : R.V. Young. We owe to Prof. Young and copyright holders immensely for subscribing the views.]

Abbreviations

APC	American Poetry Criticism
AT	Allen Tate
CB	Cleanth Brooks
JCR	John Crowe Ransom
MB	Monroe Beardsley
NC	New Criticism
RPB	R.P. Blackmur
RPW	Robert Penn Warren
TSE	T.S. Eliot
WE	William Empson
WW	William Wimsatt

6

New Historicism

Basically, New Historicists and Cultural Materialists both are interested in recovering lost histories and in exploring mechanisms of repression and subjugation. The major difference is that New Historicists tend to concentrate on those at the top of the social hierarchy (i.e. the church, the monarchy, the upper-classes) while Cultural Materialists tend to concentrate on those at the bottom of the social hierarchy (the lower-classes, women, and other marginalized peoples).

Also, though each of the schools practices different kinds of history, New Historicists tend to draw on the disciplines of political science and anthropology given their interest in governments, institutions, and culture, while Cultural Materialists tend to rely on economics and sociology given their interest in class, economics, and commodification. New Historicists are, like the Cultural Materialists, interested in questions of circulation, negotiation, profit and exchange, i.e. how activities that purport to be above the market (including literature) are in fact informed by the values of that market. However, New Historicists take this position further by then claiming that all cultural activities may be considered as equally important texts for historical analysis: contemporary trials of hermaphrodites or the intricacies of map-making may inform a Shakespeare play as much as, say, Shakespeare's literary precursors.

New Historicism is also more specifically concerned with questions of power and culture (especially the messy commingling of the social and the cultural or of the supposedly autonomous self and the cultural/ political institutions that in fact produce that self). Part of the difficulty of introducing this school is that a number of different approaches to history and culture often get lumped together under the category of "new historicism." The sheer number of historical and cultural studies that have appeared since the early 1990s, including the dominance of the still-larger umbrella term, Cultural Studies, makes the cordoning off of a group of critics as "New Historicists" difficult.

The effort to do so is certainly not helped by the fact that some of the most prominent New Historicists, like Stephen Greenblatt and Alan Liu, either reject or critique the very term, "New Historicism." Nonetheless, this critical school and those scholars commonly associated with the school have been hugely influential on scholarship of the last decade, so it's important to come to grips with some of the general trends and common practices of this critical approach.

We here also provide Modules on individual theorists in order to give a somewhat more detailed introduction to a few influential figures. We have chosen to offer one important precursor, Michel Foucault, as well as one exemplary practitioner, Stephen Greenblatt (who applies the methods of the school to Renaissance texts).

Notable Critics

It is pertinent to note that Michel Foucault is quite possibly the most influential critic of the last quarter-century. His interest in issues of power, epistemology, subjectivity, and ideology have influenced critics not only in literary studies but also political science, history, and anthropology. His willingness to analyze and discuss disparate disciplines (medicine, criminal science, philosophy, the history of sexuality, government, literature, etc.) as well as his questioning of the very principle of disciplinarity and specialization have inspired a host of subsequent critics to explore interdisciplinary connections between areas that had rarely been examined together.

Foucault also had the ability to pick up common terms and give them new meaning, thus changing the way critics addressed such pervasive issues as "power," "discourse," "discipline," "subjectivity," "sexuality," and "government." Stephen Greenblatt's brilliant studies of the Renaissance have established him as the major figure commonly associated with New Historicism. Indeed, his influence meant that New Historicism first gained popularity among Renaissance scholars, many of whom were directly inspired by Greenblatt's ideas and anecdotal approach.

In fact this fascination with history and the minute details of culture soon caught on among scholars working in other historical periods, leading to the increasing popularity of culturally- and historically-minded studies. This general trend is often referred to as Cultural Studies. Notably, there are a number of similarities between this school and the following one, Cultural Materialism.

The major difference is that New Historicists tend to concentrate on those at the *top* of the social hierarchy (i.e. the church, the monarchy, the upper-classes) while Cultural Materialists tend to concentrate on those at the bottom of the social hierarchy (the lower-classes, women, and other marginalized peoples). Also, though each of the schools practices different kinds of history, New Historicism tends to draw on the disciplines of political science, government, and anthropology while Cultural Materialism relies on economics, sociology, and cultural studies. Cultural Materialism is primarily concerned with issues of class, economics, and commodification.

New Historicists are, like the Cultural Materialists, interested in questions of *circulation, negotiation, profit* and *exchange,* i.e. how activities that purport to be above the market (including literature) are in fact informed by the values of that market. However, New Historicists take this position further by then claiming that all cultural activities may be considered as equally important texts for historical analysis: contemporary trials of hermaphrodites or the intricacies of map-making may inform a Shakespeare play as much as, say, Shakespeare's literary precursors. New Historicism is also more specifically concerned with questions of power and *culture.*

Major Concepts

(1) *Economic stages of development:* In fact, this term is used mostly by Cultural Materialists and refers to Marx's dialectical theory of historical development. According to Marx, society has progressed through various stages of development, each determined by the predominant mode of economic production. Though there are others, the main transition is the one from a feudal social order to a capitalist one. In a feudal system (predominant, for example, during the middle ages), vassals gave a percentage of their crops to their lord (who was generally a member of the aristocracy—people who earned their right to rule by blood lineage). Peasants paid this "tribute" to their lords often in exchange for protection from

invaders. The primary form of exchange is the barter system, which means that one must place value on individual objects based on their inherent worth. (Is the new table that vendor has built worth three or four of my chickens?). In the capitalist system, workers are no longer valued for the quality of the things they produce, but for "work" understood as an abstract quantity. Such a system relies on the process of commodification, explained directly below.

(2) *Class (proletariat, bourgeoisie, aristocracy):* This is a more specifically Cultural Materialist concept, since New Historicists might suggest that all levels of society share in the circulation of power through the production and distribution of the most elementary cultural and social "texts." The proletariat refers to the "lower" or "working classes" and the bourgeoisie to the "middle classes"; the aristocracy is a residual throw-back to an earlier stage of economic development: feudalism.

(3) *Power:* Although this term seems as if it should be self-explanatory, it has in fact been inflected by its re-definition in the work of an important precursor for New Historicism: Michel Foucault. In his work, Foucault argues that power is not merely physical force but a pervasive human dynamic determining our relationships to others. (One need only think of how one acts differently the moment someone enters a room in which one had previously been alone.) Power is also not necessarily "bad," since it can also be productive. (We may be willing, for example, to assign to certain people the power to organise an activity because we know they are capable of helping us actually accomplish the task at hand.) We could

also say that power is essential to a just society; all people exert a certain power over us insofar as we defer to their needs and desires. The moment we cease to acknowledge this power an other has over us, then we deny that other's humanity (his/her human rights.) However, power also refers to the (often surreptitious) ways in which a dominant group exerts its influence over others. Though this hegemonic power may (at some end point) rely on the threat of punishment, it does not necessarily rely on actual physical enforcement on a day-to-day basis. (Imagine this scenario, for example: you are driving over a flat country landscape at night and you reach a stop light. There is no one else that you can see for miles, and yet do you not feel obliged to stop for the light?)

(4) *Commodification:* This term refers to the subordination of both private and public realms to the logic of capitalism. In this logic, such things as friendship, knowledge, women, etc. are understood only in terms of their monetary value. In this way, they are no longer treated as things with intrinsic worth but as commodities. (They are valued, that is, only extrinsically in terms of money.) By this logic, a factory worker can be reconceptualized not as a human being with specific needs that, as humans, we are obliged to provide but as a mere wage debit in a businessman's ledger.

(5) *Hegemony: the processes by which dominant culture maintains its dominant position:* For example, the use of institutions to formalize power (see directly above); the employment of a bureaucracy to make power seem abstract (and, therefore, not attached to any one individual); the inculcation of the populace

in the ideals of the hegomonic group through education, advertising, publication, etc.; the mobilization of a police force as well as military personnel to subdue opposition.

(6) *Historicity of texts / textuality of history:* These catch-phrases follow from the previous points. All texts may be examined for their historicity, just as any historical phenomenon (e.g. Madonna videos or Nazi transvestite films) can be analysed much as one would a literary text. The New Historicists take this latter precept much further by examining the import of what might be considered rather minor and unimportant daily facts and events, e.g. the cultural and socio-political import of miniature portraiture in Renaissance England.

(7) *Histories not History:* Cultural Materialists reject along with the New Historicists the Western tendency to write history from the top down (e.g. political history) and in grand narrative strokes. Cultural Materialists are interested in the points of rupture in the grand narratives of Western historians, i.e. points where dissension, transgression, uncertainty, etc. open up the possibility for social upheaval or where "heroic" narratives in fact hide moments of exploitation and terror (e.g. the Columbus controversy; compare, for example, the two recent films, *Christopher Columbus and 1492*). New Historicists would look at these same moments of rupture to examine how forces of rebellion are still able to be co-opted by the powers that be (e.g. how Public Enemy's message in "Fight the Power" is compromised and even nullified by the group's desire for capital profit).

(8) *Consolidation, subversion, containment:* Cultural Materialists would be more interested in subversion, whereas New Historicists will look more specifically at forces of containment and the ways hegemonic forces consolidate the status quo.

(9) *Ideology:* The major thing to remember is that to recognize your own ideology is like pushing the bus you're riding on, since it is so much a part of the way you perceive the world and its workings.

(10) *Text always related to context:* Cultural Materialists and New Historicists both reject the New Critical precept that texts are autonomous units that should be examined without bringing in what has been termed the "intentional fallacy" (i.e. biographical criticism) or the "historical fallacy."

Remarkably, New Historicism explained new historicism occurred in response to:

(a) Large numbers of literature professors being trained who came from backgrounds (female, working class, Italian-American, African-American, and, increasingly, Asian American and Latino American) not previously represented at the PhD level.

(b) "New" Criticism's tendency to treat works of literature in a historical vacuum, as if a poem or novel had no relation to its historical context whatsoever.

(c) Political developments in the 1960s, especially a desire on the part of literature professors to figure out how understanding literature might help in understanding social problems.

(d) An influx of Continental professors and literary theories into Britain and the United States.

New Historicist premises:

(1) New Historicists also tend to stress that authors and poets are not secular saints—that even though they may be more circumspect about their societies than the average citizen, they nonetheless participate in it. Consequently, New Historicist critics often point out places in artists' work where their attitudes do not anticipate our own, or may even be distasteful to us.

(2) Images and narratives do important *cultural work*. They function as a kind of workshop (or playroom) where cultural problems, hopes, and obsessions are addressed or avoided.

(3) New Historicist criticism tries to relate interpretive problems (such as why Hamlet doesn't kill Claudius as he prays) to cultural-historical problems (such as contemporaneous debates about purgatory, transubstantiation, and salvation, as well as anxieties about what constituted legitimacy in the church, the monarchy, and succession to the throne).

(4) Consequently, New Historicists argue that the best framework for interpreting literature is to place it in its historical context: what contemporaneous issues, anxieties, and struggles does the work of literature reflect, refract, or try to work through?

Criticism

New historicism is critised by many scholars. The major disagreements and limitations put forward by them are as fellows:

(1) Frederick Jameson argues that much New Historicist criticism lacks a *theory* of history. That history, to

paraphrase the bumpersticker, "just happens," without explaining why it happens in the way that it does and who is affected.

(2) That it tends to reduce literature to a footnote of history, and neglects the uniquely literary qualities of the work in question.

(3) At its worst, New Historicism's emphasis on connecting literature to politics can resemble what Eve Sedgwick calls "good dog/ bad dog" criticism, where critics praise artists for their progressive views and chastise them for reactionary ones, instead of accepting that cultures have problems, those problems are complicated, and we can learn from how artists tried to grapple with those problems without giving them a grade card.

It is pertinent to note that Steven Greenblatt has been the guiding force in New Historicist criticism, and since he writes in the field of Renaissance studies, that was the first period to generate lots of New Historicist criticism. It has since become important in criticism of Medieval, and nineteenth century British and American literature, and is working its way through criticism of modernist literature and eighteenth century literature.

As such, Post-modernism, by its very nature, tends to have identifiable, but often obscure connections to contemporary history, challenging new historicist critics to be extremely sophisticated about how history is represented in a postmodernist works of literature.

7

School of Russian Thought

"We must hate—hatred is the basis of Communism. Children must be taught to hate their parents if they are not communists."

—*Nikolai Lenin*

First every student of literature must know that. Russia does not really have a philosophical tradition in the same sense that other European cultures do. If you were looking into the subject for the first time and went to one of the English-language anthologies of Russian thinkers, you would be amazed to see, first, that almost no one who lived before the late eighteenth century was represented and, second, that most of the writers who were represented were not philosophers at all. If you had ever had a course in Russian literature, you would be surprised to recognize in the anthology the names of a great many writers you had heard of as either novelists—Dostoevsky and Tolstoy have earned the distinction of being considered "thinkers"—or literary critics.

There would be political writers and social critics (which in nineteenth-century Russia often mean the same thing as literary critics), and there would be religious thinkers. But almost none could be classified as philosophers in the same way we classify, say, Kant or Hegel as philosophers.

Historians, in their search for themes and patterns, have not yet been able to decide whether the characteristic style of Russian thought is secular, religious, or a maddening, Dostoevskian hesitation between the two. For that matter they have not been able to decide which writers to include in books on the history of Russian thought (or philosophy, when they insist on using the word).

It is significant to mention that Polish scholar Andrzej Walicki, has written a book titled *A History of Russian Thought from the Enlightenment to Marxism,* which, though it certainly includes sections on the important religious thinkers of the nineteenth and early twentieth centuries, leaves the reader with the impression that the greatest contribution of Russian thought was in the area of social and political criticism. The bulk of his discussion of the twentieth century is devoted to the evolution of political thought that results in Leninism.

The reader would have a much different impression from reading another of the standard works on the subject, N.O. Lossky's *History of Russian Philosophy*. Lossky was himself a religious man who emigrated to USA country and spent the last years of his scholarly career at the Saint Vladimir Russian Orthodox Seminary of New York. Although he mentions most of the social and political thinkers that Walicki discusses, he devotes more than half his book to mystical and religious thinkers of the early twentieth century. One is likely to come away from Lossky's book with the idea that the religious current in Russian thought is central and the political current an aberration.

Of course, it would be foolish to pretend that either current, the religious or the secular, exists to the exclusion of the other. Russian culture contains a great many dualisms, and this is one of them. But it distorts matters to decide with Walicki that the early twentieth century in Russia is largely the affair of Marxism simply because Marxism triumphed in the end. As it happens, the late nineteenth and early twentieth centuries were an extraordinarily rich period for religious thought in Russia.

Naturally, few of the strictly religious ideas of this period caught on or had any obvious lasting effect in postrevolutionary Soviet culture, and many of the most important writers of this era, like Lossky, emigrated to the West shortly after the revolution. Nonetheless, this is precisely the period when a great creative upheaval took place in Russian culture, the brief interlude of freedom that produced many influential works in Russian arts and letters.

It is the period of the transformation that Eagleton speaks of, a period that yields an uncanny number of isms in an amazingly short time: symbolism, Acmeism, Futurism, Formalism, and on and on. It is also the period that produced the young Roman Jakobson. There is no doubt that Marxism triumphed politically in Russia, even if we countenance the argument that Soviet Marxism is merely another form of religious faith.

But the mass emigration of intellectuals who found by the late 1920s or earlier that the new regime had no place for them—and Jakobson was among these—brought to the West the legacy of centuries of religious thought, often in covert form. A critical moment for Russian culture occurred before there was any such thing as Russia and more than two centuries before the country that later became Russia converted to Christianity.

It has to do with the church father Saint John of Damascus, who led the theological battle in the eighth century against the forces of iconoclasm in the Byzantine Empire. Images representing religious figures had been in use among Christians for some time before the days of Saint John, but there had been opposition to them among certain believers on the grounds that worshiping them meant worshiping false gods. Iconoclasm gained political force by the eighth century, and in 754 Emperor Constantine V convened a church council in Constantinople at which the veneration of icons was declared both heretical and illegal.

Similarly, John of Damascus was a theologian who devoted much of his life to defending icons against the iconoclasts. Since he lived first in Syria and then in Palestine, under the protection of a Moslem caliph, he was free to write in defense of icons at a time when Christians elsewhere were having difficulty embracing that position. When the Ecumenical Council of Nicaea was convened in 787 to condemn iconoclasm and reverse the position of the Council of 754, church authorities used many of the arguments that John had presented in his defense of icons.

The case for the defense of icons rests on the analogy between icons and the Incarnation. God is invisible, immaterial, immeasurable. By the Incarnation, however, God became visible in his Son and thereby partook of the flesh and blood of corporeal beings. This meant that through Christ men were able to have a limited understanding of the intangible, since visible things serve as corporeal models of the invisible (DI, p. 20). The Son is therefore an image (eikon in Greek) of the invisible God, since an image is defined as the result of God's having become visible by partaking of flesh and blood (DI, p. 19; PG, 94:1240c).

John's purpose was specifically to refute the iconoclasts' notion that venerating icons meant venerating false gods.

The iconoclasts wanted to prohibit the worship of icons because they regarded such worship as idolatry, and idolatry (eidololatreia) implies the adoration (latreia, a form of respect due only to God) of idols (eidola) . Adoring idols thus meant considering them as gods, in the view of the iconoclasts. But venerating icons is different from idolatry, says John.

For one thing, the form of respect is not the absolute adoration that should be reserved for God alone; it is, literally, a bowing down before (proskynesis), a form of obeisance that one makes to people or things to whom honor is due. But more important is that images are not held to be gods. One cannot make an image of the invisible, immeasurable God, says John, and it is therefore absurd to suppose that in bowing down before an image one is bowing down before a god different from the one, immeasurable God.

In fact, the consequences of this doctrine are incalculable for Eastern Orthodox theology. The fundamental idea is the act of condescension or humiliation by which God became flesh in his Son. The Greek word for this act is kenosis, which means an emptying and refers to the way in which God emptied himself of his divinity to take on the form of man in his Son. The condescension is seen in many different realms of being and is thus essential to the broadness of the doctrine that John outlines. A Christ is God made flesh and represents a humiliation of God the Father.

Images are visible things, and "visible things are corporeal models which provide a vague understanding of intangible things"; so images, too, are a humiliation (p. 20). In fact, all creation is the result of the same kind of humiliation, and thus, says John, to prohibit the veneration of images is to assume that matter itself is despicable. If the iconoclasts were afraid that Christians were worshiping inanimate objects with pictures drawn on them, John felt he could allay their fears by pointing out one of the most important facts of icon veneration: the honor given the image is transferred to the prototype, to what the image stands for (p. 40). God himself is never represented in icons; icon painters had at their disposal a limited number of subjects, usually Christ, the Mother of God, and a few saints. But by the doctrine of God's condescension an image of any of these subjects is an image of God incarnate, and so the prototype of an icon is ultimately the divinity.

The essential thing about icon veneration is that the image is an incarnation and that one venerates the image not as God but as the image of God incarnate (p. 40). "We see the invisible made visible through the visible representation," in the words of Simeon the Great, as John cites them (p. 104).

In fact this is the doctrine that was adopted in the final definition (horos) of the Council of Nicaea in 787, and it is the one that has been in force ever since. That definition begins by recognizing the two natures of Christ—one divine, one earthly. The two natures are united in one person, or hypostasis. We make iconographic representations, the council members said, "for the purpose of ascertaining the incarnation of God the Word." "He who venerates the icon venerates the hypostasis of the person depicted on it." There is thus an implicit epistemology in this doctrine of icon veneration, if epistemology is the right word. The doctrine of prototypes means that the worshiper has to see the icon in a different way from that in which he or she sees other objects.

An ordinary act of seeing an object is not accompanied in most people by an idealist sense that the object they are perceiving is not physically real, that it is merely an intuition of an object that can never really be known in itself. But the perception of the icon apparently must be accompanied by such a sense because the physical object, the piece of wood adorned with colors and lacquers forming a picture of the Mother of God, is understood as a mere facade for the grace that stands behind it.

One has to look through the wood and paint into the invisible and immaterial, into something beyond that cannot be seen. The icon is like Christ: it has two natures united in one object. Christ's two natures meant that through him mere mortals could participate in the grace of God the Father, in a limited way, because they shared with Christ at least his physical nature. The icon performs the same service: it allows the worshiper a limited contact with the immeasurable through the intermediary of sensible matter.

So icon veneration has a kind of idealism built into it that operates in the mind of the ordinary worshiper. Plenty of things happened in the history of Russian Orthodoxy to insure that this doctrine would subsist and that it would be intuitively accepted by as many people as possible. For instance, the Orthodox church required that icon artists work anonymously. The main idea was that they were to work for God's glory, not their own. But the requirement was also founded on the belief that the icon artist contributed nothing of his own to his pictures.

Every iconic image was meant to be an imitation of a previous image, which was itself an imitation of a previous image, and so on, back to an image based on an actual physical view of the person represented. Icons were thus never designed to be appreciated for their beauty. The "aesthetic" posture of the viewer was discouraged by the prominent sense that the picture was authorless and not "real": it always pointed back either to a tradition or to an invisible prototype. The principles of icon theology were destined to become widely known as icons themselves became increasingly common. By the sixteenth century they were already frequently displayed in private homes, and thereafter they became a fixture.

Notably, Christian theology the expression Word of God refers to the Second Person of the Trinity, or Christ. Christ is the Word (Logos) made Flesh. Icon and Logos are thus closely related concepts, since the nature of the icon derives from the Incarnation of the Word. Logos is a complicated term. In Greek it refers to a whole range of things, from spoken discourse in general, to narrative, to thought, to the New Testament Word of God. In theology the chief ambiguity of the Logos is between its sense as Son of God and the ordinary sense having to do with language.

Because of the intimacy of the concepts icon and logos, because of the hesitation of logos, or word, between theological and other meanings, philosophy of language in Russia has generally been explicitly or implicitly a kind of theology. The late nineteenth century brought a revival of theological thought in Russia together with a surge in philosophical activity. But philosophy and theology were characteristically not entirely distinct in this period just as in others, and one result of the revival of both disciplines was the appearance in the early twentieth century of an Orthodox philosophy of language.

Naftali Prat, a Russian scholar living in Israel, has investigated this often-neglected episode in the history of the early modern era in an article titled "Orthodox Philosophy of Language in Russia." Prat identifies several sources of this trend: Platonism as it traditionally dominates Orthodox theology, German idealism, Husserlian phenomenology, and Russian poets. The dominant source, however, is Platonism, and Platonism implies the doctrine of the logos. Prat shows that logos in this tradition has to do with the unity of thought and language and the notion of adequately expressing a thought by means of the word. In the Russian philosophico-theological tradition the message of Plato's Cratylus is not the conventionality of language but rather that part of the name that is given by nature. Names express the essence of named objects through the eidos, or idea, of that object, Prat says (p. 3).

In a strictly religious arena, in the early years of the twentieth century, language and the nature of names were the subject of an intense debate. At issue was the doctrine of imjaslavie, or glorification of the name, according to which God is immediately present in his name. Prat believes that the dispute over this Christian Platonic doctrine gave the "decisive impulse" to establishing an Orthodox philosophy of language in this century. If the logical origin of icons is in the doctrine of the logos, then it is not surprising that the two concepts should have analogous natures or that the logos should suggest an epistemology similar to the one we saw in the icon. The icon contains its reference to an invisible prototype. The logos contains its invisible essence or idea, whether by "logos" we mean the Second Person of the Trinity or simply a name.

Icon and logos require a similar act of seeing, one that goes beyond the physical object toward an immaterial essence, idea, or grace, and thus they come together in the notion of idealism. Neither concept can exist without the ultimately Platonic sense that the physical thing stands for, or points to, something purely ideal. Early modern literary aesthetics in Russia is completely dominated by this kind of thinking.

Even the most "scientific" writers, like Jakobson and his precursors the Formalists, perpetuate the idealist assumptions underlying Orthodox theology and language philosophy. Russian literary aesthetics in this period and the related disciplines that have fostered so much of our subsequent thinking about literary texts in the twentieth century are really an iconology, a logology, an Orthodox Christology, if only in disguise. But sometimes it is not in disguise at all.

We have an entirely false picture of the intellectual climate of turn-of-the-century Russia because all we ever hear about is the ostensibly secular and scientific thinkers that have been adopted by later twentieth-century schools of criticism. There is a whole range of immensely important and influential thinkers who unabashedly used the language of Orthodox theology. Some were genuinely religious; others were not (or were less so). Some continued to write until well after the revolution, although for those who had not emigrated it became difficult toward the end of the 1920s to write anything that sounded like theology.

If we take a look at what some of the more overtly religious writers were saying about art and language, then we can see that they did not form an obscure, deviant branch of philosophy in an otherwise secularized age.

On the contrary, they are the ones that set out the terms of the discourse; the "secular" thinkers appropriated those terms. There is a great deal more coherence in this age than we might think. After all, was it merely an accidental combination of words that Shklovsky, the great Formalist, hit upon when he titled one of the central aesthetic proclamations of the day "The Resurrection of the Word"? Now we will describe some notable Russian thinkers.

Vladimir Solov'ev

Like so many other Russian thinkers, Solov'ev was not only religious but fundamentally ambivalent about Russian Christianity, flirting at various stages of his life with Orthodoxy's two greatest temptations, atheism and Catholicism. He was staggeringly precocious, beginning his mature writing career when he was in his twenties. He was astonishingly versatile, writing philosophy, poetry, and humorous theatre. And he was enormously influential: the whole symbolist movement in Russian letters finds the source for much of its essential thinking in him. The root of Solov'ev's thought is the same as for John of Damascus and the same as for the entire Russian kenotic tradition. It all goes back to Christ, the Word incarnate: two natures, one person.

Solov'ev's *Lectures on Godmanhood,* which he began writing at the age of twentyfour and which contain many of the principles he was to write about for the rest of his career, take their point of departure in the notion of Christ's—and consequently man's—dual nature. Duality underlies everything for Solov'ev, who is an idealist in virtually every sense of the term. There is God and his creation; God and man; Christ's divinity and Christ's humanity; the world of ideas and the world of matter; the absolute, permanent, objective idea in the individual and the purely subjective, personal idea; and on and on. History is the dynamic process of the unfolding of the world spirit, which Solov'ev defines as the "tendency toward the incarnation of the Godhead in the world" (SS, 3:145).

The Incarnation of the Word is the last link in a long chain of physical and historical incarnations. It is the crowning event in history because through it Christ abdicates his divine glory, thus simultaneously divinizing his humanity and humanizing his divinity. With the Incarnation it is no longer a question of simply a transcendent God: we now have the God-Logos, the personal incarnation of God. The Incarnation points up the duality of man's own nature and makes possible Solov'ev's dream of Godmanhood, by which he means an assertion of the divine and absolute that inheres in each of us (as it did in Christ through the miracle of the Incarnation). Solov'ev's dualism is thus not the dualism of radically separate entities; the whole point of Lectures on Godmanhood and the underlying doctrine of the Incarnation is to show the original unity and the continuity of God and nature. God inheres in nature; the ideal inheres in the material. This is how we get to Solov'ev's doctrine of beauty and art. Beauty in nature and beauty in art are not different in kind for Solov'ev. Art is not an imitation of nature or even a mere duplication of nature's work; it is rather a continuation of what is begun by nature.

What is begun by nature is the same kind of incarnation we found in the Godman. Beauty in nature is "the transformation of matter through the incarnation in it of another, supramaterial principle," Solov'ev says in an essay called "Beauty in Nature." Thus beauty in nature is ultimately the expression of a purely ideal content. It is the "incarnation of an idea" (SS, 6:43) or, as Solov'ev puts it later on in the essay, the "sensible incarnation of a certain absolutely objective, completely single idea" (SS, 6:73).

A diamond, for example, is an object of beauty because it represents an almost perfect embodiment (incarnation) of an idea, namely the idea of illuminated stone. The beauty of a diamond resides neither exclusively in its substance (coal) nor exclusively in the light it reflects and refracts, but in both. The substance provides a means for embodying the supramaterial, ideal agent of light, and this very embodiment embodies the idea of illuminated stone.

In an essay titled "The General Meaning of Art" Solov'ev shows where nature leaves off and art picks up. "The beauty of nature," he says, "is merely a veil cast over evil life and not a transfiguration of that life. Man, therefore, with his rational consciousness, must be not only the end of the process of nature but also the means by which an ideal principle can exert an inverse, deeper, and fuller influence on nature" (SS, 6:78). Man enhances and furthers the work of the ideal in nature by creating artworks, and this act of creation consists precisely in the type of incarnation whose result we see in diamonds and other objects of natural beauty.

Beauty always represents the incarnation of an idea. The artistic activity of man incarnates an idea by uniting "a spiritual content and a sensible expression"; thus, through the "mutual penetration" of this content and this idea, "a material phenomenon that has truly become beautiful, that is, that has truly incarnated in itself an idea, must become just as enduring and immortal as the idea itself". The repeated use of the word incarnate and its various related forms in this essay is sufficient to show the theological character of Solov'ev's thought.

The root notion is always condescension or kenosis, which translates, in aesthetics, as any process by which something that is not physical gets expressed in something that is.

The triple task of art, says Solov'ev, consists in "(1) the direct objectificarion of those deepest internal determinations and qualities of the living idea that cannot be expressed by nature, (2) the animation of natural beauty and, through this, (3) the immortalization of the individual phenomena of that beauty" (SS, 6:84).

It is almost senseless to speak of an iconology in Solov'ev, if by iconology we refer to a separate science of icons. Everything is iconic for him. All creation is pervaded with the ideal, and almost everything would seem to invite the kind of perceptual act I just described. But artworks are even more iconic than other things because in them the work of the ideal has been enhanced by man. More than other things, presumably, artworks highlight their own iconicity.

Andrei Bely

It is pertinent to note that Bely's most ambitious essay from his symbolist period is "The Emblematics of Meaning." There is little likelihood that many of Bely's contemporaries (or successors, for that matter) bothered to read through and understand the whole thing, and so it is equally unlikely that one can speak of any direct impact the essay had on subsequent thought. And yet the essay contains perhaps the essence of Bely's whole doctrine. That essence is hinted at in the way the fields of language theory and theology usually overlap in Bely's thought. In "The Emblematics of Meaning," however, Bely has stepped back from language theory to confront a more general area, one that subsumes language theory. His concern in this essay is meaning, understood in its broadest sense.

Meaning is involved in virtually every realm of human endeavor, so Bely's essay of logical necessity takes account of not only language, art, and artistic language but also many other fields.

His approach to meaning amounts to a kind of formalistic, secularized, twentieth-century version of Orthodox iconology.

There are two broad categories of meaning, as Bely sees it: symbolic meaning and emblematic meaning.

Symbolic meaning is meaning presented in images; emblematic meaning is meaning presented in concepts. Symbolic meaning corresponds to creation, emblematic meaning to cognition. But the formal process by which both types of meaning are apprehended is identical, and since Bely could find no generic term to cover the two species symbolic and emblematic, he simply used the word emblematics in his title. "The Emblematics of Meaning" means that meaning is emblematic, which means that it comes into being by the formal process Bely defines in his essay. Bely calls that formal process symbolization, by which he means something very similar to incarnation. Symbolization starts with an ideal quality and embodies (incarnates) that quality in some intelligible medium (an image or a concept). The result is a symbol or emblem. Bely was so pleased with his description of the logical origins of all meaning that he made a diagram of the various fields of human endeavor to show how they stack up in relation to one another. The diagram is a large triangle subdivided into many small triangles, each standing for a field of human knowledge (S, p. 639; SE, p. 145).

The schema is hierarchical: the closer a field is to the ideal, which appears at the summit of the triangle, the farther up on the triangle it is located. The farther it is from the ideal, the lower down it appears. "Higher" fields are thus characterized by meanings with a greater ideal component, lower ones by meanings with a lower ideal component, which is to say that their meanings are more concrete.

Any field on the triangle is in a sense derived from the one immediately above it by the same process of symbolization that yields all objects of meaning, and thus it stands in relation to that superior field as an object of meaning stands in relation to its ideal content. The higher field supplies the ideal for the lower field, and the lower field then "symbolizes" that ideal. What is peculiar about Bely's system is how he appropriates the fundamental terms of Russian Orthodox iconology and logology but corrupts them by integrating into his system a set of godless philosophical concepts taken from some of the neo-Kantian thinkers then in vogue in Russia. What is the prototype for Bely?

We can find it by looking at the summit of his triangle since the summit shows what is symbolized by everything beneath it. The highest small triangle on Bely's diagram bears the inscription Value . At the summit of this triangle, which is also the summit of the entire diagram, are the words Symbol Embodied (or Symbol Incarnate —there is no distinction in Russian).

Basically, the term value comes from the epistemological system of Heinrich Rickert. Rickert had reformed the Kantian theory of knowledge by asserting that values are the true objects of ordinary acts of cognition (see above, p. 51). Values are apprehended by an act of the will because for Rickert ordinary cognition has come to be based on a kind of ethical affirmation of truth. In connecting the ethical element with the will, Rickert was simply following Kant, for whom the will is the faculty that comes into play in our decisions of right and wrong.

But for Kant the will connects us with the realm of freedom, and freedom is a transcendental idea (like the idea of God or the idea of immortality), something we cannot "know," something metaphysical that is not accessible to ordinary knowledge. Oddly enough, however, Rickert was antimetaphysical and saw his theory of knowledge as entirely scientific. His whole system was meant to reject the Kantian notion that there is a suprasensible world existing beyond the world of appearances.

In fact, the modern notion of value philosophy, something that had just come into fashion at the end of the nineteenth century, represented an effort to provide secular and relativistic answers to traditional ethical questions. So when Bely jumps on the value bandwagon, he is for all intents and purposes committing himself to an antireligious philosophy. But the structure of Bely's system is the structure of Orthodox iconology, and Bely is not in the least troubled by the easy mingling of religious and nonreligious terms that characterizes his essay. The summit of the value triangle, I said, is labeled Symbol Embodied . Bely often refers to this supreme term simply as the Symbol (with a capital S to distinguish it from ordinary symbols). What he appears to mean by it is the prototype of all symbol-forming activity, together with the reminder that such activity is a type of incarnation (embodiment). The ultimate, prototypical principle of value, and thus of everything meaningful, is the Symbol.

How does the Symbol come to be expressed? Bely uses the example of the three triangles situated immediately under the value triangle: metaphysics, theosophy, and theurgy. "The Symbol is expressed in symbolizations," he says, "and, in the present case, metaphysics, theosophy and theurgy are such symbolizations" (S, p.101; SE, p.160).

What is symbolization?" Here we can see how closely bound Bely is to his theological tradition. Remember that "embody" translates the Russian word that is used for the theological sense of "incarnate." Symbolization is the same sort of thing as incarnation. The last sentence of the passage I just quoted should leave no doubt about the analogy.

How does God come to be "seen as an existing something"? Through his creation, or through his Word—that is, through the condescension that occurs in the act of Incarnation. A few sentences after this one Bely says, "The reality created by God is a symbolic reality" (S, p. 106; SE, p. 164). Thus symbolization is like God's creation, which is like the Incarnation of the Word.

This brings us back to the epistemology of icon worship. Bely chooses to call his objects symbols instead of icons, but the posture of the perceiver is the same in both instances. Like the Christian worshiper venerating icons, the perceiver of symbols is always looking through a level of concretion to something invisible beyond, and Bely has seen fit to call that something value (or the Symbol Embodied). Symbols can be all sorts of things, associated with all sorts of fields of endeavor. If they are associated with art, then we have a theory of aesthetics that is clearly traced on the original of Orthodox iconology. Has Bely theologized aesthetics or aestheticized theology? It doesn't make much difference.

Sergei Bulgakov

It is remarkable that twentieth-century thinker who most successfully blurred the boundary between language philosophy and theology was probably Sergei Nikolaevich Bulgakov (1871–1944). Bulgakov is a Platonist in the grand tradition of Orthodox theology. "What is the Word?" is the title of the first chapter of Philosophy of the Name, and the answer has to do with essence. The essence of a word is its eidos, says Bulgakov. As usual, Bulgakov gives an Orthodox coloring to a Platonic notion. The idea or eidos of a word is the same as the "inner word," the "sense" of the word (FI, p. 21), and this gives rise to a peculiar property of words. "Logos," says Bulgakov, switching freely into the Platonic-theological idiom (and using the actual Greek letters, too), "has a double nature: in it the Word and the thought, the body and the sense, are inseparably and unamalgamatedly fused" (FI, p. 19).

If we didn't know this was a book about words we might simply think Bulgakov was explaining the Orthodox doctrine of the Logos. The Logos is Christ, and Christ has two natures in one person. In Christ the fleshly and the divine are inseparably united, just as body and sense (which is the same as the inner essence or Platonic idea) are united in Bulgakov's word. Christ is the Word incarnate, and Bulgakov naturally resorts to the Orthodox concept of the Incarnation to describe things that initially appear to have to do only with language. Meanings, he says, are ideas that become incarnate by means of words (FI, p. 21).

Bulgakov's subject is ambiguous from the outset. By calling his book Philosophy of the Name, instead of, say, Philosophy of Language or even Philosophy of the Word, Bulgakov is placing himself squarely in the same theological tradition that generated so much speculation about God's presence in his name.

When Bulgakov comes to talk about language in an apparently grammatical context, he plays on the possible confusion between linguistics and theology by using the Russian word for "name" as the central term in his discussion. He can do so because several of the Russian words for parts of speech contain the word "name" (imja), instead of the word "word" (slovo). The expression for "noun" in Russian, for instance, means something like "essential name" or "being-name" (imja suscestvitel'noe).

In fact, the transition from word to Word and from word to name is thus an easy one for Bulgakov. So, for that matter, is the transition from word to icon. Bulgakov is one of the few thinkers of the era to give explicit formulation to the analogy of word and icon and to locate the source of the analogy in the doctrine of kenosis. "Every icon is a name that has taken root and sprouted," he says (FI, p. 182). God's name is a "verbal icon of the Godhead" (FI, p. 184). The name of God "reveals itself in the word, our human word made up of sound," and this human word, declares Bulgakov, is an icon (FI, p. 190).

God comes to be present in his name and in the names of human language through precisely the same kenosis as allowed for the Incarnation of the Word of God in God's Son. There is an implicit hierarchy in Bulgakov's conception, not unlike the one we find in Bely. At the top is God, in the sense of the idea of God, who is present in his own name. Next there is Christ, the humiliated divinity. The name of Jesus reflects this status, Bulgakov says; it is the name of God, but with a human element. At the next level down we have the words of human language. Each new type of name, from the name of God down to the names, or words, of human language, represents an additional stage of concretion, of condescension, just as it had in Bely's pyramid. All names or words ultimately have a prototype, as they do for Bely. For Bulgakov this prototype is God, not value, but that does not alter the basic model.

The same epistemology is implicit in Bulgakov's scheme. In Bulgakov, as in Bely, the act of apprehending an object of meaning is the same as the act of worshiping an icon: it means looking through and beyond to something that cannot be apprehended by fleshly beings. The most curious thing about Bulgakov in this regard is that he is part of the same European linguistic tradition as Jakobson and all other early twentieth-century linguists. In the notes and appendixes to Philosophy of the Name we find references to Humboldt, Max Müller, Heymann Steinthal, Michel Bréal, and a host of other nineteenth-century philologists and linguists.

So it is not true that Bulgakov was a theologian and nothing more, approaching the study of language from the perspective of a tradition buried in the recesses of Orthodox church history. On the contrary, he was quite a modern man, almost as much of one, in fact, as Roman Jakobson. Nor is it true that Bulgakov took his modern linguistic heritage and gave it a surprising and ungainly twist to make it fit his theology. Bulgakov's view of language is not substantially different from the prevailing Russian view of language.

The theology that appears to the Western mind to be artificially superimposed on modern linguistics fits in a way that is completely natural for the Russian tradition of language philosophy. The proof is that we find the theology in Jakobson, too.

Pavel Florensky

A versatile genius, Pavel Florensky (1882–1937) was so many things that it would be hard to decide which to list as his principal occupation: theologian, priest, mathematician, scientist, inventor, or philosopher. He wrote on art, language, organic chemistry, mysticism, Kant, sculpture, Dostoevsky, Flaubert, Aegean culture, arithmetic, idealism, iconography, electromagnetism, microscopy, carbolic acid, asbestos, Pythagorean numbers, Aleksandr Blok, ecclesiology, and an absurd variety of other topics.

After the revolution he was one of the few intellectuals with conservative views to be permitted to remain professionally active in the country, at least for a time. His training in science made him useful in the early years of the Soviet Union, when he applied his expertise as an electrical engineer to various public-works projects. It is a testimony to the enforced, selective blindness of Soviet history that until recently the achievement for which Florensky was perhaps best remembered officially in his own country was his invention in 1927 of a noncoagulating machine oil. Before the revolution, in a climate that was more receptive to the full range of Florensky's interests, he was not obliged to concern himself with asbestos and machine oil. His most important writing is a monstrously large book called The Pillar and Ground of the Truth, an attempt to elaborate an entire Orthodox metaphysics based on the ideas of love and friendship.

Florensky was also a leading figure in the cult of Divine Wisdom, or Sophia, a movement initiated by Solov'ev. Sophia was seen as various things: a kind of supreme prototype in the universe, a fourth member of the Trinity, the church, God's love, and another expression for the Mother of God. The point of departure for Florensky's thinking shows what a Platonist and essentialist he was. The basic truth for Florensky is the existence of two worlds, a visible one and an invisible one. The first chapter, or "letter," of The Pillar and Ground is called "Two Worlds," and Florensky's long essay on icons, "Iconostasis," begins with reflections on the division of the world into visible and invisible. I have referred repeatedly to kenosis, the condescension of God in the Incarnation. Florensky describes kenosis as the entering of God into flesh, of one "I" into another "I" (SU, p. 92). This then serves as an analogy for a number of fundamentally related concepts: love, too, is the entering of an "I" into another "I."

The condescension of God into human flesh thus becomes

an act of love linking the invisible with the visible. Human cognition bears a significant analogy to love and kenosis because it consists in "the real going-out of the cognizing [subject] from himself or—what is the same—the real entering of the cognizing [subject] into the cognized [object]—the real union of cognizing [subject] and cognized [object] " (SU, p. 73).

This means that cognition has to do with truth, which is the subject of Florensky's big book. "The essential cognition of Truth," he says, "that is, a communion with Truth itself, is, consequently, a real entering into the depths of the Divine Triunity . . . Therefore, true cognition—the cognition of Truth—is possible only through the transubstantiation of man, through his deification, through the acquisition of love as Divine essence . . . In love and only in love is the actual cognition of Truth thinkable" (SU, p. 74).

Love, truth, cognition, kenosis, and, by implication, the Incarnation are thus all profoundly linked together. All either actually or by analogy bridge the gap between the visible and the invisible worlds.

Florensky came to the attention of literary scholars in recent years because of his writing on language and art. Members of the Tartu school of structuralism and semiotics, a group of Soviet scholars working at the University of Tartu in Estonia, rediscovered Florensky's writings some twenty years ago and, in the early 1970s, published several of them with footnotes and commentary. One of these is titled "Iconostasis."

The iconostasis is a screen in Orthodox churches that separates the sanctuary from the nave and is covered with icons arranged in prescribed, complicated patterns. The essay is about icons, and it gives one of the most extended and complete philosophical treatments of the subject in the history of Russian iconology. It was written in 1922 but never published until 1972. Much of what Florensky says about icons fits the standard formulations. In some cases, however, he has come up with novel ways of thinking about icons and novel terms in which to conceptualize them. He starts out by pointing to the truth underlying the existence of icons, namely the existence of a visible and an invisible world.

Florensky says that the iconostasis represents the border between these two worlds. Icons are not art, they do not represent things, and icon painters do not create anything. Instead, icons are the means by which the prototype "witnesses" itself. When he turns to language the Platonic essentialism and a Humboldtian myth of origins persist in Florensky's conception, but with a twist that is entirely new. There are two important places where we can learn Florensky's thoughts on language. There is The Pillar and Ground of the Truth, which contains numerous etymological excursuses on various concepts.

And there is a short article titled "The Construction of the Word," which Florensky wrote sometime before 1922, but which was not published during his lifetime.

In *The Pillar and Ground* Florensky shows a fondness for philological speculation that anticipates Heidegger. We find the same simple faith in the myth of original purity, the same sense that a primitive, essential core dwells in a word over the centuries and continues to have signifying force for the speakers of a particular nation. In his chapter on truth, for instance, Florensky examines the words for "truth" in a number of different languages and includes an analysis of the Greek word aletheia similar to Heidegger's celebrated treatment in his 1943 essay "Aletheia."

We find, too, the same willingness to cross the boundary between sober scholarly accuracy and pure fancy in his etymological work. In fact, Florensky openly acknowledges and even justifies his transgressions in a footnote to one of his etymological analyses in The Pillar and Ground : "Philosophy creates language, not studies it." He then strangely cites as his authority Humboldt and the theory that language is a dynamic process (SU, p. 786).

Notably, "The Structure of the Word" contains a theory of language that is extraordinary for the way it combines the traditional romantic myth of origins with a more "modern," contextual theory. Florensky's point of departure is the observation that a basic antimony underlies language. Every word, he says, derives at once from a set of primary elements common to all speakers and from the mind and thoughts of the individual speaker. The word is thus both public and private. It contains elements that must not change from utterance to utterance in order for a community of speakers to have a fixed means of communication.

At the same time, since the word is used in actual utterances, it contains elements that are peculiar to those utterances and to the speakers making them. Florensky then builds on this antinomy a theory of inner and outer form clearly derived from Potebnia, except that he performs a fascinating reversal of Potebnia's terms. Outer form, according to Florensky, is what he calls the body of the word. It is the word's unchanging composition, which serves common reason. Inner form, by contrast, is the very soul of the word.

It is constantly changing, always being born anew, and it serves individual reason. Potebnia, remember, had equated the inner form of the word with its closest etymological meaning. Florensky retains both the idea of inner form and the idea of a closest etymological meaning, but he changes things around and associates the closest etymological meaning, what he calls the etymon, with outer form. That's because the etymon, which is the true flesh of the word, provides the constant element in a word, the element that does not appreciably change from one utterance to the next. Florensky uses the same terms as Potebnia to describe this changeless element in a word. It is the old etymological myth of origins. The etymon for Florensky is the word's "original [pervonacal'noe] or truthful [istinnoe] meaning."

Florensky gives an example of a word with its etymological derivation to illustrate what "primeval [pervobytnyj] man" thought about the object designated by that word. But Florensky's conclusion is entirely different from Potebnia's. For Florensky, the etymon is merely part of the outer form of the word, that is, the form that serves the needs of the community of speakers. It is not the soul of the word. The notion that speech is, at least on one level, linked with inner, private experience leads Florensky to the following bold observation: "Words are unrepeatable; in every instance they are spoken anew, that is, with a new sememe, and in the best case this will be a variation on an earlier theme. . . . Only the outer form of a word can be objectively one and the same thing in a conversation, but never the inner form."

What do we make of an assertion like this? There is no doubt that the Platonist and essentialist impulse is there. The whole doctrine of inner form as it was modified by Potebnia was Platonic because it linked the essence of the word with something basically ahistorical. Florensky may have seen himself as returning to Humboldt's notion of inner form, which had to do with the dynamic nature of language and not with frozen, ahistorical meanings. But there is an important difference here, too.

For Humboldt, the dynamic, generative nature of language had to do with a concept of nationhood. It was the Volk with all its generative cultural energy that was responsible for the constant process of renewal that languages undergo. With Florensky, however, the emphasis is on the individual utterance, on the implicit isolation and uniqueness of any act of speech.

His use of the word context, the idea that speech can be understood only in relation to a total "lived" set of circumstances, is particularly striking since it anticipates all those lonely twentieth-century postmodern theories of language, which see language as ultimately unstable because it is always "implicated" in a ceaselessly changing historical context.

This contextuality is what Florensky appears to regard as essential in language. But the most Platonic and essentialist concept in Florensky's theory of language is associated for him with the aspect of language that is least essential, namely its outer form.

Bulgakov was an important figure not because of any impact his writings had on his contemporaries or on future generations but because his thinking arises from the same tradition as the thinking of figures that did have an enormous impact on future generations in the West. This is true of Florensky, too. But with Florensky we can speak of a few actual points of contact with his contemporaries.

Most important of all, however, is the connection with Mikhail Bakhtin. In Bakhtin's theory of discourse all speech is part of a dialogue. The word never exists in isolation but gets its meaning from the context in which it is uttered. Thus for Bakhtin, too, words are unrepeatable, since contexts are unrepeatable. Bakhtin spent most of his life in obscurity or in internal exile in the Soviet Union, and his writings were not widely known even abroad until the 1970s. But he has since become popular in the academic literary establishment. As it happens, Florensky and Bakhtin were part of the same intellectual circle in the 1920s, and there are affinities between their ways of thinking that can perhaps be explained by the circumstance that Bakhtin was, to a surprising extent, a religious man in the Orthodox tradition.

Katerina Clark and Michael Holquist, who have written the standard biography of Bakhtin, show the religious bases of his theory of language. There are two concepts, both deriving from the familiar doctrine of kenoticism. The first is something called sobornost ‘, which Clark and Holquist translate as "communality."

It refers to the brotherhood on earth of Christian worshipers, and it derives from the idea of the shared experience with Christ that was made possible by the kenosis. As Clark and Holquist explain, this idea serves as a foundation for Bakhtin's notion of the dialogic. Dialogic communication rests on the fundamental act by which one consciousness recognizes another. All human interaction is an example of this kind of self-other relation. In his earliest work Bakhrin explicitly makes the connection between this model of human interaction and the idea of Christian community. The second concept, Clark and Holquist say, is "a profound respect for the material realities of everyday experience." Since the kenotic tradition emphasizes the Incarnation so strongly, it has always insisted on the miracle of creation itself as another instance of incarnation and thus has always revered the material world. This was the injunction of John of Damascus, who cautioned men not to despise matter. Bakhtin, as Clark and Holquist explain, was fascinated with the material dimension of language for precisely this reason. But he also reverted to the standard terms of Orthodox logology to describe the word, referring to the two-sided nature of the word and implicitly confusing "word" (a unit of human language) and "Word" (the Word of God that was made flesh).

Thus it is easy to see the resemblance between this idea and the doctrine that Florensky has briefly elaborated in "The Construction of the Word." Bakhtin's communal conception of language would later develop into a full-fledged theory of linguistic contextuality, and that is exactly what Florensky proposes in his essay. And Bakhtin's point of departure is the recognition of the fundamental duality of language, a recognition that comes from the way the kenotic tradition views the relation between the visible and the invisible.

8

Psychoanalytical Criticism

> "The artist is one who is urged on by instinctive needs which are too clamorous; he longs to attain to honor, power, riches, fame and the love of woman; but he lacks the means of achieving these gratifications. So like any other with an unsatisfied longing, he turns away from reality, and transfers all his interest, and all his libido too, on to the creation of his wishes in the life of phantasy."
>
> —*Sigmund Freud*

As we know Sigmund Freud propounded the theory of 'psychoanalysis'. The school of psychoanalytical literary criticism is based on the dictum given by Freud.

First it is apt to quote Derrida suggests that we conceive of the play of *différance* before thinking of or as prior to such oppositions as absence/presence or subject/object; this différance "holds us in a relation to what exceeds . . . the alternative of presence or absence. A certain alterity—Freud gives it a metaphysical name, the unconscious."

If we move to Lacan's reading of Freud, we find the self articulated as or through the discourse of the Other (via unconscious activity that indicates the difference within consciousness between consciousness and itself). Lacan offers a way to envision the social and linguistic construction of the self: We become social by appropriating language, or rather, it (also) appropriates or constitutes us as subjects (selves).

The individual and society appear in opposition but should not be dichotomized: social discourses inhabit each subject (self). But such discourses work largely through unconscious activity that remains untranslatable; we can only diagnose and infer the structuring process of this language-like activity from the perspectives of "consciousness"—again, these are unconscious processes that Lacan compares to the structuring activity of language. This relation and this figure (linguistic metaphor/comparision) are particularly apt for literary studies, especially in terms of the analyst/critic's interpretation of the analysand's narrative/story and the attendant disguises/displacements of meanings (repression). Language is the condition for unconscious activity, producing its figurative detours and deferrals of signification (for example, via metaphoric condensations of meaning and metonymic chains of part for whole associations).

The Oedipus complex and its resolution mark a transition for a child into a cultural arena where he (she?) becomes self-aware, conscious of an identity and a position or name in relation to family and others—ultimately a place within culture and its laws, discourses, and organisation, but also a position disrupted by possibilities that seem to exceed and to challenge predominant ways of naming and knowing (for example, the rule/Name-of-the-Father, illusion of 'phallic' power, authority figures who supposedly have the power to name and to recognize one).

Hence, for Lacan the Subject ('self') is always split by that which is Other, which the Subject experiences as something lacking/missing, which in turn creates desire (compare this to the Derridean move to supplement lack on the part of the signifier/signifying). Desire is not primarily literal or only sexual: it describes a struggle for wholeness, a pursuit of fullness of meaning and being. The Subject projects desire onto an(Other), who also tends to see him/herself in the Subject. The unconscious is that which the Subject does not recognize to be himself and which he experiences as other from himself. Thus the way that the Subject (reader/critic/writer/text?) projects upon and views an Other will yield clues concerning his or her relationship to unconscious wishes and desires (lack). The unconscious is thus often in the place of the Other, the place where the subject does not recognize herself. Unconsciousness emerges as otherness within consciousness. Instead of the rational, autonomous assertion of the unified Cartesian self—"I think, therefore I am"(*cogito ergo sum*) —Lacan announces that "I think where I am not, therefore I am where I do not think," or "I think where I cannot say I am."

Our largely unwitting dependence upon others (texts too) for self-recognition can become threatening, prompting aggressive self-assertion or a pursuit of Mastery over others even as we may also long poignantly for full intersubjectivity, for complete understanding and union with others (a wish-fulfillment that we could identify with Dr. Spock's Vulcan mind-meld).

As Hegel argued, desire is directed towards another's desire, another (desiring and desired) Subject. Desire reveals our desire to be desired, to be valued and recognized by another, perhaps by the way another's desire will be seen to confirm or to subtitute metaphorically for our own (for us). Desire proceeds from unconscious activity and the lack that it generates (or by which it is comprised and construed, its condition for being). We may demand recognition/love/

meaning from others (texts), but we can never be certain that others recognize or speak to us in particular, though we try metaphorically and metonymically to compensate for such lack; desire is insatiable, and we may feel subordinated to the symbolic order and activity of language, as it produces desires for particular meanings that continue to elude us, alienating us from ourselves and others even as our relation to others informs and creates our desires.

Finally, all of the arguments above suggest that as we read literature, we locate meaning in the text as Other, which we then hope to master through our interpretation. Interpretation supposes "if not a conception of the unconscious itself, then at least some mechanism of mystification or repression in terms of which it would make sense to seek a latent meaning behind a manifest one" (Jameson, The Political Unconscious 60). A conventional "Freudian" reader would then supply the answer to the text that has evidenced its "sexual frustration and repression." But a Lacanian reading recognizes that what one discovers within the discourse of the other—the unconscious—is a discovery of what is actively reading within oneself, just as, for example, Freud read his own unconscious reading him within the hysteric's discourse. In effect, the text reads the reader who unconsciously repeats its structure and thereby dismantles distinctions between subject/object, master/slave, reader and that which is read.

The text's untranslatability, its silence, is what it won't tell and what the reader cannot tell himself. The structure of such narrative is transferential, with reading presented as the repetition of a love story "addressed to and directed toward the knowledge of the Other". To attempt to master such knowledge is to blind oneself (like Oedipus?), to repress the divisions within meaning (self,unconscious), and to disguise the will to power as a will to knowledge. *[Courtesy: Stephan Flores]*

Freud was a cultivated man and, while not entirely approving of artists, did take a close interest in artistic production and appreciation. Psychic energy (libido) was sexual at base, but was not channelled wholly into sexual activity. Amongst its expressions were dreams, fantasies and the personality disorders that arose when instinctual drives were constrained by exterior reality: the pleasure principle versus the reality principle.

Desire was the motivating force of the artist — an inordinate desire to win honour, power, wealth, fame and the love of women with a corresponding lack of means of doing so. Notoriously, the artist was an introvert, and not far removed from a neurotic.

Nonetheless, Freud did not confuse daydreams and artistic creation, did not reduce aesthetics to wish fulfillment, and admitted that psychoanalysis could not say how the artist achieved his successes. Dreams and art both employed strategies to transform primitive desires into the culturally acceptable, and indeed the artist masked and sweetened his daydreams with aesthetic form. Even Freud's much-criticized essay *Leonardo and a memory of his childhood* is more a psycho-biography than art criticism.

Freudian literary analysis comes in various degrees of subtlety. At its most elementary, the novel or poem may be analyzed simply in terms of phallic symbols: the assertive male organ or receptive female organ. More usually there is some attempt to see these as the secret embodiment of the author's unconscious desires. More penetrating is the psycho-biographic approach which seeks to explain an artist's life and work through childhood events, the Oedipus conflict and repression. Sometimes the psychic energy is regarded as the life-force, as in D.H. Lawrence's study of American nineteenth century literature, where a lust for power is attributed to a repressed Puritan conscience.

Different again is ego-analysis, which attempts to show that the pleasure of artistic creation and performance lies in the *controlled* play with primitive material, both artist and audience entering into the process. Art for Kleinians continues the encounter between infant and mother, contentment at the breast and separation, harmony and rebellion: the unconscious creates the form of the artwork through the interaction of artist with medium.

Anton Ehrenzweig saw the work of art as a womb which received fragmented projections of the artist's self. Julia Kristeva talks of a "potential space" leading to language acquisition. André Green extended analysis to reader and writer, so involving two sets of conscious and unconscious minds. There are many schools, of varying plausibility, which lead to or become involved in Structuralism or Post-structuralism. The straightforward psychological approach is unpopular. The New Critics concentrated on textural analysis, and declared biography to be irrelevant. The Poststructuralists believe that authors have less control over their writing (or at least the import of their writing) than is supposed: all that authors can do is manipulate a language fraught with ethnic and political repressions, with indeterminacy and cultural imperialism.

Even among traditional critics, psychology has earned itself a bad name by crudely fitting the novel or poem into some straight-jacket of psychoanalysis. The terminology of psychoanalysis is abstruse and/or repugnant. Too many of the psychoanalytic critics have no literary sensibility. {8} More damaging still is the plethora of psychoanalytic theories:

all wildly different and all claiming the truth. Perhaps none is acceptable, as psychoanalysis evades scientific testing and has an indifferent therapeutic record.

Sexual Symbols

Readers may wish to analyze themselves, or their whole body of work, dwelling in particular on obsessions and any favourite or repetitive imagery. But for the limited purposes of this exercise, it may be best to adopt something basic to Freud and start with a crude stocktaking.

Condensation

It is apt to note than in condensation, two or more elements combine in a composite image. The first such image here is buildings. They seem unusually important, indeed the whole poem on one level is about buildings. We learn they have much of the North Sea in them, being composed of aggregates that derive from the land they occupy. That North Sea is somehow oppressive. When the aggregate is heaped up in cliffs, those cliffs become burdensome, underwritten by past days. Not created, note — which is literally true — but in some way guaranteed by past, stormy days. That past, moreover, spreads into and colours the present.

It is glinting, obdurate and part of the stony lives of bureaucrats who occupy the levels of our modern buildings, described here as concrete pallets. The word "silicates" is another composite image. Silicates are minerals making up all rocks except limestones, and thereby enter into the great mass of buildings, even those of glass, which is of course silica.

But silicates, which have a complex crystal structure, are also used as an image for the rigid and unfeeling lives (tough, distant and intricate) of the bureaucrats who inhabit the buildings. Not just their inhabitants, moreover, but the buildings themselves are also seen as dead.

Finally, the buildings are regarded as whales, not only large and isolated (Caulked like great whales about us) but taking on their behaviour — their attitudes (pleading and flailing) and their sonic signalling to each other (placid but unbearable melodies). There are many other condensations, but let us concentrate on those above and ask: what psychological purposes do they serve, i.e. why were they written? The author will initially say that he does not really know: they seemed intriguing at the time, and even now, after extensive analysis, they continue to carry some emotional charge. Attempts to make them more rational and explanatory led to what seemed to be a weakening of the poem. Perhaps the reason is inaccessible to us. But note the preoccupation with sea and death. The buildings have something of the sea in them, but it is of past days. The bureaucrats' activities are likened to inert minerals. The buildings are described as concrete pallets or as possessing bare rib-bones.

Even the whales are doomed animals, pleading and flailing (close to failing). The death instinct seems very strong. Now look at the sexual symbols. The male symbols (buildings, grit, pebbles, obdurate) all carry something of the detrital, of a resistance to being worn down. They are not permanent or life-enhancing. The female symbols (surf, sea, burdensome, vacuumed, webs, deep, incurved) are again heavy and unregenerative. The images of sexual congress (impatient, flurrying, fill) are certainly not lusty and confident. In all there seems an air of sadness, even dejection, about the poem's symbolism. Only "impatient" runs against this trend, and that impatience, if buildings to reassumed the restless past of their constituents, would end in the buildings shaking themselves to pieces.

Displacement

It is worth mentioning that the second of Freud's processes was displacement, whereby an image is replaced by a psychologically more significant one. We have one in the bureaucrats' lives, which are replaced by a silicate frigidity. We have another in vacuumed — the afternoons being not merely clear but evacuated, vacuum-cleaned. And the buildings that metamorphose into whales is perhaps another displacement.

Indeed, in some ways, the whole process noted above is an extended displacement — of the useful (buildings), orderly (bureaucrats), structurally necessary (rib-bones) and purposeful (constructing these webs of buildings) by the defeated, the inert, the wearing away to nothing. Is this symbolism maintained? It seems to be. The bureaucrats are time-wasters (awaiting the post and the department meeting).

They are not aware either of the past history of the materials making up their building, or that their own lives are intricate but life-denying. Even the light-headedness of living in high buildings (the bureaucrat's, presumably, or just possibly the personified afternoon's: the syntax is confused) is not exhilarating, but brings on a neuralgia described either as troublesome and inconvenient (Calling at random like frail relations) or pointless.

Representation

Freud's representation, in which thoughts take the form of images. We have seen that the poem views the world as inert, cyclic and pointless, so that we need to investigate the images employed. Why were they chosen? Are they apt? What deeper psychological need is served by them? As to the first, the author replies that he cannot remember. The work is unusual for him, but was no doubt an attempt at making the worlds of rocks, natural processes and construction into a poem.

There are no early drafts to hand, so that he cannot now see how the work progressed. But very probably it was from the first line, which then lead him into thinking about the constituents of buildings — natural for someone who spent many years as a professional geologist. But that is not a very full answer. The natural world is not necessarily sad. Indeed, for most who study it, even geology is immensely fascinating and invigorating.

The trail again ends in matters not understood — unless the author was writing of his dissatisfactions with geology and reasons for leaving it, which is possible. Are the images apt? If the poem intended was a sort of Arnold's Dover Beach, but without the sustaining power of love, then the answer is surely "no". There is imagery much closer to home than this — more vital, better grasped, impinging more directly on lives. If the poem is an oblique criticism of the stultifying way geology is addressed, then the answer is again "no." The approach is very obscure indeed. But if the poem is an attempt to extend the content of poetry and see the world as the product of forces that carry meaning and emotional significance, then analysis moves to another sphere, to the subject of poetry, where psychoanalysis does not pretend to arbitrate.

Secondary Revision

Freud's fourth process was secondary revision, where the disparate elements are combined into an intelligible, coherent whole. Freud's terminology of course applied to dreams rather than literature, but it is noteworthy that the poem does have a dreamlike quality. The content appears by image association, and there are sudden shifts: from "they" to "we", and from buildings to whales. More pertinently, the need for an intelligible, coherent whole is the old demand for artistic autonomy and form. This fourth requirement is better examined under other approaches: traditional, textural or stylistic criticism.

All we need do here is to summarize those findings and note that the poem is unbalanced, unnecessarily dreamlike and requires more suspense in plot and argument. Psychoanalysis does not have an aesthetic remit. Its claims are for a psychological truth; if a poem seems significant and carries a strong emotional cnarge, then the poem is operating on the hidden drives of the unconscious.

The writer created the work in answer to some deep personal instincts, and the work appeals because it finds similar or equivalent instincts in the reader. There are no corrections indicated by psychoanalysis, only the proviso that the writer must ensure that in correcting along other lines that his corrections do not weaken that appeal. Further than that, of course, he has an obligation to examine what psychoanalytical criticism is suggesting, about his work, and about his fundamental nature.

It is obvious from the above discussion that psychoanalytical literary criticism is an important school of thought, no doubt it has also some limitations.

9

Modernism and Postmodernism

Now we will discuss modernism and post-modernism schools of literary thought. First it is apt to quote Berger who says, "Historically, the modernizing institutions par excellence have been modern industrial capitalism and the modern bureaucratic state." These modernizing factors have contributed to a shift in the understanding of concepts such as authority and truth a shift similar to that experienced in philosophy which has moved from an emphasis on universal essence to the existing individual. Sociologically these factors can be seen primarily in the political and economic arena in which power is no longer vested in the divine right to rule but with the consent of the governed. The rise of capitalism has dramatically changed the old hierarchical institutions controlled by church and king and has given rise to modern democracy.

Capitalism's ability to "universalize" the market has undermined the hierarchy of the past and brought about a new world.

Jane Tompkins catalogs the change in literature, with specific reference to her reader-response perspective, as a result of the changed social order brought on by capitalism:

> But, once authors become dependent for their means of support upon the sales of their printed work, the personal relation to their audience is severed and the relationship becomes more purely economic. Manuscripts no longer circulate by hand among a coterie of friends and associates; poems are no longer read aloud in groups; sonnets are not exchanged among acquaintances. Instead, literature assumes the fixed condition of print. The literary work becomes endlessly reproducible, available to anyone who can read. Hence, the possible distance in time and space between the originator of the work and its readers becomes virtually limitless.

Remarkably, Anthony Thiselton commenting on the rise of reader-response theory says, "In a commercial world too, the *consumer* decides what is to be offered and what is marketable, and *what is marketable becomes 'what is'*." What the consumer wants becomes what is true as the power lies with the purchaser, the demand with the consumer. This brings us to the influences of democracy which follow upon capitalism and bring another set of factors to bear on the interpreter. But first let us examine some of the influences of modernity on truth and authority.

It is a political Democracy that most accurately reflects the conventional beliefs regarding language and truth as its laws and social mores are, at least theoretically, determined by consensus. Capitalism and Democracy having brought about the demise of the old order based on a transcendent authority, promote an authority rooted in the people. It is an authority that is universal and like the marketplace rests on capital. Thus, the old authority rooted in God, in transcendent unchanging principles, has given way to a new order founded upon rationality which in a Democratic society often degenerates into popular opinion, a fear with which Plato was not unfamiliar.

The new order stands against the old with its authority rooted in the transcendent. It rebels against any sort of hierarchy either in society, the market, or the academy. As Gadamer has pointed out, the denigration of authority was a prejudice established in the enlightenment.

But this anti-hierarchical sentiment finds expression in philosophical terms through the death of the Author. Nietzsche proclaimed that God was dead and it was not long after that the notion of an author lost its meaning. Thus the demise of the Author has led to the demise of the author in the field of literature.

Roland Barthes has written that "to refuse to fix meaning is, in the end, to refuse God...." The post-modern society would prefer an unfixed, conventional view of language and truth because what is not "fixed" can be changed. And it can be changed because the power to do so resides with the society or the interpretive community. Thus Fish is able to claim with Foucault that the author is a creation of the reader. He is a fiction which is easier to live with than without. But ultimately Fish would claim there is no author because to quote Barthes, "To give a text an Author is to impose a limit on that text, to furnish it with a final signified, to close the writing."

In fact, once an author is conceded then an authority figure stands over the reader, alternately approving or condemning whatever meaning the reader takes from the text. She is no longer free and equal but instead subordinate to the will of the author, an authority figure reflective of Western patriarchal society. Conversely, to deprive a text of its author is to deprive it of its intentionality as well as its meaning which makes it easier for a hermeneutic such as Fish's to appear.

Democracy is a value laden institution. It consciously promotes individual freedom, self rule, and equality and these values in turn affect the way we look at the world. America, especially, has seen an increased emphasis placed on individual freedom, the ability to choose one's own destiny, with its right to "life, liberty, and the pursuit happiness" often to the detriment of social responsibility. These values affect the way we look at the world and produce an anti-hierarchical and anti-authoritarian *zeitgeist* as the power resides with the people.

David Wells says that it is "not simply a political system but an entire worldview and for whom, therefore, culture and truth belong to the people." In Berger's analysis of modernity he contends that the individual in modern society lives in a "*plurality of life-worlds*," by which he means that one's life is fragmented into various differing parts without the ability of each of those parts to interact with one another. Therefore the typical worker's occupation will seldom if ever come into contact with his family life.

This scenario can be, and is, multiplied in a world of increasing complexity. "A fundamental aspect of this pluralization is the dichotomy of private and public spheres." One of the effects of pluralization is, in Berger's analysis, secularization and the privatization of religion. Because religion cannot compete in a pluralistic society, while maintaining peace and harmonious relationships, it becomes increasingly a matter for discussion at home, although this is more the case for American than European communities. The same processes at work to take religious discussion out of the public arena (freedom of religion as seen in the separation of church and state is one of our most cherished values) have also worked to take notions of "truth" from the public arena.

As with religion, "truth" has become privatized and expressions like "what is true for me" become commonplace. The very idea that one religion could be true for me while another is true for you, undermines the concept of truth as an objective reality, something which was highly prized under the rubric of modernism. Thus in the post-modern world, the concept of truth becomes private property or immanent.

The privatization of which I am referring goes hand in hand with the values of a democratic institution. One of the results of "cognitive bargaining" in the modern world as a result of the dichotomy between public and private worlds is the subjectivization of truth. One may wonder whether the roots of existential thought cannot be traced to the rise of modernity, which is not to say that it is an asymmetric relationship. Referring to the fragmentation of the modern identity due to the loss of a cohering world, Berger says, "The modern individual's experience of a plurality of social worlds relativizes every one of them. Consequently the institutional order undergoes a certain loss of reality. . . . the individual's experience of himself becomes more real to him than his experience of the objective social world.

Therefore, the individual seeks to find his 'foothold' in reality in himself rather than outside himself." This puts the modern emphasis on existence over essence in a new light. It is not surprising then to find religion, philosophy, and literary theory placing the emphasis more on subjective experience and working to validate that experience.

In this connection it is apt to quote W. John Harker.

> So it was that the world seemed less certain. The philosophical reality of logical positivism the psychological

> certainty of behaviorism, the linguistic "common sense" of sensorially received language, and even the unassailable objectivity of scientific method all fell before competing movements in their respective disciplines, movements which had in common an appeal to the inner consciousness of man as the determiner of relative meaning, rather than an appeal to external observable, analyzable phenomena as the determiners of an objective reality.

Whereas at one time truth belonged to the transcendent realm that was fixed and unchanging, it has in the post-modern world become immanent. Knowledge, as with everything else in a capitalistic society, is spoken of in terms of "ownership."

This is not a coincidence. Whereas democracy begins with an ontological egalitarianism when transcendence is lost, epistemological egalitarianism results, in which each person has an equal right to make truth claims. Thus the proliferation of opinion polls in which the opinions of those less "informed" are equal to those more "informed," in which the unreflected upon opinions are weighted equally with those that are carefully considered. And it is often these kinds of opinion polls that determine, indirectly, public policy. Likewise, talk shows have become increasingly popular as they have become increasingly ludicrous and regardless of their claim, each one is on an equal footing epistemologically as "everyone has a right to an opinion."

Again, Thiselton referring to the rise of reader-oriented hermeneutics says, "Such a move also coheres too neatly with the trend towards social egalitarianism in an age which transfers any notion of 'privileged' knowledge on the part of an author or a sacred text to the shared contributions of pluralist reading communities."

It is exactly this privilege knowledge that Stanley Fish's

theory transfers to the possession of the reading community. For Fish it is the reader's perspective within his own context that is normative. As the concept of "author" has gone by the wayside there is therefore no longer any need to access what the meaning was in its original context, the reader's context takes precedent. Indeed, for Fish the reader's context is all that is accessible. It is not surprising therefore that Fish's theory would be labeled subjective by his critics, a criticism Fish strongly denies.

Peter Kivy maintains that subjectivity is exactly one of the consequences of Fish's critical theory. Reason is just another attempt at "metanarrative," another attempt by the powerful to control societal values. Instead truth is a socially constructed cultural given. Truth becomes immanent residing in each individual culture or person. No one has any greater claim to truth than any other as each is on an equal status epistemologically.

It is apt to quote Stanley Fish who says,

> . . . the claims of objectivity and subjectivity can no longer be debated because the authorizing agency, the center of interpretive authority, is at once both and neither. An interpretive community is not objective because as a bundle of interests, of particular purposes and goals, its perspective is interested rather than neutral; but by the very same reasoning the meanings and texts produced by an interpretive community are not subjective because they do not proceed from an isolated individual but from a public and conventional point of view.

Basically, language and literature become a means of promoting ideology as each community represents its own *interested* viewpoint. Eagleton, a Marxist, claims that literature has always been the means of enforcing a particular ideology on a people for the purposes of exploitation.

"Literature, in the meaning of the word we have inherited, *is* an ideology. It has the most intimate relations to questions of social power." And he discerns this perspective in the work of others such as Jacques Derrida, "deconstruction is for him an ultimately *political* practice, an attempt to dismantle the logic by which a particular system of thought, and behind that a whole system of political structures and social institutions, maintains its force."

If nothing else, at least *literary criticism* has become an arena in which ideological warfare is waged. Thus Marxist, feminist, African-American and every other interpretive grid competes for validity in the democratic market. It is probably no mistake that each has seated itself in a pedagogical role because in a democracy legitimation comes through the will of the people and education is one of the principle keys to that will.

Berger states that "*pluralization has a secularizing effect*" because the individual is forced to take cognizance of others who do not believe what he believes and whose life is dominated by different, sometimes contradictory, meanings, values and beliefs." These differing if not contradictory meanings, values, and beliefs lead to a cognitive bargaining in which each one's beliefs become less certain, in which more latitude is given to opinions that differ and which leads to the notion that truth is relative to one's socio-historical perspective. Thus, much of the Western ideology has come under attack, ironically from those within the culture.

Pluralism and relativism have produced a widespread hesitancy to affirm anything whose origin is in Western culture while at the same time maintaining an obsequious posture toward minority and non-Western ideas. Berger calls this a "failure of nerve" and maintains that, "It is not the first time in history that a cultural elite has stood in the forefront of those who would give up their society." It is by no means accidental that Fish's reader-response thesis has arisen in such a pluralistic age. Even in the academy there are numerous and competing schools of thought.

Graff comments that "Fish's concept of interpretive communities was enormously suggestive. . . particularly in an age of competitive academic interpretive schools. . .". As this cognitive bargaining takes place between cultures and viewpoints a certain leveling occurs on the epistemological plain. It becomes more plausible to maintain such a thesis as Fish's. Harker in chronicling the decline of New Criticism due to its narrow views of literature and heavily pedagogical nature makes an insightful statement. "Yet these internal flaws may not in themselves have been sufficient to bring down the New Criticism had they not become increasingly apparent during a period when public verse and public criticism were becoming antithetical to the increasingly introspective, relativistic spirit of the times."

Fish's critical theory accurately reflects this relativistic spirit of the times. The idea that truth is an historically conditioned notion that does not transcend cultural boundaries is by definition relativism. Within a community, however, a standard of right (and wrong) can always be invoked because it will be invoked against the background of a prior understanding as to what counts as a fact, what is hearable as an argument, what will be recognized as a purpose, and so on.

The point, as I shall later write, is that standards of right and wrong do not exist apart from assumptions, but follow from them, and, moreover, since we ourselves do not exist apart from assumptions, a standard of right and wrong is something we can never be without. Fish's writing smacks of relativism and indeed it is something of which he has often been accused. James Battersby points this out in his article "Professionalism, Relativism, and Rationality" published by the Modern Language Association. It is interesting to note however that Fish believes that he has insulated himself from the critique of relativism by positing his interpretive community theory. In an introduction to one of his reprinted articles in *Is There a Text in This Class?* he maps some of the course his mental activities have gone through over the years.

He says, "I was thus flirting with a relativism that would be removed only when the notion of interpretive communities, grounded in a bedrock of belief, allowed me to preserve the distinction between the fictional and the true by understanding it as a conventional or community-specific distinction rather than as one rooted in nature and eternity." As relativism as a philosophical perspective or hermeneutic presents a number of other problems. David Hackett Fischer in his book *Historian's Fallacies* shows even less patience with this form of error than he does most others. Fish's argument for the ungroundedness of the interpretive community, which takes full flower in his article entitled, "Anti-Professionalism," leaves itself open to the critique of historicism, that whatever is is right. And Gerald Graff levels this very critique against him in his response to "Anti-Professionalism."

But Dr. Fischer appropriately comments that the end result of such a view is that, "It would prevent any moral judgment against the filth which flowed from 'the innermost individual character' of many Nazi beings." Relativism, regardless of the form, comes under the age old criticism of being a false objectivity. As Battersby has said, "the view that all our ideas are historically or professionally conditioned is itself not historically or professionally conditioned." In other words, relativism claims that all truth is relative except for the claim that "truth is relative." And here we are in the same predicament the post-modern critics want to free us from, that is a metanarrative, a story that explains all other stories. But maybe Fish will argue that of course relativism is only my socially constructed reality, true only for the culture in which I live. This then is an agnostic position regarding possibility of knowing truth instead of the claim to knowledge which relativism definitely makes. Fish's response to this criticism of his position is to argue again that the critic is hopelessly mired in his own foundationalist paradigm.

His claim is that it is illegitimate for the foundationalist to criticize his position because the foundationalist belongs to a different community with different interpretive assumptions and his position can only be understood from *within* Fish's position. Battersby responds, My answer. of course, is that self-refutation owes no special allegiance to foundationalism or essentialism. As a standard, it serves many causes on many fronts. It belongs to the class of transparadigmatic criteria. . . . it has our interest because it is a strong standard, capable of leading to a deep objection.

Notably, one of dangerous aspects of relativism is that it bears an element of truth. It is certainly true that one's perspective and context controls, to a large extent, one's opinion. It is also true that different cultures and time periods emphasize different standards depending again on their cultural context. It does not however follow that all truth is relative. The relativist attempts to reason from what appears true in specific cases to what is true universally. This is both fallacious and self-stultifying.

Berger draws an interesting insight in *The Homeless Mind* that I believe applies to philosophical relativism and post-modern thought. His thesis is that modernity has caused a homelessness that is deeper than social dislocation. The 'homelessness' of modern social life has found its most devastating expression in the area of religion. . . . The age-old function of religion—to provide ultimate certainty amid the exigencies of the human condition—has been severely shaken. Because of the religious crisis in modern society, social "homelessness" has become metaphysical—that is, it has become "homelessness" in the cosmos.

Remarkably, Post-modern literary criticisms fit nicely into the new intellectual paradigm. While Deconstructionism works to undermine classical Western thought based on the principle of non-contradiction, reader-response theories serve to legitimate whatever interpretive paradigm a particular "interpretive community" brings to the text. Thiselton writes, "If reader-oriented literary theory has become entangled with philosophical contextual relativism and post-modernism, meanings of texts are not only contingently plural in the history of interpretation and textual reception; they are irreducibly plural in principle as a hermeneutical axiom."

Basically, Postmodernism is an aesthetic, literary, political or social philosophy, which was the basis of the attempt to describe a condition, or a state of being, or something concerned with changes to institutions and conditions (as in Giddens, 1990) as postmodernity. In other words, postmodernism is the "cultural and intellectual phenomenon", especially since the 1920s' new movements in the arts, while postmodernity focuses on social and political outworkings and innovations globally, especially since the 1960s in the West.

The *Compact Oxford English Dictionary* refers to postmodernism as "a style and concept in the arts characterized by distrust of theories and ideologies and by the drawing of attention to conventions." Notably, term postmodern is described by Merriam-Webster as meaning either "of, relating to, or being an era after a modern one" or "of, relating to, or being any of various movements in reaction to modernism that are typically characterized by a return to traditional materials and forms (as in architecture) or by ironic self-reference and absurdity (as in literature)", or finally "of, relating to, or being a theory that involves a radical reappraisal of modern assumptions about culture, identity, history, or language".

The American Heritage Dictionary describes the meaning of the same term as "Of or relating to art, architecture, or literature that reacts against earlier modernist principles, as by reintroducing traditional or classical elements of style or by carrying modernist styles or practices to extremes: "It [a roadhouse] is so architecturally interesting ... with its postmodern wooden booths and sculptural clock".

Postmodernism literally means 'after the modernist movement'. While "modern" itself refers to something "related to the present", the movement of modernism and the following reaction of postmodernism are defined by a set of perspectives. It is used in critical theory to refer to a point of departure for works of literature, drama, architecture, cinema, and design, as well as in marketing and business and in the interpretation of history, law, culture and religion in the late 20th century.

Postmodernism was originally a reaction to modernism. Largely influenced by the Western European "disillusionment" induced by World War II, postmodernism refers to a cultural, intellectual, or artistic state lacking a clear central hierarchy or organizing principle and embodying extreme complexity, contradiction, ambiguity, diversity, interconnectedness or interreferentiality, in a way that is often indistinguishable from a parody of itself. It has given rise to charges of fraudulence.

Postmodernity is a derivative referring to non-art aspects of history that were influenced by the new movement, namely developments in society, economy and culture since the 1960s. When the idea of a reaction or rejection of modernism was borrowed by other fields, it became synonymous in some contexts with postmodernity. The term is closely linked with poststructuralism (cf. Michel Foucault) and with modernism, in terms of a rejection of its bourgeois, elitist culture.

The term was first used around the 1870s in various areas. For example, John Watkins Chapman avowed "a postmodern style of painting" to get beyond French Impressionism Then, J.M. Thompson, used it to describe changes in attitudes and beliefs in the critique of religion: "The raison d'etre of Post-Modernism is to escape from the double-mindedness of Modernism by being thorough in its criticism by extending it to religion as well as theology, to Catholic feeling as well as to Catholic tradition" ('Post-Modernism, J.M.Thompson, *The Hibbert Journal,* Vol. XII, No. 4, July 1914, p. 733).

In fact 1917 Rudolf Pannwitz used the term to describe a philosophically oriented culture. Pannwitz's idea of post-modernism came from Nietzsche's analysis of modernity and its ends of decadence and nihilism. Overcoming the modern human would be the post-human. But, contrary to Nietzsche, Pannwitz also includes nationalist and mythical elements. It was used later in 1926 by B.I.Bell in his "Postmodernism & other Ess."

In 1925 and 1921 it had been used to describe new forms of art and music. In 1942 H. R. Hays used it for a new literary form but as a general theory of an historical movement it was first used in 1939 by the historian Arnold J. Toynbee: "Our own Post-Modern Age has been inaugurated by the general war of 1914-1918." In 1949 it was used to describe a dissatisfaction with modern architecture, leading to the postmodern architecture movement. Postmodernism in architecture is marked by the re-emergence of surface ornament, reference to surrounding buildings in urban architecture, historical reference in decorative forms, and non-orthogonal angles. It may be a response to the modernist architectural movement known as the International Style. The term was applied to a whole host of movements, many in art, music, and literature, that reacted against modernism, and are typically marked by revival of traditional elements and techniques. Walter Truett Anderson identifies postmodernism as one of four world views.

These four worldviews are the postmodern-ironist, which sees truth as socially constructed, the scientific-rational in which truth is found through methodical, disciplined inquiry, the social-traditional in which truth is found in the heritage of American and Western civilisation and the neo-romantic in which truth is found either through attaining harmony with nature and/or spiritual exploration of the inner self.

Postmodernist ideas in philosophy and the analysis of culture and society expanded the importance of critical theory and has been the point of departure for works of literature, architecture, and design, as well as being visible in marketing/business and the interpretation of history, law and culture, starting in the late 20th century. These developments — re-evaluation of the entire Western value system (love, marriage, popular culture, shift from industrial to service economy) that took place since 1950's and 1960's, with a peak in the Social Revolution of 1968 — are described with the term postmodernity, as opposed to postmodernism, a term referring to an opinion or movement. Whereas something being "postmodernist" would make it part of the movement, its being "postmodern" would place it in the period of time since the 1950s, making it a part of contemporary history.

Notwithstanding the foregoing distinctions, both terms can be synonymous and interchangeable in common parlance, given the fluidity and ongoing evolution of their definitions.

Whether 'postmodernism' is seen as a critical concept or merely a buzzword, one cannot deny its range. Dick Hebdige, in his 'Hiding in the Light' illustrates this:

When it becomes possible for a people to describe as 'postmodern' the décor of a room, the design of a building, the diegesis of a film, the construction of a record, or a 'scratch' video, a television commercial, or an arts documentary, or the 'intertextual' relations between them, the layout of a page in a fashion magazine or critical journal, an anti-teleological tendency within epistemology, the attack on the 'metaphysics of presence' a general attenuation of feeling, the collective chagrin and morbid projections of a post-War generation of baby boomers confronting disillusioned middle-age, the 'predicament of reflexitivity, a group of rhetorical tropes, a proliferation of surfaces, a new phase in commodity fetishism, a fascination for images, codes and styles, a process of cultural, political or existential fragmentation and/or crisis, the 'de-centring' of the subject, an 'incredulity towards metanarratives', the replacement of unitary power axes by a plurality of power/discourse formations, the 'implosion of meaning', the collapse of cultural hierarchies, the dread engendered by the threat of nuclear self-destruction, the decline of the university, the functioning and effects of the new miniaturised technologies, broad societal and economic shifts into a 'media', 'consumer' or 'multinational' phase, a sense (depending on who you read) of 'placelessness' or the abandonment of 'placelessness' (critical regionalism) or (even) a generalised substitution of spatial for temporal coordinates: when it becomes possible to describe all these things as 'postmodern' (or more simply using a current abbreviation as 'post' or 'very post') then it's clear we are in the presence of a buzzword.

Emergence and Growth

The movement of Postmodernism began with architecture, as a reactionary movement against the perceived blandness and hostility present in the Modern movement. Modern Architecture as established and developed by masters such as Walter Gropius and Philip Johnson was focused on the pursuit of an ideal perfection, harmony of form and function and dismissal of frivolous ornament. Critics of modernism argued that the attributes of perfection and minimalism themselves were subjective, and pointed out anachronisms in modern thought and questioned the benefits of its philosophy. Definitive postmodern architecture such as the work of Michael Graves rejects the notion of a 'pure' form or 'perfect' architectonic detail, instead conspicuously drawing from all methods, materials, forms and colors available to architects.

Postmodern architecture began the reaction against

the almost totalitarian qualities of Modernist thought, favoring personal preferences and variety over objective, ultimate truths or principles. It is this atmosphere of criticism, skepticism and subjectivity that defines the postmodern philosophy. Certain interpretations of Søren Kierkegaard, Karl Marx, and Friedrich Nietzsche are important precursors to postmodernism. With their emphasis on skepticism, especially concerning objective reality, social morals, and societal norms, all three philosophers, for the postmodernists, represent a reaction to modernism ending in Georg Wilhelm Friedrich Hegel. Other notable influences on postmodernism include Laurence Sterne's novel *Tristram Shandy*, Alfred Jarry's 'Pataphysics, and the work of Lewis Carroll.

Art and literature of the early part of the 20th century play a significant part in shaping the character of postmodern culture. Dadaism attacked notions of high art in an attempt to break down the distinctions between high and low culture; Surrealism further developed concepts of Dadaism to celebrate the flow of the subconscious with influential techniques such as automatism and nonsensical juxtapositions (evidence of Surrealism's influence on postmodern thought can be seen in Foucault's and Derrida's references to Rene Magritte's experiments with signification). Some other significant contributions to postmodern culture from literary figures include the following: Jorge Luis Borges experimented in metafiction and magical realism; William S. Burroughs wrote the prototypical postmodern novel *Naked Lunch* and developed the cut up method (similar to Tristan Tzara's "How to Make a Dadaist Poem") to create other novels such as *Nova Express*; Samuel Beckett attempted to escape the shadow of James Joyce by focusing on the failure of language and humanity's inability to overcome its condition, themes later to be explored in such works as *Waiting for Godot*.

Karl Barth's fideist approach to theology and lifestyle, brought an irreverence for reason, and the rise of subjectivity. Postcolonialism after World War II contributed to the idea that one cannot have an objectively superior lifestyle or belief. This idea was taken further by the anti-foundationalist philosophers: Heidegger, then Derrida, who examined the fundamentals of knowledge; they argued that rationality was neither as sure nor as clear as modernists or rationalists assert.

It is with the end of the Second World War that recognizably postmodernist attitudes begin to emerge. It is possible to identify the burgeoning anti-establishment movements of the 1960s as the constituting event of postmodernism. The theory gained some of its strongest ground early on in French academia.

In 1971, the Arab-American theorist Ihab Hassan was one of the first to use the term in its present form (though it had been used by many others before him, Charles Olson for example, to refer to other literary trends) in his book: *The Dismemberment of Orpheus: Toward a Postmodern Literature*; in it, Hassan traces the development of what he called "literature of silence" through Marquis de Sade, Franz Kafka, Ernest Hemingway, Beckett, and many others, including developments such as the Theatre of the Absurd and the nouveau roman. In 1979 Jean-François Lyotard wrote a short but influential work *The Postmodern Condition: A report on knowledge*. Richard Rorty wrote *Philosophy and the Mirror of Nature* (1979). Jean Baudrillard, Michel Foucault, and Roland Barthes are also influential in 1970s postmodern theory.

Postmodern Music

The postmodern impulse in classical music arose in the

1970s with the advent of musical minimalism. Composers such as Terry Riley, John Adams, Steve Reich, Phillip Glass, and Lou Harrison reacted to the perceived elitism and dissonant sound of atonal academic modernism by producing music with simple textures and relatively consonant harmonies. Some composers have been openly influenced by popular music and world ethnic musical traditions. Though representing a general return to certain notions of music-making that are often considered to be classical or romantic, not all postmodern composers have eschewed the experimentalist or academic tenets of modernism. The works of Dutch composer Louis Andriessen, for example, exhibit experimentalist preoccupation that is decidedly anti-romantic. Eclecticism and freedom of expression, in reaction to the rigidity and aesthetic limitations of modernism, are the hallmarks of the postmodern influence in musical composition.

Deconstruction

It is pertinent to note that the term "deconstruction" comes from Martin Heidegger, who calls for the destruction or deconstruction (the German "Destruktion" connotes both English words) of the history of ontology. The point, for Heidegger, was to describe Being prior to its being covered over by Plato and subsequent philosophy. Thus, Heidegger himself engaged in "deconstruction" through a critique of post-Socratic thought (which had forgotten the question of Being) and the study of the pre-Socratics (where Being was still an open question). Deconstruction is a term which is used to denote the application of postmodern ideas of criticism, or theory, to a "text" or "artifact", based on architectural deconstructivism.

A deconstruction is meant to undermine the frame of

reference and assumptions that underpin the text or the artifact. In later usage, a "deconstruction" is an important textual "occurrence" described and analyzed by many postmodern authors and philosophers. They argue that aspects in the text itself would undermine its own authority or assumptions and that internal contradictions would erase boundaries or categories which the work relied on or asserted.

Poststructuralists beginning with Jacques Derrida, who coined the term, argued that the existence of deconstructions implied that there was no intrinsic essence to a text, merely the contrast of difference. This is analogous to the idea that the difference in perception between black and white is the context. A deconstruction is created when the "deeper" substance of text opposes the text's more "superficial" form. This idea is not isolated to poststructuralists but is related to the idea of hermeneutics in literature; intellectuals as early as Plato asserted it and so did modern thinkers such as Leo Strauss. Derrida's argument is that deconstruction proves that texts have multiple meanings and the "violence" between the different meanings of text may be elucidated by close textual analysis. Popularly, close textual analyses describing deconstruction within a text are often themselves called deconstructions. Derrida argued, however, that deconstruction is not a method or a tool but an occurrence within the text itself. Writings about deconstruction are therefore referred to in academic circles as deconstructive readings. Deconstruction is far more important to postmodernism than its seemingly narrow focus on text might imply.

According to Derrida, one consequence of deconstruction is that the text may be defined so broadly as to encompass not just written words but the entire spectrum of symbols and phenomena within Western thought. To Derrida, a result of deconstruction is that no Western philosopher has been able to escape successfully from this large web of text and reach that which is "signified", which they imagined to exist "just beyond" the text. The more common use of the term is the more general process of pointing to contradictions between the intent and surface of a work and the assumptions about it. A work then "deconstructs" assumptions when it places them in context. For example, someone who can pass as the opposite sex may be said to "deconstruct" gender identity, because there is a conflict between the superficial appearance and the "reality" of the gender of persons.

Social Construction, Structuralism, Poststructuralism

Often opposed to deconstruction are social constructionists, labeled as such within the analytic tradition, but not usually in the case of the continental tradition. The term was first used in sociologists Peter Berger and Thomas Luckmann's book *The Social Construction of Reality*. Usually in the continental tradition, the terms structuralism or poststructuralism are used. Maurice Merleau-Ponty is seen as the biggest contributor to structuralism, which is epitomized in the philosophy of Claude Levi-Strauss.

Michel Foucault was also a structuralist but then turned to what would be termed poststructuralism, although he himself declined to call his work either poststructuralist or postmodern. Structuralism historically gave way to poststructuralism; often the role of postmodernism within the analytic tradition is played down, although works by major figures of the analytic tradition in the 20th century, including those of Thomas Kuhn and Willard Van Orman Quine, show a similarity with works in the continental tradition for their lack of belief in absolute truth as well as in the pliability of language. In the continental tradition, most works argue that power dissimulates and that society constructs reality, while its individuals remain powerless or almost powerless.

Often, both continental and analytic sources argue for a renewed subjectivity, borrowing heavily from Immanuel Kant, while they largely reject his a priori/a posteriori distinction. They both minimize discussions of practical ethics, instead borrowing heavily from post-Holocaust accounts of the need for an ethics of responsibility, which is very rarely practically defined.

Notably, one of the large differences between analytic postmodern sources and continental postmodern sources is that the analytic tradition by and large guards at least some of the tenets of liberalism, while many continental sources flirt with, or completely immerse themselves in, Marxism. Recently, it is noticeable that some of the ideas found in poststructuralism and postmodernism, as the lack of belief in absolute truth or the idea of a reality *constructed*, is promoted in a new paradigm within constructivist epistemology.

An Analysis

As noted above, the term postmodernism, when used pejoratively, describes tendencies perceived as relativist, counter-enlightenment or antimodern, particularly in relation to critiques of rationalism, universalism or science. It is also sometimes used to describe tendencies in a society that are held to be antithetical to traditional systems of morality. Elements of the Christian Right, in particular, have interpreted postmodern society to be synonymous with moral relativism and contributing to deviant behavior. The criticisms of postmodernism are often complicated by the still-fluid nature of the term, and in many cases the criticisms are clearly directed at poststructuralism and the philosophical and academic movements that it has spawned rather than the broader term postmodernism.

The criticism of elements of postmodernism as sophism or obscurantism was played out in the Sokal Affair, where Alan Sokal, a physicist, delivered for publication an article about interpreting physics and mathematics in terms of postmodern theory, which he had deliberately written to mock postmodernist views on objectivity, determinism and the social construction of scientific truth. It was published by *Social Text*, a cultural studies journal active in the field of postmodernism. Sokal arranged for the simultaneous publication of another article describing the former as a successful experiment to see whether a postmodernist journal would publish it, triggering an academic scandal. Sokal later published a book with Jean Bricmont called *Intellectual Impostures,* which expands upon his criticism of postmodernism. The celebrated linguist Noam Chomsky has suggested that postmodernism is meaningless because it adds nothing to analytical or empirical knowledge.

He asks why postmodernist intellectuals won't respond as "people in physics, math, biology, linguistics, and other fields are happy to do when someone asks them, seriously, what are the principles of their theories, on what evidence are they based, what do they explain that wasn't already obvious, etc? These are fair requests for anyone to make. If they can't be met, then I'd suggest recourse to Hume's advice in similar circumstances: to the flames."

"There are lots of things I don't understand — say, the latest debates over whether neutrinos have mass or the way that Fermat's last theorem was (apparently) proven recently. But from 50 years in this game, I have learned two things: (1) I can ask friends who work in these areas to explain it to me at a level that I can understand, and they can do so, without particular difficulty; (2) if I'm interested, I can proceed to learn more so that I will come to understand it. Now Derrida, Lacan, Lyotard, Kristeva, etc. — even Foucault, whom I knew and liked, and who was somewhat different from the rest — write things that I also don't understand, but (1) and (2) don't hold: no one who says they do understand can explain it to me and I haven't a clue as to how to proceed to overcome my failures. That leaves one of two possibilities: (a) some new advance in intellectual life has been made, perhaps some sudden genetic mutation, which has created a form of "theory" that is beyond quantum theory, topology, etc., in depth and profundity; or (b) ... I won't spell it out."

Michel Foucault rejected the label of postmodernism explicitly in interviews but is seen by many to advocate a form of critique that is "postmodern" in that it breaks with the utopian and transcendental nature of "modern" critique by calling universal norms of the Enlightenment into question. Giddens (1990) rejects this characterisation of modern critique by pointing out that a critique of Enlightenment universals were central to philosophers of the modern period, most notably Nietzsche. What counts as "postmodern" is a stake in political struggles where the method of critique is at issue. The recurring themes of these debates are between essentialism and anti-foundationalism, universalism and relativism, where enlightenment thinking is seen to represent the former and postmodernism the latter. This is why theorists as diverse as Nietzsche, Lacan, Foucault, Derrida, and Butler have been labeled "postmodern", not because they formed a historical intellectual grouping but because they are seen by their critics to reject the possibility of universal, normative and ethical judgments. With some exceptions (e.g. Jameson and Lyotard), many thinkers who are considered 'postmodern' or 'poststructuralist' see these characterizations merely as labels of convenience and reject them altogether.

Fredric Jameson, American literary critic and Marxist political theorist, attacks postmodernism (or poststructuralism), what he claims is "the cultural logic of late capitalism," for its refusal to critically engage with the metanarratives of capitalization and globalization.

Alex Callinicos, a leading member of the Socialist Workers Party (Britain) - a Marxist organisation of the International Socialist Tendency - argued against what he calls "the idealist irrationalism of post-structuralism", the "existence of any radical break" from modernism to postmodernism, and the socio-economic developments of the late 80s and early 90s (the height of postmodernism's popularity) actually representing "any fundamental shift from classical patterns of capital accumulation (surplus value)." Callinicos attacks notable postmodern thinkers such as Baudrillard and Lyotard, arguing postmodernism "reflects the disappointed revolutionary generation of '68, (particularly those of May 68) and the incorporation of many of its members into the professional and managerial 'new middle class'. It is best read as a symptom of political frustration and social mobility rather than as a significant intellectual or cultural phenomenon in its own right."

REFERENCES

1. Barthes, "Death of the Author," p. 143.
2. Berger, *The Homeless Mind*, p. 9.
3. Gadamer, *Truth and Method*, p. 279.
4. Thiselton, *New Horizons*, p. 503.

10

On Language

Language and diction is one of the most important criteria to assess the literary work of any genre. It is language which has last long impression on the reader.

Here in this chapter we will elucidate the issue of myth about language.

It is significant to note that it has been an age-old problem with language: since it has never done what it was meant to do, since no one has ever established a lasting notion of what it was meant to do, and since it has never submitted to any plausible account of why it functions in the inadequate way it does, the only way out has been to resort to myths. Most of these myths are myths of origin: language today is imperfect in performing its assigned task, but in the beginning it was different in a way that can be ideally hinted at but not fully described.

This is the way Rousseau sees it. "The first language of man," he says, "the most universal, the most energetic language, and the only one he needed before it became necessary to persuade men in an assembly, is the cry of Nature." In those early days "people spoke only in poetry." Man had not yet learned to reason, but that was fine since his life was an unspoiled vision of simplicity and his needs were few. Some myths are not quite like this one. The myth about language that has served as a point of reference for almost all philosophy of language in the West is a myth of the present, and it belongs to Cratylus in the dialogue of that name by Plato. Cratylus is a naive etymologist who thinks that language is meant to name things and that names consequently bear a necessary connection with the things they designate.

But even Cratylus's argument requires an appeal to an unknowable and ideal past, a past when the words of language sprang into existence by a kind of natural necessity. The distance of the myth, whether it's a distance in time or just a distance in thought, a sense of distinctness from the way things are today, is essential. It is a correlate to the present inadequacy of language: if language is imperfect today, it must be that it has fallen from grace, from some distant Eden where it did all the things it no longer does. But language is inadequate only in relation to a standard that has been assumed, often without any explicit argument, from the outset.

Thus the pure, natural language that Rousseau's primitive man spoke—or sang—in that idyllic landscape of uncorrupted, precivilized virtue was ideal because Rousseau expects from language a perfect medium for the expression of man's passions. Love, hate, pity, and anger are the things that first raised men's voices, and this is why the first languages were "singing and passionate" rather than "simple and methodical."

The birth of language in the passions has to be accepted before the myth makes sense. And the pure language that Cratylus sees in operation in the present is pure because he expects from language a perfect medium for the transmission of things in nature. The primacy of this function of language has to be accepted before his myth makes sense. Of course, we can see what makes myths about language so valuable. It is not at all important to ask whether the authors of these myths (if there is such a thing as the author of a myth) really believe them to be plausible, historical accounts of the emergence or origin of language. It is important only to ask what the myths tell us about their authors' notions of language in the present—for instance, that Rousseau saw the unity of speaker and speech as a fundamental obligation of human language, whereas Cratylus saw the unity of name and thing (signifier and signified) as an equally fundamental obligation. The question arises why does this need to be said? Because the history of the theory of literary language in modern times is a history of the attempted flight from Eden and the subsequent, irresistible pull of Eden.

This history parallels, in fact is intertwined with, the history of modern linguistics, a distinctly modern product that is modern precisely because it has tried to be "scientific" and dispense with disobedient, metaphysical ideas like myths of the origin of language. But modern linguistics, for all its efforts to demythify, hasn't resisted the temptation of the traditional myths any more than Rousseau or Cratylus did; or any more than the visionary poets of the late nineteenth and early twentieth centuries who dared, in what appeared to be a last, desperate appeal for the metaphysical integrity of the human spirit in a scientific and skeptical age, to propose their own myths about the nature and origin of language. It wasn't really a last, desperate appeal, because the myths were carried on—by even the scientifically inclined literary theorists.

And it wasn't an appeal for the metaphysical integrity of the human spirit either, because the myths served the same function for the visionary poets as for the theorists. The myths were there to be rejected in favor of a far lonelier view of language. At least that's what they all thought. The only problem was that the myths never really went away as of now too. The curious thing is that there is more than one myth—or more than one level of myth. There are the various myths about language, its primeval unity, its innate expressiveness, its state of perfection in some other time and place than now and here. But there is also the myth of how these myths came to be abandoned.

For modern criticism not only has perpetuated many of the myths of its predecessors but also has told its own story with a pretty fair mythical imagination of its own. It is the significant to note that the story of one of the most fundamental and "radical" tenets of modern criticism and linguistics is a perfect illustration of this point. The lost unity of language in the early modern era was most forcibly asserted by the Swiss linguist Ferdinand de Saussure, who used the expression l'arbitraire du signe (the arbitrariness of the sign).

This cardinal concept, the concept of Saussure's Cours de linguistique générale (Course in general linguistics, 1916), the frontal assault on the myth that the sign, or word, bears a motivated connection with the thing it designates, has been seen as a necessary condition for modern linguistics and criticism. It is the cornerstone of the "lonelier" modern view of language. Surprisingly , the myth of modern criticism is that this concept was new. It was not. Eugenio Coseriu, a Romanian linguist teaching at Tübingen, wrote an article in the 1960s in which he demonstrates first, how pervasive the belief is that the theory of l'arbitraire du signe originated in the twentieth century and, second, how far this belief is from the truth.

In fact, Coseriu shows, the notion has to be traced back to Aristotle. For one thing, Aristotle sees language from a purely functional rather than a Cratylic point of view, rejecting the Cratylic idea of any sort of motivated or necessary connection between words and the things they stand for. For another, the very concept of arbitrariness and the expressions in Latin, French, German, and English to convey it can themselves be traced back to Aristotle and a troublesome little two-word phrase he used in his treatise On Interpretation . The phrase in Greek is kata syntheken, and in Coseriu's understanding it means something like "through what is already established."

In a famous passage from On Interpretation Aristotle defines language as "sound that is meaningful kata syntheken, " which is to say that the words of language have meaning not through any kind of natural necessity, as Cratylus believed, but through historical necessity, through tradition, through what is already established. Further, Coseriu says, the concept of kata syntheken is adopted by a long line of Western philosophers and translated into various modern languages by a number of different phrases.

What is striking is that if one is willing to accept Coseriu's idea that the various words and phrases (ad placitum, institutio, and conventio in Latin, arbitraire in French, Willküur in German, arbitrary/arbitrariness in English) are equivalent, a great many thinkers steadily from the seventeenth century up until Saussure had already proposed the notion of the arbitrariness of the sign. In fact, many of them had done so without any particular claim to originality, in some cases treating the idea as a self-evident truth. Coseriu lists about twenty philosophers, among them Hobbes, Locke, Leibniz, Christian Wolff, Berkeley, Condillac, Lessing, Fichte, and Hegel. Coseriu, whose business it is to know the facts about the history of language philosophy, expresses shock and indignation at this common oversight. And who can blame him?

After all, Hobbes, Locke, and Leibniz are not insignificant thinkers. The writers whose ignorance is in question are not insignificant in their fields either; they are prominent linguists and historians of linguistics. Is the problem that Coseriu's list of names is largely restricted to philosophers who were known less for language philosophy than for other things? This may well be part of it. The twentieth-century philosopher and historian of philosophy Ernst Cassirer devotes a brief section of his monumental work *The Philosophy of Symbolic Forms* to the history of language philosophy, mentioning a good many of the same names as Coseriu does. But then Cassirer is hardly a standard to measure others by, since he was enormously erudite and saw everything in such broad terms as only his uncannily vast learning permitted.

The fact remains that Coseriu's list does not look like the list of figures one would include in a history of language philosophy, linguistics (to the extent that these two are different), or modern literary theory. But something else is going on here, something that Coseriu doesn't mention and that he really has no reason to mention.

Look at the writings of the literary theorists who wrote in the years right after Saussure and to whom the notion of the arbitrariness of the sign (to choose just this one concept of "modern" language theory) may be attributed, of any theorist who is committed to undermining the notion that language functions because of a mystical unity between sign and world (or sign and speaker, or sign and national spirit). What about the Russian Formalist critics, who for instance, in the 1910s and the 1920s were so intent on rejecting the old myths and retaining only the most functional, "scientific" view of language?

How many of them cite Hobbes, Locke, Leibniz, Wolff, Berkeley, Condillac, Lessing, Fichte, or Hegel as their models and predecessors? These names almost never appear in the writings of the Formalists or in writings about them. The names that do appear are either from the tradition that still entertained the old myths, and are thus cited antagonistically, or from a new, revolutionary tradition, and are thus cited favorably.

Viktor Shklovsky, one of the most famous members of this group, in his early writings uses a critique of the nineteenth-century philologist Aleksandr Potebnia to launch his own theory of poetic language, citing the contemporary Russian Futurists as illustrations of the "new" ideas he is advocating. When the renowned linguist Roman Jakobson, whose early career is an integral part of the history of Russian Futurism and Formalism, comes to talk about the formative influences in his early linguistic theories—the principle of relativity and the belief that everything in language "is based on relationship"—he mentions not the linguists or philosophers of language but "the great men of art born in the 1880's": Picasso, Joyce, Braque, Stravinsky, Khlebnikov, and Le Corbusier. It was in studying Khlebnikov's poetry, Jakobson says, that he first tested one of his most basic concepts, that of the phoneme.

Is this preference for recent thinkers just a manifestation of the cult of the new that is a trademark of modernism, a bold refusal to acknowledge any predecessors except either the latest ones or those who are to be discarded for having old, worn-out ideas? Maybe. Is it simple ignorance? Possibly in some cases, though certainly not in the case of Jakobson. But two things are clear. One is that the ideas of the

Formalists (to take just this one example) were not as new as the Formalists' mythical account of their own ideas made them out to be.

The other is that the Formalists, while perpetuating the myth of the novelty of their own ideas (the myth of the rejection of myth in favour of functionalism and science), were still holding on to precisely those myths they claimed to be rejecting. In fact , L'arbitraire du signe is only one idea that the twentieth century has canonized, and canonized as specifically new. The Russian Formalists are only one group of critics and did not, besides, explicitly propose a doctrine of the arbitrariness of the sign. It would be wrong to suggest that their failure to recognize predecessors in this doctrine is by itself evidence of much of anything. Still, there is a pattern here.

Modern literary theory and criticism has always promoted its own novelty in cases where it is not completely novel. It has defined itself by a relation of antagonism with its past while continuing a great many of the myths it rejects. The whole process appears to be one vast evolutionary rejection of the myths. When Shklovsky criticizes Potebnia for overlooking the formal elements of language in his distinction between poetic and prosaic language, for ignoring the "facts" of sound and rhythm and thus being unscientific, there are two things he doesn't realize (apart from the circumstance that what he says about Potebnia isn't really true): first, that Potebnia, like Shklovsky himself, is engaged in a valiant attempt to reject the old, unscientific myths about poetic language and, second, that he, Shklovsky, was just as unsuccessful as Potebnia.

Both merely perpetuated the myths they sought so earnestly to overturn. Over and over again modern criticism, like a neurotic lover foolishly, ridiculously vowing every day to escape the clutches of the abusive and overbearing tyrant who was once a source of tenderness and security, seeks a radical break with the myths of the past, only to find itself helplessly drawn back to them.

The poets I've chosen as characters in this story define the terms of the whole ritual. They supply the idea of the break, and they sustain the myths to run back to. One of the most prominent myths is precisely that there is no myth, that we have finally made that break. We haven't.

Before we describe this history, we need to have a sense of where it goes. How will this struggle for freedom from the old myths play itself out in twentieth-century criticism? I've used the word break to describe the desired liberation from mythical forms of thought. As it happens, the notion of a break or fracture comes to be an integral part of the very theories that seek that break with the past.

Now, however, the break has to do with language itself, not just the relation of theorists and poets to their past. The late French philosopher Michel Foucault has described the modern view of language in Les mots et les choses (Words and things, translated into English for some reason as The Order of Things) in a way that is useful, although his context is different from ours. For Foucault, a view of language is part of an episteme, by which he means an entire way of understanding and knowing in a given epoch.

An episteme is different from a worldview or Weltanschauung in that it has as its specific object the human, social world. The three broad classifications into which the objects of a single episteme can be divided are life, work, and language. Amaringly, Foucault is interested in three epistemai, the most recent of which extends from shortly before the beginning of the nineteenth century to the present.

The big change that begins to occur in the thinking about language early in this period is the change from a view of language as a representational medium to a view of language as functional. In the period of Foucault's first episteme, roughly corresponding to the sixteenth century, the prevailing notion of language is of a medium that operates through a principle of resemblance between words and designated objects.

Notably, in the period of the second episteme, comprising approximately the seventeenth and eighteenth centuries, the notion of resemblance is rejected in favor of a binary notion of language. That is, language is seen as a neutral and conventional means for representing—rather than imitating—the world, and the emphasis is on the split between representing word and represented world.

In the modern period representation gives way to a notion of pure function, as philologists discover laws of similarity among the Indo-European languages, particularly those laws that show resemblances among such purely grammatical attributes of languages as inflectional endings. "Language is no longer composed only of representations and sounds that, in turn, represent these representations and order themselves as strings of thought require. It is instead composed of formal elements that are grouped in a system and that impose on the sounds, the syllables, and the roots an order that is not that of representation." This is how there comes to appear in the modern age a "dimension of the pure grammatical."

Consequently, language in the modern age takes on a kind of opacity and becomes an object in its own right, instead of being merely a transparent, representational medium. It "folds back on itself, acquires its own density, displays a history, laws, and an objectivity that belong to it alone." Language exists now only in a "dispersed mode." "For the philologists, words are like so many objects composed and passed on by history; for those who wish to formalize, language must rid itself of its concrete content, leaving only the universally valid forms of speech to appear. If one wishes to interpret, then words have become a text to be fractured in order that one can then see the emergence of this other meaning they hide." Foucault's presentation of the modern episteme goes a long way toward describing the status of language in the writings of twentieth-century literary critics, theorists, and aestheticians. But critics, theorists, and aestheticians are not Foucault's subject, at least not exclusively or even prominently.

Foucault speaks largely of the professional philosophers—in addition to speaking of authors and poets from time to time—and thus provides a perspective similar to the one we find in Coseriu's article on the arbitrariness of the sign. When Foucault speaks of Mallarmé, saying that with him (and Nietzsche) "thought was led, and violently so, back towards language itself, back to its unique, difficult being," thus making Mallarmé a crucial figure in the twin processes of the "fracturing of language" and its transition to a state of "philological objectivity," he speaks almost as though the whole question had been settled with Mallarmé. But the value of Foucault's discussion of language for us lies in its capacity to describe the limits of the trend he is talking about, to describe a view of language that has come to dominate much twentieth-century thinking.

The term fracture is apt, and it certainly gives a good idea of the situation in which language finds itself in the twentieth century. The fracture operates on levels that Foucault does not enumerate (this is not his purpose). But one may classify a great many twentieth-century theories of language according to the terms in which they formulate a fracture. Its most basic sense may be found in the Saussurian doctrine of l'arbitraire du signe, in which the fracture severs the sign from its referent. Any aesthetics that is formalist in the general sense—any aesthetics emphasizing functions and relations over elements (in this case words)—will accept this doctrine as a self-evident truth.

Other schools of criticism, aesthetics, and language theory have seen the fracture as operating at a higher level than sign and referent, namely the level of the extended utterance. Theorists loosely grouped under the rubric of phenomenology tend to see the problems of language arising not out of the relation between words and things, or signs and referents, but instead out of the relation between larger signifying units and a newly problematized entity called meaning. Edmund Husserl, the founding father of this movement in philosophy, had initiated this trend in his Logische Untersuchungen (Logical investigations, 1900–1901) by referring to meanings as an independent class of ideal objects that don't need to have anything to do with the signs associated with them.

In fact, the nature of this association is far less simple than has commonly been supposed, Husserl thinks. Signs may well be signs for something, he says, but they do not in all cases possess a meaning or sense that is "expressed" by them. When Roman Ingarden, a Polish pupil of Husserl, comes to talk specifically about literary texts in the late 1920s, he organizes language into what he calls meaning units, or unified utterances. Like Husserl before him,

Ingarden distinguishes sharply between meanings, which are created by subjective acts of consciousness, and the units of language associated with those meanings.

The meaning function of language—the function, that is, that associates a meaning with a particular meaning unit—is conferred on that meaning unit from without by a subjective act of consciousness and can therefore in no way be considered as automatic or absolute. The very premise of Ingarden's theory is thus that there is no necessary, simple, or natural relation between language and its meanings.

Three decades later the French phenomenologist Maurice Merleau-Ponty also was to insist on the lack of a necessary and direct relation between utterances (by which Merleau-Ponty understands units larger than individual words) and their associated meanings. For him, meanings are ideas that cannot be directly expressed but can only be approached through a series of "adumbrations" (Abschattungen, a Husserlian term).

In his essay "On the Phenomenology of Language" (1951) he describes how the adumbrations in a given utterance suddenly "contract into a single meaning" by a process that can't even be described. For Merleau-Ponty, there can never be any question of a direct signifiedsignifying relation because the signified always "surpasses" the signifying. A much more radical fracture, however, is the one we find in the work of Jacques Derrida and his many American epigones. In fact, the whole trend known as postmodernism, which helped set the tone for literary studies in the 1970s, is dedicated to an idolatrous fascination with the lonely, nihilistic worldview that is implicit in Derrida's fractured theory of language.

For Derrida, language can be characterized only as a play of differences among an intricate network, or "tissue," of signs. Language is marked by the "impossibility for a sign, for the unity of a signifier and a signified, to occur in the plenitude of a present and an absolute presence."

There is no present or absolute presence in any sign other than the divine logos, and the logos is a purely metaphysical, "infinitist" notion. In the language of man, meaning is always in flight, always beyond the horizon; there is no presence, no unity, only the trace of what was just there. Thus language is not only the differences at play in a tissue of signs; it is also différance (with a instead of e), a word Derrida invented to combine the two principal senses of the French verb différer, "differ" and "defer." In the intricate complex of differences that is language, meaning is always deferred, put off, scattered. Derrida introduces the concept of the trace to describe the way in which language is never fully present (as we would like to think it is) but exists instead in a state that looks back to something that was already there.

The trace, always flitting ahead of the presence that it leaves behind, thus describes a double process of "retention" (since it retains what has been present) and "protention" (since it tends forward, away from that present). Signification is born at this juncture of retention and protention, and Derrida finds in the French language a word that happily combines the notion of juncture and rupture he sees united in the trace—brisure, which means "hinge," as in the hinged articulation between two parts of a shutter (this definition, of course, allows Derrida to exploit the double sense of "articulation"), and "fracture." There is another kind of fracture that at one time had become canonical in literary aesthetics, and that is the fracture that separates speaker from language.

This fracture is the premise of any objectivist literary aesthetic, any aesthetic that regards the word as independent of its speaker and the literary work of art as independent of its creator. Such a view had become virtually an article of faith in the teaching of literature in many of the most respected American universities in the 1960s and 1970s, when it was fashionable for professors to shock undergraduate students by telling them that inquiries into an author's life or into the author's avowed understanding of his or her own work were irrelevant to a true understanding of that work—hence the license to throw lecture notes away and spend hours of class time in an exercise known as close reading, wherein students, with their instructor's minimal participation, take a piece of writing, like a bit of organic tissue, pick it into tiny bits, and comment on how those bits interact either with each other (the bits) or with them (the students). Objectivist criticism became entrenched in the 1950s, when many of the next decade's academics were still in graduate school. Cleanth Brooks published The Well Wrought Urn in 1947, proposing a view of literary artworks as organic structures whose constituent parts were to be understood and judged only in terms internal to the artwork as a totality.

In "The Intentional Fallacy," (1946) and then again as a chapter of The Verbal Icon in 1954, W. K. Wimsatt and Monroe Beardsley had argued that consulting an author to discover the meaning of that author's words was illegitimate. "Critical inquiries are not settled by consulting the oracle," the essay ends.

And in Aesthetics: Problems in the Philosophy of Criticism (1958), a work designed as an introductory college textbook in aesthetics, Beardsley forcefully espoused objectivism as a principle of all art criticism. Notably Wimsatt and Brooks, in their Literary Criticism: A Short History, published in 1957, trace the origins of the objectivist aesthetic, or "impersonality," as they put it (since the author's "person" does not appear in his works). Credit goes to T. S. Eliot, they say, not because he was the first to come up with the idea but because it was he who "brought this matter of impersonality squarely to the attention of his generation."

Eliot's position in separating the personal experience of the poet from the poem itself is stated in 1919 "with almost shocking emphasis," as Wimsatt and Brooks put it. The idea of severing the speaker from his words is by no means restricted to such New Critics as Wimsatt and Brooks. Nor am I persuaded that Eliot is the one who brings it into the open. It is implicit in any formalist or structuralist view of language (in the general sense of those terms), where the emphasis is on relations between words rather than on their expressive qualities. And it emerges in the phenomenological views of language I mentioned a moment ago, since for thinkers like Ingarden and Merleau-Ponty the meanings of language escape and surpass the speaker as much as they escape and surpass language. But no matter what the specifics of the view are, language is a long way from the organic unity it enjoys in the myths—unity with man in Rousseau and many of the romantics, unity with God in the Gospels. Many of the relativizing tendencies in the twentieth century are evidence of a fracture in the primitive unity of language. This notion is true of any theory asserting that the meanings of language are determined by a context of some sort.

It is essential to the thought of Mikhail Bakhtin, the Russian philosopher and literary theorist whose works became immensely fashionable in the 1980s. One of Bakhtin's central notions is raznorechie (translated as "heteroglossia"), which describes the necessary interaction in verbal utterances between the fixed system of a given language and the context of a particular utterance. It is certainly there in E. D. Hirsch, who, some twenty years before he gained notoriety for his *Cultural Literacy* (a kind of companion best-seller to Allan Bloom's Closing of the American Mind in 1987), wrote a book in which he gave a theory of literary interpretation.

Hirsch distinguishes between the "meaning" of a literary work as a fixed thing established in the context of its writing, and the "significance" of a literary work as something that changes over history as a function of the contexts of future generations of readers.

It is there in so-called reception theories, which see the meaning of language as largely determined by characteristics of the listener (or reader). And it is there in Marxist theory, which views consciousness and, consequently, language as determined by social existence. The twentieth century is not responsible for inventing the skepticism necessary to produce language theories as lonely and unsettling as some of these.

But it is never asserted wholeheartedly. Instead, the old myths dwell side by side with the fractured notion of language. And the forum that allows for this cohabitation is the one where the distinction between poetic language and ordinary, or prosaic, language is investigated. The typical symptom of the surviving neurotic attachment to the old myths is the tendency to distinguish between two types of language, the language of poetry and the language of prose (or whatever you want to call language that is not poetic), and to assign a privileged, Edenic status to poetic language in true sense.

Perhaps it would be most accurate to say simply that the whole poetryprose distinction is a myth, at least as it is framed in this period. Whether or not this is true, the distinction presents a problem since so much of modern literary criticism and language theory has been intent on fostering an image of itself as the product of rational reflection, of a carefully, thoughtfully elaborated "methodology".

In fact, it has in many cases sought to earn itself a place next to the other "human sciences," which are also a product of modern times and whose central obsession has been with their place next to the methodologically more secure natural sciences. The scientifically inclined schools of literary criticism, the formalisms and the structuralisms, have ridden the coattails of twentieth-century linguistics, something that is evident not only because modern criticism has often borrowed the methods and terminology of linguistics but above all because it has focused on the same object of study, namely language. Even where the notion of science and scientificity has not had an overriding appeal, the concern has been with detachment, with sober and impassive judgment—hence the preference for a spirit of objectivism in so much twentieth-century criticism. But literary criticism is of necessity either implicitly or explicitly an aesthetic.

Its object of study is not language in general, signifying objects in general, or meaning in general; it is specifically literary language, literary signifying objects, literary meaning. The problem has been, then, to account for the specific "literariness" of literary language (what Jakobson called literaturnost'), but to do so without abandoning the highly esteemed posture of scienrificity. It is questionable whether modern criticism or modern linguistics has successfully done this, though both have certainly tried.

The task presents some significant difficulties. For to set aside a certain body of written texts and call them literary is to assume the existence of an aesthetic value, some quality that mysteriously places these texts in an entirely different category from the ones in which we place "ordinary" written texts. And the minute we start talking about values, we are talking about murky, essentialist, metaphysical qualities whose existence is suspect and whose functioning is hopelessly obscure, at least from a "scientific" viewpoint.

Nonetheless, modern thinking has had trouble abandoning the romantic notion that literary texts are somehow the object of reverence and awe. It has also not quite been able to abandon the notion that poetic literary texts are more literary than prose texts and that they are, consequently, more the object of reverence and awe.

And there is an assumption, usually unwritten, that literary works of art owe the specificity they possess as works of art to qualities in the language that composes them. It follows that there must be a difference between literary language and "ordinary" language and that this difference accounts either entirely or in part for the difference between, say, a poem by Blake and a paragraph from a car repair manual. Even deconstructionist thinkers like Derrida and Paul de Man, for all their skepticism about language and meaning, retain a faith in the specificity of poetic language.

Derrida drew a clear distinction between literary and philosophical texts, and de Man, as I mentioned in my introduction, used the term rhetoricity for his version of the specificity of poetic language. And so we see in modern criticism the complicated situation I described earlier. The myth subsists that there is an intrinsic distinction between poetic and prosaic language.

I use the word myth not because we wish to assert that the poetry-prose distinction is false in all of its versions (although we do happen to believe it is false when it is expressed as a distinction between two types of language); I use it because belief in the poetry-prose distinction is framed as a myth, usually a Rousseauistic myth of original purity. But as literary aesthetics and its corresponding philosophy of language grow increasingly "scientific," there is an increasing tendency toward formalism in philosophy of language, and with formalism comes a tendency to demythify.

Hence the coexistence, in the early modern period, of the myth itself (that is, the myth of the poetry-prose distinction) and the myth that there is no myth. The idea of poetry (a term that can mean anything from imaginative writing to specifically lyrical verse) as a distinctive form of verbal expression that stands in natural opposition either to other forms of expression or to whole ways of apprehending the world is an idea of long standing.

Aristotle, in the Poetics, had opposed poetry (understood in its broadest sense as what we might call today simply literature) to history, saying that poetry is more philosophical, indeed is "greater" than history, because poetry expresses universals whereas history expresses particulars. The more familiar distinction since Aristotle has been between poetry and prose, poetry being understood in a more specific sense than the one it has in Aristotle. This distinction is standard in the poetics of romanticism. Rousseau sets the tone for the entire era in his "Essay on the Origin of Languages," where poetry is identified as the earliest and, of course, most natural of languages.

The English and German romantics return again and again to the same theme: poetry, specifically as distinguished from prose, is the purest, the most original (in the sense of being close to the origin) form of verbal expression. The German romantic critic Johann Gottfried von Herder, in his essay on the origin of language, asserts, like Rousseau before him, that poetry is older than prose and that in its capacity to express passions in all their immediacy lies the primitive source of all verbal communication. By the late romantic era in England something new has happened: the poetry-prose distinction has given way in a great many instances to a distinction between poetry and science. M. H. Abrams, in his classic work on English romanticism The Mirror and the Lamp, documents this transition, citing Thomas Babington Macaulay's 1825 essay on Milton as evidence that Aristotle's poetry-history distinction had been converted into the distinction between poetry and science.

But the poetry-science opposition does not arrive directly from a rejection of Aristotle; it comes along instead to replace the distinction that was dominant at the time, namely the distinction between poetry and prose.

This, at least, is how Wordsworth sees it. As early as 1800, in the preface to the Lyrical Ballads, he goes so far as to say that "there neither is, nor can be, any essential difference between the language of prose and metrical composition." Then, in a footnote, he says that "much confusion has been introduced into criticism by this contradistinction of Poetry and Prose, instead of the more philosophical one of Poetry and Matter of Fact, or Science."

The poetry-science opposition in most cases does not represent an abandonment of the poetry-prose distinction; it represents merely a clarification, in epistemological terms, of the perceived province of prose, since science in the new opposition corresponds to prose as the vehicle exclusively suited to its methods and worldview. Thus poetry is to prose as feeling is to intellect, or as expression is to description, or as emotion is to scientific cognition.

This view is taken over in the work of Wilhelm von Humboldt, author of the highly influential über die Verschiedenheit des menschlichen Sprachbaues und ihren EinfluB auf die geistige Entwicklung des Menschengeschlechts (On the diversity of human speech structure and its influence on the spiritual development of the human race, published 1827–29) and in many ways a pivotal figure both for the history of language philosophy and for our story here. Humboldt divides the territories of poetry and prose in a manner similar to that of the romantics. Poetry apprehends reality in its sensible (sinnlich) manifestations; it is "inseparable from" music and is thus more appropriately the vehicle of aesthetic beauty than is prose.

It is given to the rendition of "individual moments" in human experience rather than to universals. Prose, by contrast, is concerned with facts and concepts rather than with ideas or sensation. Since it is suited to the rendition of ordinary life, it is the province of the objective, of science and scientific terminology; and where poetry "belongs to the individual moments of life," prose accompanies man "in all the expressions of his spiritual activity."

But there is a significant difference between the opposition that Humboldt makes and the one the romantics made, and that is that for Humboldt the opposition does not of necessity entail the privileging of poetry over prose. Humboldt's distinction is simply descriptive, and this is because his approach to language is in certain fundamental respects different from that of the romantics.

Humboldt sees language above all as a function of our inner being. It is an organic medium, representing the perpetual spiritual activity of an entire nation (not the individual). As Humboldt put it in his famous formulation, language is not a mere dead created thing (ein totes Erzeugtes) but an ongoing creation (eine Erzeugung); it is not (finished) work (he uses the Greek word ergon) but ceaseless activity (energeia).

Any definition of language must, then, be a genetic one, that is, one that sees language not as the product of an act of genesis in some distant, mythic past but as a continuing genesis in the present. Thus Humboldt has taken the romantic myth of origin, by which language is a creature fallen from the grace it had "in the beginning," and replaced it with a myth of origin where that origin is always now. The secret to the creative, perpetually generative force of language in the present is what Humboldt calls the inner form of speech, a notion that will be taken over by the Russian philologist Potebnia, with lasting consequences for the Russian tradition.

Inner form is the thing that makes language what it is. It is the key to the connection between language production and the sound of language. It is what allows language to express those thoughts that the greatest minds entrust to it. Language deals not with objects but with concepts. Its principal task is to mediate between objective reality and subjective inwardness, and it successfully accomplishes this task when sound and inner form are harmoniously joined. At that moment the process of language production and the external sound qualities of language work together to form a language that is living and rich, particularly in metaphorical content.

This happens especially in the works of poets and philosophers, who contribute to the development of a nation's language by infusing its words with spiritual content. The success of a language for Humboldt is always measured by the progress of that language through history, and this notion leads him to mention a phenomenon that Potebnia and the entire Russian tradition later canonize. Harmony of inner and outer form is lost when a language stagnates. At that moment metaphors that had previously had a "youthful sense" become, through daily use, "worn out" so that they are "barely perceived anymore." To the question 'Why is Humboldt a pivotal figure?' he has sought to abandon all forms of naive Cratylism and romantic primitivism in his approach to language. If Humboldt believes in the specificity of poetic language, it is not because he sees poetry as based in some mystical unity of either word and object or word and speaker. For him, poetic language is distinguished from prosaic language more by its function, by the way it is used, than by any intrinsic properties.

The nonexistence of a necessary or motivated connection between signs and the things they designate in language in general, whether that language is poetic or prosaic, is already implied in the subject of Humboldt's work. Humboldt's point of departure, as the title of his work suggests, is precisely the fact of the diversity of human speech, the obvious fact that, owing to the existence of a multitude of human languages, there is no single, universal, and necessary way of saying any one thing. The flight from Cratylism or natural-sign language is further signaled by Humboldt's insistence that language has to do not with things but with concepts. This is because language does not spring into existence ready-made to serve poets as a vehicle for the expression of their feelings; on the contrary, we ceaselessly create language for the purpose of meaningfully organizing our own experience.

And since Humboldt was a good Kantian, believing that conscious beings can never "know" things in and for themselves, to him language, like any activity that generates meaning, cannot deal directly with objects. Humboldt's Kantianism is another reason for his status as a pivotal figure. Ernst Cassirer writes about it in the brief history of language philosophy that he includes in the first volume of the Philosophy of Symbolic Forms .

As Cassirer sees it, Humboldt betrays his underlying Kantianism in at least two ways. The first is in the notion of language as a subjective medium whose function is to objectify sensory impressions, thus serving as a kind of bridge between subjectivity and the objectivity that, according to Kant, we can never know in and for itself. The second is in the distinction between the matter (namely sound) of language and its form.

In Cassirer's reading of Kant form is "the truly objectifying principle of knowledge" because it is the source of unity in our apprehension of objects. The function of form in Humboldt is entirely analogous since inner form for him is exactly what serves as a mediating function between subjectivity and the objective world of phenomena. Humboldt's entire conception of language thus appears in Cassirer's eyes to be founded in the "basic principle of the transcendental method" (the method in Kant by which the philosopher logically deduces the categories that the mind uses to order experience). Cassirer calls this principle "the universal application of philosophy to science." Humboldt's innovation consists in making language the object of that "universal application" rather than mathematics and mathematical physics, as Kant had. The Russian tradition begins in the shadow of Humboldt, with a bow to Humboldt, but also, strangely enough, with a reassertion of some of the older myths Humboldt had apparently rejected—the myth of origin, for instance, which now shows itself in a slightly new form. The Russian tradition that is central to the development of language theory in modern literary aesthetics begins precisely in the context of the transition that Cassirer identifies in the work of Humboldt.

11

Role of Theology

First it is pertinent to note that one of the cleverest and funniest accounts of literary criticism in the twentieth century is Marxist critic Terry Eagleton's *Literary Theory: An Introduction.* Eagleton's project is to discredit most of the major schools of twentieth-century literary criticism by exposing for each one the underlying, untested assumption that must be accepted on faith in order for the whole system to stand. Eagleton has an extraordinary gift for this kind of analysis. He shows, for instance, how T. S. Eliot's notion of a Tradition in literature is based solely on authoritarian judgments handed down by Eliot himself and then given the status of absolute, almost divine principles. Similarly, the critical program of New Criticism, with its intensive focus on the poem itself, starts by imbuing the poem "with an absolute mystical authority". Like Eliot's doctrine of the great Tradition, New Criticism is at bottom a religious system in disguise. Phenomenological criticism, with its habit of reducing everything to pure subjective consciousness, is authoritarian, too, because it depends heavily on intuition.

And so it goes for virtually all schools of modern criticism: if you look closely at them, they all turn out to be authoritarian, mystical, religious. A moderately skeptical mind will find Eagleton's debunking easy to accept. But Eagleton comes close to wrecking his entire enterprise at the end of the book when having proclaimed with great satisfaction the death of literary studies, he proceeds with the blind faith of a true ideologue to outline for the reader the sole realms of criticism worthy of being practiced.

These are ones that pursue the goal of "human emancipation, the production of 'better people' through the socialist transformation of society" (p. 211). What exempts socialist and feminist criticism from the charges Eagleton levels at all other types of criticism is that they are categorically different, and this because they "define the object of analysis differently, have different values, beliefs and goals" (p. 212).

In other words, once the activity of literary criticism rests on the solid bedrock of a political program dedicated to the destruction of social inequality, it is beyond reproach from any quarter because no one can possibly question the assumption that inequality is bad (and that the elimination of privilege and private property are the solution to it). Hence the need for humanists in our day to turn their attention to areas of cultural endeavor whose worth, Eagleton feels, cannot logically be disputed, areas, that is, where "cultural and political action have become closely united" (p. 215).

And Eagleton lists these areas: the culture of "nations struggling for their independence from imperialism," the women's movement, the "culture industry" (culture of minorities), and working-class writing (pp. 215–216). Eagleton has asked us to take the skeptical line throughout his book and decry the clandestine articles of faith in each of the systems he talks about. He then asks us to regard another system as not just another system but as something different in kind from all the systems he disdains.

But isn't there an untested, authoritarian principle here, too? "Men and women do not live by culture alone; the vast majority of them throughout history have been deprived of the chance of living by it at all, and those few who are fortunate enough to live by it now are able to do so because of the labour of those who do not. Any cultural or critical theory which does not begin from this single most important fact, and hold it steadily in mind in its activities, is in my view unlikely to be worth very much" (p. 214, emphasis added).

Does Eagleton have any more right to tell us what the "single most important fact" is than Eliot does to tell us which are the most important texts? Eagleton is asking us to accept on faith, first, that the humanities are tools of capitalism, second, that they have an intrinsic responsibility to devote themselves to political change, and, finally, that the form of political change to which they must devote themselves is the "socialist transformation of society." So Eagleton has his untested assumption, too, and he has introduced it with the same slippery logic as his predecessors, hoping in the end that a universal sense of social justice will persuade his readers to accept principles that in fact are merely handed down by authoritarian fiat. The social-activist theory of literary criticism begins to look a little like theology, as well. But social-activist literary criticism is not my subject. After all, if a critic like Eagleton, whose basic motivating force is precisely a resistance to arbitrary expressions of authority, does not escape the cancer of mystical authoritarianism, then who can?

Eagleton says at one point that there is "no need to

drag politics into literary theory. As with South African sport, it has been there from the beginning" (p. 194). This is one of his most basic beliefs. In fact, however, he has demonstrated the truth of another statement, a paraphrase of that one: There is no need to drag theology into literary theory; it has been there from the beginning, and it lives on in the theory of Eagleton himself.

But we need to examine Shklovsky's predecessors and contemporaries to understand what sort of transformation had taken place. It rums out that the transformation was not so marked as we might think, that the origins of Shklovsky's type of literary theorizing go deep into the theological history of Russia, and that these origins are never entirely abandoned. Yet even this is only part of the story, for there are two theologies. There is Russian Orthodox theology, which threads its way through a millennium of Russian culture and into the early twentieth century, when all the major Russian literary thinkers of the early modern period share its heritage. The Russian whose impact on succeeding generations was the most direct was not Shklovsky or any of the other Formalist critics; it was a linguist, Roman Jakobson. In spite of his reputation as a guiding force in the modern "science" of language, Jakobson operates in an old system of religious language philosophy that in many ways has simply been dressed up in the more modern fashion of scientific terminology. The other theology is a Western, largely Catholic one. It can be seen in French writers like Mallarmé, although the content of Catholic theology is obscured by Mallarmé's constant urge to satirize and profane the same religious principles he surreptitiously adopts.

Theology has a great deal to do with language: it is, in its root sense, "God-talk" (theo-logos), as the Heideggerian theologian John Macquarrie puts it in the title of his book on the subject; and, since Christian theology is talk about the Christian God, it is also talk about God's Word. In some ways this brings us back to the subject of Part I. But in this part we will move on from language to the question of artworks, specifically artworks made out of language, and see how the hidden god has affected our thinking about them in modern times. We don't usually think of Sartre as a funny man, but when he turned his attention to literary subjects, he was capable of being quite a joker. The first section of "L'engagement de Mallarmé" is called "Les héritiers de l'athéisme" (The inheritors of atheism), and it starts out like this:

> 1848: the fall of the monarchy deprives the bourgeoisie of its "cover"; with a single stroke Poetry loses its two traditional themes: Man and God.
>
> First God: Europe had just heard a stupefying piece of news, still contested by some today:"God dead. Stop. Intestate." When it came time to divide up the estate, panic reigned: what had the Deceased left? (p. 15)

Sartre views the whole phenomenon of Mallarmé as essentially a late reaction to the recent "death of God." "Les héritiers de l'athéisme" paints a sweeping picture of European culture in the wake of this event. Sartre then turns his attention to Mallarmé, in a section called "L'élu" (The chosen one). With the same kind of licentiously creative psychological analysis that he was to employ in his later monumental work on Flaubert, L'idiot de la famille, Sartre picks through the spiritual world of Mallarmé, revealing to his eager readers all the exciting details of the great artist's sexual and religious life. The sexual life need not concern us (it is largely the invention of Sartre, who was fond of doing that sort of thing).

But what Sartre says about Mallarmé's religious life is extraordinarily clever, especially because it has a direct bearing on the philosophy of art that Sartre finds in Mallarmé. Mallarmé's peculiar aesthetics, it would appear from Sartre, actually has a double source. There is the spiritual desolation in Europe caused by the death of God, something that allows Sartre to talk in general about what it means to be a poet in the late nineteenth century. And there is the personal desolation caused in Mallarmé by the death of his own mother (when he was five).

The way Sartre sees it, both deaths produced in Mallarmé a strange cult of absence, negation, and nonbeing, which in turn produced a religion and an aesthetics that are intertwined. The religion is a sort of obverse Christianity. Sartre describes Mallarmé's grief over yet another death, that of his sister, when he was sixteen. "It's the death of his mother all over again," Sartre says. "This mystery of the Disincarnation, the union of a myth and a ritual, seems to found a Christianity in reverse. It's not the Parousia, but Absence that is the hope and aim. What 'was in the beginning' was not the logos, but the vile abundance of Being, Vulgarity; it is neither Creation nor the passage of the Word into the World that we adore, but instead the passage by emaciation of Reality into the Word" (p. 113). For Mallarmé, religion had become an interrogation into being, and all the traditional absolutes had been replaced with negation and absence. The departed mother and sister become the emblems of this absence. "The young priest of the new religion does not address God; he reserves his prayers for a Great Goddess who will be the image of everything a woman can be for a man apart from carnal love, a white goddess of chastity mingling mother and sister in a single absence" (p. 114).

From the absence of God (and mother) the natural

place to turn to was poetry, which is how religion and aesthetics are connected for Mallarmé. But the connection is not what we might expect. After all, wouldn't it be natural to seek in poetry a replacement for the lost God (and the lost mother's love)? This is apparently what Mallarmé did, but he faced an irreconcilable contradiction. "After having killed God with his own hands," says Sartre, "Mallarmé still wanted a divine guarantee; Poetry had to remain transcendent, even though he had eliminated the source of all transcendence" (p. 152). So poetry, too, becomes a place where strange ontological impossibilities reign, just as they do in religion it becomes "pure Negation" (p. 141). It is "a hole bored into Being, the establishment and delimitation of an absence that, bit by bit, from one allusion to the next, turns out to be the world. Through the poem, on a single point in the world, the total absence of the world is realized" (p. 162).

The poem "displays the world and everything that's in the world; not in order to give us things, but in order to take them away from us. . . . Meaning is a second silence in the heart of silence; it is the negation of the word-thing" (p. 160).

Precisely because poetry could not be the replacement for religion, it became essentially the same thing as religion. But religion, after the death of God, had become a religion of absence, and so poetry became a poetry of absence. There is much truth in what Sartre says. Not always, of course, in the sense of factual truth: how can Sartre pretend to know about things like Mallarmé's sexual habits? There is truth in Sartre's clever way of contextualizing Mallarmé's religious attitude, and there is truth in the way he links that same attitude with Mallarmé's aesthetics.

He certainly tends to conceptualize the figure of Mallarmé

in characteristically Sartrean terms (speaking of the engagement, or commitment, of Mallarmé, the emphasis on his existential "situation"), but he has refrained to a surprising degree from the kind of doctrinaire and heavy-handed treatment we might expect from him, especially in the early 1950s. In an era when language was increasingly viewed as a functional system, as something with its own objectivity, Mallarmé had played a crucial role in leading thought violently "back towards language itself," Foucault said. But an era for Foucault here means an entire episteme, which implies a certain universal way of understanding, and he credits Mallarmé with a major change in that universal way of understanding. Sartre, too, sees Mallarmé as a pivotal figure, and, like Foucault, he considers Mallarmé's view of language to be the critical thing. But Sartre is interested in it not solely for its impact on the way people think about language but also for its impact on the way people are.

Mallarmé, as Sartre saw it, created a whole new man. "Ever since he decided to write in order to launch the Word [Verbe] on an adventure from which there is no return, there is no writer, no matter how modest, who will risk himself in a book without risking the Word [Parole] at the same time. *The Word or Man:* it's all the same thing. . . . With Mallarmé a new man is born, reflective and critical, tragic, whose life line reveals a decline." This new man, Sartre continues, "surpasses himself and totalizes himself in the fulgurating drama of the incarnation and the fall, he cancels himself and exalts himself at the same time, in a word, he makes himself exist through the realization of his own impossibility". Perhaps Sartre is just indulging in rhetorical excess. It is one thing for Foucault to say that Mallarmé was responsible for a new conception of language. But can we really assert that Mallarmé gave birth to a whole new man? This is a natural way for Sartre to think, reluctant as he was to separate art from life, the artistic calling from one's calling as a man. These days people have grown tired of Sartre's pedantic ideas about commitment in art and the greater, human vocation of the writer.

Maybe Mallarmé didn't create a whole new man. In almost every Dostoevsky novel, it seems, there is an exchange between two characters in which one, often without warning and always without apology, bluntly asks the other if he believes in God (or if there is a God). Every Dostoevsky character is torn between the twin temptations of faith and faithlessness. Nonetheless, the answer is almost always as blunt and unhesitating as the question: Yes, there is a God, or No, there is no God. Period. Imagine Mallarmé, arch-ironist of French letters, the man who cultivated the art of politesse to the point where he lavished praise on the most tasteless rubbish written by his friends; imagine this man assaulted by one of Dostoevsky's shaggy, maniacal heroes with this question: Do you believe in God, yes or no, answer at once! What would he have said? Did he believe in God?

The question of Mallarmé's religious thought is complicated. The beginnings are not entirely clear. We read that his father and stepmother were both Catholic. His maternal grandparents continued to play an important role in the boy's life after his mother had died. His grandmother appears to have been religious, whereas his grandfather was something of a skeptic. Mallarmé was sent to a boarding school run by a religious order, where he consistently received poor to passing grades in religion. What Gill says may be true. Does it settle the question of Mallarmé's belief or nonbelief? Not convincingly. Another commentator, L.-J. Austin, in an article that presents a kind of spiritual biography of Mallarmé, says that Mallarmé was quite traditionally and sincerely religious as a child. He cites as evidence several of Mallarmé's juvenile creations in which the word Dieu is used. Some undoubtedly see raillery where Austin sees piety and would conclude from this and other material that Mallarmé was a skeptic from an early age.

To attribute great religious devotion or great skepticism to a teenager strikes me as placing undue importance on thoughts that have not yet matured. As it happens, most biographers and commentators do not see things Gill's way and insist that Mallarmé was unquestioningly religious as a boy, just because he was raised to be that way. Some of the best evidence on the question of Mallarmé's religious attitude comes later. Every artist needs to have a metaphysical crisis at some point, and Mallarmé had his when he was in his early twenties. He made three related discoveries at that time: Nothingness, Hegel, and the idea for his future creation called the Book. His correspondence charts the progress of this strange episode.

The central experience seems to have been an encounter with Nothingness (le Néant), followed by a revelation about Beauty and the Absolute. "I will tell you that for the past month I have been in the pure glaciers of Aesthetics—that after finding Nothingness, I have found Beauty," he writes to his friend, the minor poet Henri Cazalis. "I have died and been reborn," he exclaims in another letter.

Mallarmé, it seems, had recently become acquainted secondhand with Hegel's aesthetics and had appropriated some of the terms and concepts as he had understood them. Once the crisis was over, Mallarmé wrote to Cazalis what was to become one of his most frequently cited letters. This letter is particularly valuable because in it, in addition to describing once again the crisis that he had been talking about for more than a year, in addition to revealing the resolution to that crisis more completely than he had done before, in addition to flaunting his Hegelian vocabulary, Mallarmé puts the whole experience in a religious perspective.

Mallarmé goes on to talk about what has replaced God. He uses the word Synthesis again, saying that he has "marked out the opus [oeuvre] that will be the image of this development." That opus will be a collection of poems, including "four prose poems on the spiritual conception of Nothingness." A little bit farther on he says, "I have made a rather long descent into Nothingness so that I can speak with certainty. Beauty is all there is—and beauty has only one perfect expression, Poetry."

As mentioned earlier that Sartre saw the death of family members as having a profound impact on Mallarmé's spiritual outlook. He talked about the death of Mallarmé's mother and sister and the way it contributed to the poet's religion of absence and Nothingness. In 1879, more than a decade after his metaphysical crisis, another death intervened that once again forced Mallarmé into an evaluation of his spiritual "situation," to use the Sartrean term.

Once again Mallarmé reacts in a way that shows the basic structure of religious thought, and once again a conscious effort is made to replace God with something else. This time it was Mallarmé's eight-year-old son, Anatole, who died. The father's memorial to his son was to be a work (oeuvre) of some sort, a tombeau like the one he had written to Edgar Allan Poe in 1876. The tombeau for Anatole never got written, and all that remains is a project for the text in the form of manuscript notes, which Jean-

Pierre Richard published in 1961 under the title Pour un tombeau d'Anatole. It's hard to make sense of these notes. Richard, in his excellent introduction, gives what interpretive insights he can on a collection of pages whose very status is ambiguous (are they plans for a poem, are they fragments of that poem, or are they something else altogether?).

One thing is clear both from the notes themselves and from Richard's commentary, and that is Mallarmé's continuing flirtation with religion—not just any religion but specifically Catholicism, the faith in which he was raised. Referring, for instance, to the various objects associated with the dead boy in the notes, Richard says that they are "reinterpreted by an entirely metaphysical imagination." The ritual gestures expressing mourning "find their complete meaning only as they are situated in a perspective of religious faith and transcendental salvation" (p. 51). All the traditional gestures, Richard says, maintain for Mallarmé their usual prestige in spite of the poet's rejection of God in 1866. Richard thinks all this represents an effort on Mallarmé's part to establish a "natural foundation" and a "human origin" for religious objects and practices, just as Mallarmé will later find a way of laicizing Catholic ritual by likening it to an ordinary Sunday concert.

But the fact is that the impulse to respond religiously remains intact. And so the death of Anatole is seen as a sort of theophany, Richard says, because it "humanly places in evidence the transcendence, present in him [the boy], of death" (p. 63). Mallarmé speaks continually in the manuscript notes of the survival of his son after death, but without ever using a word for "soul." As Richard points out, however, even though Mallarmé had for some time separated himself from the church and its beliefs, "all the images or expressions he uses to evoke the survival after death of Anatole represent little more than hesitating approximations of this word [that is, soul]."

Richard sees other evidence of a Christian doctrine of resurrection in Mallarmé's notes, which show a faith in the process by which "bodily decomposition prepares the release of the spirit" (p. 72). Mallarmé begins to look a bit more like a Dostoevsky character torn between the temptation to believe and the temptation to renounce. The solution he finds to his dilemma, however, is the same one he had found to his actual crisis of 1866. It is a solution that will allow him to live the resurrection myth, but without giving up the religious skepticism and doubt he had embraced twelve or thirteen years earlier. The only trouble is that the secular solution he envisioned was not realizable.

In the crisis letter of 1867 Mallarmé had talked about a work of some sort that would reflect the new supreme synthesis he had arrived at. The solution to the new dilemma in 1879 will be the work I mentioned, a book that will allow the "spiritual essence of his son," as Richard calls it, to endure (p. 84). There is not much in the manuscript notes to specify what sort of oeuvre Mallarmé had in mind this time.

As we'll see, though, the whole project of a work or a book for Mallarmé was always conceived from the outset as something that could not be actualized. Mallarmé's characteristic procedure thus seems to be to move from religious crisis—brought on by the contemplation of death or Nothingness—to a religious structure in which the divinity has been replaced by an aesthetic quality or object. It may be a Hegelian term like Beauty or the Idea, or it may be a mysterious object like the "work" or "Book" that Mallarmé so often talks about. It thus makes sense to speak of a religion of aesthetics or an aesthetics of religion, as many Mallarmé scholars have done. This brings us to a curious series of prose pieces that Mallarmé published between 1892 and 1895 and then grouped under the title "Offices" (Religious services). There are three of them: "Plaisir sacré" (Sacred pleasure), "Catholicisme" (Catholicism), and "De même" (The same [that is, the same subject as in the previous essay]). The theme throughout is Catholic rites, the liturgy specifically, treated in a mock-serious way. Mallarmé's conceit is that the liturgy resembles drama or any kind of performance, even a Sunday symphony concert.

What is especially valuable about these pieces is that, better than almost any of his other writings, they show Mallarmé straddling the neighboring territories of religion and art. And his rhetorical device for doing so is the use of religious terms in a dual, religious-secular sense. Consciousness lends permanence to this fear by expiring (that is, breathing out) the abyss (eternity in its most fearsome aspect as Nothingness) into future ages. This process permits a race, like the French, to endure. Such a race would be ordinary and vague unless life, reconquered (as it is in the Resurrection), is allowed to blossom. And so church ritual becomes mere show—or mere show becomes church ritual.

Religion becomes aestheticized, and art becomes divinized. Religious words become secular, and secular words become religious. "Our communion or share of one to all and of all to one, thus, removed from the barbarous food that the sacrament designates—in the consecration of the host, nonetheless, the Mass, prototype of ceremonials, in spite of the difference with a tradition of art, asserts itself" (OC, p. 394). In the rest of the paragraph where this statement comes from, Mallarmé sets up a confusion between

Catholic mass and tragedy. Liturgy fades into drama, participants become actors, and the presence of Christ becomes the presence of the pagan god. " 'Real presence': or that the god should be there, long-winded, complete, mimed from afar by the unobtrusive actor" (OC, p. 394), the poet says in a mocking reference to belief in the actual presence of Christ in the consecrated host.

What goes on in a church is described repeatedly in these writings as a mystery, and here, too, Mallarmé is being intentionally ambiguous. Does he mean mystery as divine truth concealed, or as a medieval mystery play, or in the ordinary sense as something obscure? The medieval mystery play had a liturgical structure, placing the actor-hero in the role of priest and the audience in the role of congregation. Mallarmé evokes this setting repeatedly. "Always that, in this place, a mystery is put on: to what degree does one remain a spectator, or does one presume to have a role in it?" (OC, p. 395). "Mystery, other than representative and [other] than, I'll say, Greek, Play, [religious] service" (OC, p. 393). But this "mystery" is clearly not a sacred event since the author continually makes us aware of a decor that is modern and very secular. We keep seeing the elegant finery of feminine toilette, and we keep being reminded that all we're really doing is going to a Sunday concert: "Performance with concert," announces the author in one paragraph, indulging his taste for desecrating art by imitating the style of an advertising poster (OC, p. 393). The "real presence" of Catholic doctrine is reduced here to "mythic presence," the priest becomes an actor, and the liturgy becomes a "divine Drama," That's if we read it as a comment on Catholicism. Read in another way, however, the passage has the effect of exalting drama (or whatever sort of performance Mallarmé is talking about). This is the source of Mallarmé's irony. Irony, after all, involves the clash of two meanings or systems of meaning in a single utterance, frequently where one meaning is serious and the other is not.

But maybe it doesn't matter whether Mallarmé thought his reflections in "Offices" were a joke. The fact is that he exerts a great deal of effort in surrounding the ceremonies of art with the rituals of religion, so that the first resemble the second as much as possible. In "L'art pour tous" (Art for everybody) the young Mallarmé had likened art to religion and had sought to establish a sacred status for art objects (see above, p. 64). As in "Offices," Mallarmé had focused on the quality of mystery, although in the earlier essay he was a little less mysterious about what he meant by mystery. The tone there was almost as skeptical as in "Offices": "Every sacred thing that wishes to remain sacred envelops itself in mystery," the poet had said in a passage strongly suggesting that religions intentionally cloak themselves in mystery just so as to project a quality of sanctity. But if the young Mallarmé was skeptical about religion, he appeared to be quite serious about art, for instance, in his admonition to the artist to "remain an aristocrat" (OC, p. 259).

Mallarmé remained a man of faith ("You can't do without Eden"); it's just that faith was a part of a religion that did not include God or personal salvation. What did it include? Delfel agrees with a great many other commentators on Mallarmé that one important ingredient was the notion of essences. He speaks of Mallarmé's tendency to renounce sensible matter in favor of the "transcendence of aesthetic essences." In L'univers imaginaire de Mallarmé (Mallarmé's imaginary universe) Jean-Pierre Richard speaks of Mallarmé's belief in the possibility of discovering, by means of some sensible form of language, an "idea" inside an object. Richard renames that idea "concrete essence." As he shows with many examples, Mallarmé frequently expressed a belief in essences, notions, and ideas.

Mallarmé certainly wrote plenty of literary works, but they are no help at all. What we are interested in is his thinking about what literary works are. The good thing is that Mallarmé wrote so much about this object called the work (I'oeuvre) or the Book (le Livre). The bad thing is that what he wrote is often indecipherable, and what isn't indecipherable leaves more questions than answers about what Mallarmé is saying.

A decade after the "Autobiography" Mallarmé published a series of four essays under the title "Quant au Livre" (Concerning the Book). Once again, it is not entirely clear what Mallarmé means by "Book." In the first essay, "L'acticn restreinte" (The restricted action), he explores the mysterious nature of the act of writing: In the second, "Étalages" (Displays), he speaks of the commercial aspects of the Book. The third, "Le Livre, instrument spirituel" (The Book, spiritual instrument), examines the dialectic between the physical book and its spiritual dimension. The fourth is a meditation on language and reading.

By far the most interesting document is Le "Livre" de Mallarmé: Premières recherches sur des documents inédits (Mallarmé's "Book": Preliminary research on some unpublished documents), edited by Jacques Scherer. This book itself requires some description. Almost half of it is a scholarly study, by the editor, of the other half. That other half is a printed version of some manuscript notes Mallarmé had made. Scherer thinks Mallarmé wrote the notes in the last few years of his life, although he may have begun them earlier. They certainly respond to ideas he had had since as far back as 1866. Mallarmé had left instructions to have these notes and other loose papers burned after his death. Perhaps we would all have been better off if those instructions had been followed, but thanks to Mallarmé's disciple, Paul Valéry, who intervened after Mallarmé's death to preserve the notes, we now have at our disposal Scherer's pile of 202 sheets of . . . well, it's hard to say what they're of.

There has been considerable controversy over what this material means. Scherer is convinced that the sheets he has selected contain plans for the Book that Mallarmé had envisioned in his other writings. Other scholars are not so sure, some because they don't see the same themes that Scherer sees in these notes, others because they don't think there was ever any such thing as a Book that Mallarmé projected but never created. But it's not absolutely necessary to settle the controversy over whether Scherer's notes have to do with the same thing that Mallarmé refers to in other writings when he uses the words book and work (or whether he always means the same thing in those writings). The notes are a fascinating document that shows, at some indefinable and prepublishable stage, Mallarmé's musings on some sort of book or work. There is much to be said about these musings, and I'm afraid I will have to say it piecemeal since the Book is central not only to religion, but also to the remaining two parts of this book. For now, let's talk about religion.

In the other writings about the Book there is not much to suggest that the concept was fundamentally religious. Certainly the idea of a Book with the kind of mystical significance Mallarmé associates with it conjures up, without much effort, the idea of the Scriptures. The title "Le Livre, instrument spirituel" has a mystical, religious ring to it. At one moment in the essay of that title Mallarmé says that the crease in the page of a book (any book) is "almost religious" (OC, p. 379). The Book as the "Orphic explanation of the earth" is clearly a religious, if not a Christian, concept.

The essays in "Quant au Livre" betray the same taste for humorous profanation as the essays in "Offices" (which, curiously, are placed directly after "Quant au Livre" in the Oeuvres complètes) . But the thing being profaned in "Quant au Livre" is not as clearly religious as in "Offices": in "Quant au Livre" it is more the commonplace idea of the sacredness of literature (which is characteristically profaned by its juxtaposition with the much more commonplace idea of the commerciality of literature).

Mallarmé appears to have in mind an elaborately planned event that by the simplest description will just be a reading of his poems (or the Work, or the Book). The event is to be presided over by an enigmatic personage named the operator. There are repeated references to various elements of the event, including where it is to take place. For instance, we read of a yacht from time to time, and there is even a page that contains the rudiments of a narrative, something like a plot for the event (169 [A]).

In the midst of these stage directions (or whatever they are) are words and phrases that suggest a religious ceremony. The phrase Messe en Musique (Mass in Music) occurs at one point (3 [A]), and passion occurs a few pages later.

The most compelling evidence of the religious nature of the event is the numerous terms that suggest a mystery play. Over and over again we see the words hero, drama, mystery, hymn, theatre, usually abbreviated and arranged in patterns on the page (rarely as part of intelligible sentences). Mystery plays were originally performed with priests and clerics before an altar. They typically represented a biblical story, like the Passion story or some aspect of it, and, as I have said, they frequently had a liturgical structure. In France, during the sixteenth century, popular audiences were fond of seeing scenes with different settings in close succession. Advances in stagecraft made it possible to rearrange the stage quickly and show a variety of scenes in a short time. Mallarmé seems to have something like that in mind in his directions. In addition to the many references to drama, mystery, and hymns, we read of a complicated scheme that will allow the reader or operator of Mallarmé's event to shuffle and redistribute pages from the Book in the place where the event is staged.

In *After the New Criticism,* Frank Lentricchia demonstrates how American literary criticism, when it imports theories from France, as it did so avidly in the last few decades, has consistently concentrated on the Platonic elements, ignoring other important aspects of the theories—for instance, their historical aspects. The implication is that the American critical mind would insist on seeing the eternal and the essential even if the eternal and the essential were not there. When French structuralism caught on in the 1960s, Lentricchia thinks, it was "mediated" by American critics in such a way as to preserve one of the most important articles of faith from the era of New Criticism, namely that literary artworks are timeless objects containing eternal and unchanging values. Now I don't believe that structuralism is entirely free of this faith any more than the New Criticism was, but Lentricchia's point is that the Americans largely overlooked those elements of structuralism that were primarily secular, namely those that stressed historical change.

Glossary

Aestheticism: A late nineteenth century movement whose characteristic slogan, "art for art's sake," stresses the uselessness of art and divorces aesthetics from any moral, social, political, or practical concerns. The work of art is viewed as being isolated from extrinsic reality or nature and as existing in, of, and for itself. Worshiping the decay and transience of things of beauty, aestheticism often incorporates decadence, seeing the accursed poet as a visionary who cultivates a systematic derangement of all the senses and makes a demented inner voyage into the dark depths of the self. Decadence luxuriates in the flowers of evil such sophisticated ennui produces. From Charles Baudelaire's demonics to the dandyism of Oscar Wilde, aestheticism leads to the modernist cult of the image and the formalist view of art as a self-enclosed universe.

Affective fallacy: A term used by W K. Wimsatt and M. C. Beardsley to describe the "confusion between the poem and its result (what it *is* and what it *does*)." According to them, the critic should regard a poetic structure as formally self-sufficient and not commit the error of considering its emotional or pragmatic effects upon a reader.

Ambiguity: A nonpejorative term for the capacity of language to sustain multiple meanings. Also called plurisignation or polysemy, ambiguity arises from what William Empson calls "any verbal nuance, however slight, which gives room for alternative reactions to the same piece of language." In literary parlance, ambiguity is not a mistake in denotation to be avoided, but a resource of connotation to be exploited. In *Seven Types of Ambiguity* (1930), Empson argues that the richness, complexity, and concentration of literary language derives from the seven types of ambiguity he discusses. The notion that ambiguity is the root condition of all literary discourse, a notion that arises from I. A. Richards's distinction between the scientific (referential or denotative) and the poetic (emotive or connotative) uses of language, is an integral aspect of the New Critical view that paradox and tension are definitive aspects of the work of art.

Anxiety of influence: A term used by Harold Bloom to describe the overriding sense of belatedness that creative writers feel when they confront the rich plenitude of a literary tradition that seems to leave little room for novelty. According to Bloom, strong writers make literary history by misreading and misinterpreting their titanic predecessors so as to clear imaginative space for themselves. Every poem is a misprision or misconstrual of a hypothetical parent poem. Bloom's theory of the genesis of poems has a self-admitted psychoanalytic resonance, Sigmund Freud's Oedipal scenario being used as an analogy for the relationship between poet and predecessor.

Applied criticism: Applied criticism; explication de texte; the analysis, interpretation, and evaluation of particular works and writings. In the New Criticism practical criticism involves the close reading of individual texts with particular attention to their intrinsic verbal texture and structure. In *Practical Criticism* (1929), I. A. Richards analyzes the responses of his students to poems unfamiliar to them in order to point out characteristic errors in interpretation: mnemonic irrelevances, stock responses, doctrinal adhesions, technical presuppositions, general critical presuppositions, and so forth.

Archetypal criticism: A form of criticism which is based on the psychology of Carl Jung, who argues that there are two levels of the unconscious: the personal, which comprises repressed memories that are part of an individual's psyche, and the archetypal, which comprises the racial memory of a collective unconscious, a storehouse of images and patterns, vestigial traces of which inhere in all human beings and which find symbolic expression in all human art. Myth criticism explores the nature, function, and significance of these primordial images or archetypal patterns. Whereas Jung focuses on the genesis of these archetypes, myth critics such as Northrop Frye focus on their analysis. For Frye, an archetype is "a symbol, usually an image, which recurs often enough in literature to be recognizable as an element of one's literary experience." Frye devises an elaborate taxonomy of modes, symbols, myths, and genres, establishing a complex and comprehensive correspondence between the basic genres — comedy, romance, tragedy, and irony — and the myths and archetypal patterns associated with the seasonal cycle of spring, summer, fall, and winter.

Catharsis: An Aristotelian term for the purgative or purifying effect that the imitation of victimage in tragedy has upon an audience. According to Aristotle, a tragedy is a dramatic form "with incidents arousing pity and fear wherewith to accomplish the catharsis of such emotion." By allowing spectators to load their emotions onto a scapegoat, tragedy cleanses them of harmful tensions which would otherwise poison their mental health. It also purifies these emotions and forces the audience to undergo a process of ethical clarification. Catharsis, therefore, is morally as well as psychologically therapeutic.

Concretization: A phenomenological term used by Roman Ingarden to describe the process whereby the reader fills in the gaps in the structure of a work by rendering concrete and determinate its "places of indeterminacy." According to Ingarden, the reader has to concretize the work, making the implicit explicit, the potential actual.

Contextual criticism: A form of criticism which views the literary text as a self-contained verbal structure. Akin to the New_Criticism contextualism holds that a work of art generates self-referential meanings within its own internal and autonomous context. Its proponents include Cleanth Brooks, Eliseo Vivas, and Murray Krieger.

Delight: A term used by classical, Renaissance, and neoclassical critics (Horace, Sir Philip Sidney, John Dryden, and others) to describe the pleasure and entertainment that artistic imitation affords. The idea of instruction with pleasure — *utile et dulce* — was introduced by Horace.

Diachrony: A term describing a mode of analysis that undertakes to construct the historical evolution of a system of thought or language. The synchronic by contrast, undertakes to describe the system as an existing whole without respect to its history. Structural linguistics rejects the diachronic assumptions of classical philology, which studies linguistic change over a long period of time, and embraces the synchronic assumptions of Saussurian linguistics, which studies language as a functioning system existing in the here and now.

Dialectical criticism: A Marxist term for the kind of criticism that explores the causal connections between the content or form of literature at a given historical moment and the economic, social, and ideological factors that shape and determine that content or form. Work and background are construed to be dialectically related.

Dialogism: A term used by Mikhail Bakhtin to describe how a literary work may incorporate a rich variety and multiplicity of voices, styles, and points of view. Unlike a monological text, which depends on the centrality of a single authoritative voice, the dialogical text allows for "a plurality of independent and unmerged voices and consciousnesses, a genuine polyphony of fully valid voices."

Dissemination: A deconstructionist term coined by Jacques Derrida to describe the necessary indeterminacy of meaning. Since any signifying system is but a system of differences without any positive terms, meaning is disseminated rather than conveyed. It disperses itself throughout the realm of *différance* the realm of endless differing and deferral, of limitless free play. Meanings are thereby dispersed or disseminated among countless and contradictory alternatives, partaking of a fundamental instability.

Episteme: A term used by Michel Foucault to describe a heterogeneous and discontinuous epistemological field which is not to be understood as a cultural totality. It is an unmasterable web of historical ideas, social practices, power relations, and discursive formations that provides an alternative to the totalizing history that seeks to draw "all phenomena around a single center — a principle, a meaning, a spirit, a world-view, an overall shape."

Genre: A term used to describe types or categorizations of literature: tragedy, comedy, epic, lyric, pastoral, novel, short story, biography, essay, and so forth. Prior to the nineteenth century, it was assumed that the laws of genre were fixed and stable and that they provided objective criteria for evaluation. Today it is commonplace to acknowledge their arbitrary, conventional, and historical nature.

Humanism: A man-centered rather than a god-centered view of the universe. In the Renaissance, Humanism devoted itself to the revival of classical culture: the life, thought, language, and literature of ancient Greece and Rome. A reaction against the divine concerns of medieval Scholasticism and, Humanism orients itself toward secular concerns and applies classical ideas to theology, church reform, government, literature, criticism, and education. In literature the main virtues are seen to be restraint, form, and imitation of the classics, the ultimate authorities being Aristotle and Horace.

Icon: Charles Sanders Peirce's term for a sign that functions by means of sharing resemblances with what it signifies. Portraits or maps, for example, are natural resemblances rather than arbitrary and conventional signs.

Impressionistic criticism: A kind of criticism that tries to convey what the critic subjectively feels and thinks about a work of art.

Irony: Recognition of the difference between real and apparent meaning. Verbal irony is a rhetorical trope wherein "x" is uttered and "not x" is meant, as when Mark Anthony says that Brutus is an honorable man. Dramatic irony occurs when characters say something and the auditors know more than they do. In the New Criticism, irony, the poet's recognition of incongruities, was thought to be the master trope in that it was essential to the production of paradox, complexity, richness, and ambiguity.

Metacriticism: A criticism of criticism, the goal of which is to scrutinize systematically the terminology, logic, and structure that undergird critical and theoretical discourse in general or any particular mode of such discourse.

Metalanguage: A language used to describe and analyze the codes, conventions, and structures of another language.

Modernism: A term used to describe the characteristic aspects of literature and art between World War I and World War II. Influenced by Friedrich Nietzsche's annunciation of the death of God Karl Marx's view of consciousness as a product of sociohistorical factors, Sigmund Freud's view of the unconscious as the determinant of motivation and behavior, and the dislocating effects of the carnage and devastation of the war, modernism embodies a lack of faith in Western civilization and culture — its humanism and rationalism. In poetry, fragmentation, discontinuity, allusiveness, and irony abound; in fiction, chronological disruption, linguistic innovation, the stream-of-consciousness device, and point-of-view narration; in art and theater, expressionism and surrealism.

Moscow Linguistic Circle: An offshoot of the Moscow Linguistic Circle, members of which included Boris Eikhenbaum, Viktor Shklovsky, and Roman Jakobson. When Formalist criticism was suppressed by the Russian government in the early 1930s, Jakobson emigrated to Czechoslovakia and became part of the Prague Linguistic Circle, members of which included Rene Wellek and Jan Mukarovsky.

New historicism: A mode of analysis that sees history as a form of writing, discourse, or language. This new historicism abandons any notion of history as an imitation of events in the world or a reflection of external reality. Instead, it regards history as a species of narrative with gaps or ruptures between epistemes — modes of thought and ways of knowing that characterize a given historical moment.

Objective correlative: A term used by T. S. Eliot in the 1919 essay "Hamlet and His Problems." According to Eliot, "the only way of expressing emotion in the form of art is by finding an 'objective correlative'; in other words, a set of objects, a situation, a chain of events which shall be the formula of that particular emotion."

Objective criticism: A term used to describe a kind of criticism that views the aesthetic object as autonomous and self-contained. Because a work of art contains its purpose within itself (is, in Eliot's phrase, autotelic), analysis and assessment of it can take place only with reference to certain intrinsic criteria — form, coherence, organic unity (the interdependence of parts and whole). Extrinsic criteria — poet, audience, sociohistorical context, external reality — are deemed to be out of order. Objective criticism thus includes the New_Criticism contextual criticism.

Old criticism: Criticism predating the New Criticism and bringing extrinsic criteria to bear on the analysis of literature. Refusing to recognize the autonomy of art, such criticism sees literature as authorial self-expression or critical sell-expression (impressionism or as parasitic upon moral or ethical absolutes (new humanism. Such criticism blithely commits the affective and intentional fallacies.

Poststructuralism: Critical theory that uses the concepts of Saussurian linguistics, signifier, signified langue, parole, and so forth) and the structuralist application of these terms to the study of literature as a system of signs for the purposes of subverting or deconstruction these concepts. Poststructuralism is thus a blanket term and refers to diverse writings such as the deconstruction of Jacques Derrida, the late criticism of Roland Barthes, the New Historicism of Michel Foucault, the psychoanalytic revisionism of Jacques Lacan, the feminist criticism of Gayatri Spivak, and so forth.

Prague Linguistic Circle: An offshoot of the Moscow Linguistic Circle, members of which included Boris Eikhenbaum, Viktor Shklovsky, and Roman Jakobson. When Formalist criticism was suppressed by the Russian government in the early 1930s, Jakobson emigrated to Czechoslovakia and became part of the Prague Linguistic Circle, members of which included Rene Wellek and Jan Mukarovsky.

Reader-response criticism: The systematic examination of the aspects of the text that arouse, shape, and guide a reader's response. According to reader-response criticism, the reader is a producer rather than a consumer of meanings. In this sense, a reader is a hypothetical construct of norms and expectations that can be derived or projected or extrapolated from the work and may even be said to inhere in the work. Because expectations may be violated or fulfilled, satisfied or frustrated, and because reading is a temporal process involving memory, perception, and anticipation, the charting of reader-response is extremely difficult and perpetually subject to construction and reconstruction, vision and revision.

Symbolism: A literary movement encompassing the work of a group of writers working in France in the latter half of the nineteenth century, a group which included Charles Baudelaire, Stéphane Mallarmé, Paul Verlaine, Paul Valéry, Arthur Rimbaud, and others. According to Symbolism, there is a magical and mystical correspondence between the natural and spiritual worlds. By exploiting the connotative, associative, and evocative power of words, the poet, through his own suggestive private language, can obliquely express this correspondence and trigger a sympathetic vibration in the reader. The Symbolists had a great influence on British and American poets, especially on William Butler Yeats and T. S. Eliot.

Textual criticism: The gathering together and collating of all the variant versions of a given text in order to arrive at an authoritative text, the one which most accurately reflects the intentions of the author.

Textuality: *Écriture*, the social institution of writing, a heterogeneous collection of texts that interanimate one other (intertextuality and that cannot be studied as autonomous objects. Textuality is an all-embracing term for the idea that the world itself is nothing but a culturally endorsed system of signs — of shared codes, conventions, and ideologies — a textual system whose free play is limitless.

Bibliography

Ahsen, A. (1985). Unvividness Paradox. *Journal of Mental Imagery* (9) 1-18.

Ahsen, A. (1993). *Imagery Paradigm: Imaginative Consciousness in the Experimental and Clinical Setting.* New York: Brandon House.

Ahsen, A. (1999). *Hot and Cold Mental Imagery: Mind over Body Encounters.* New York: Brandon House.

Baddeley, A.D. (1976). *The Psychology of Memory.* London: Harper.

Blake, A. & Yuille, A. (Eds.) (1992). *Active Vision.* Cambridge, MA: MIT Press.

Bower, K.J. (1984). Imagery: From Hume to Cognitive Science. *Canadian Journal of Philosophy* (14) 217-234.

Brown. Peter (2008) *Encyclopaedia of World Great Literary Critics,* (2 vols). Anmol, New Delhi.

Bugelski, B.R., Kidd, E., & Segmen, J. (1968). Image as a Mediator in One Trial Paired Associate Learning. *Journal of Experimental Psychology* (76) 69-73.

Burnham, J.C. (1968). On the Origins of Behaviorism. *Journal of the History of the Behavioral Sciences* (4) 143-151.

Chandra, Suresh (1998), *Essays in Comparative Literature,* Anmol, New Delhi.

Cohen, D. (1979). *J. B. Watson — the Founder of Behaviorism: A Biography.* London: Routledge & Kegan Paul.

Danesi, Marcel & Perron, Paul. (1999). *Analyzing Cultures: An Introduction and Handbook.* Bloomington: Indiana UP.

Danesi, Marcel. (2002). *Understanding Media Semiotics.* London: Arnold; New York: Oxford UP.

Durgin, F.H. (2002). The Tinkerbell Effect: Motion Perception and Illusion. *Journal of Consciousness Studies* (9, v-vii) 88-101.

Fodor, J.A. (1975). *The Language of Thought.* New York: Thomas Crowell. (Paperback edition: Harvard University Press, 1980).

Giaquinto, M. (1993). Visualizing in Arithmetic. *Philosophy and Phenomenological Research* (53) 385-396.

Hauck, P.D., Walsh, C.C., & Kroll, N.E.A. (1976). Visual Imagery Mnemonics: Common vs. Bizarre Mental Images. *Bulletin of the Psychonomic Society* (7) 160-162.

Holt, R.R. (1964). Imagery: The Return of the Ostracised. *American Psychologist* (19) 254-266.

Jay, M. (1993). *Downcast Eyes: The Denigration of Vision in Twentieth-Century French Thought.* Berkeley, CA: University of California Press.

Kakkar, Rita (2004), *Critical Theories of I.A. Richards*, New Delhi: Anmol.

Kosslyn, S.M. (1983). *Ghosts in the Mind's Machine: Creating and Using Images in the Brain.* New York: Norton.

Ledger, Gerard R., 1989, *Re-Counting Plato: A Computer Analysis of Plato's Style*, Oxford: Oxford University Press.

Marks, D.F. (Ed.) (1986). *Theories of Image Formation.* New York: Brandon House.

O'Regan, J.K. (1992). Solving the "Real" Mysteries of Visual Perception: The World as an Outside Memory. *Canadian Journal of Psychology* (46) 461-488.

Paivio, A. (1977). Images, Propositions and Knowledge. In J.M. Nicholas (Ed.). *Images, Perception and Knowledge.* Dordrecht/Boston, MA: Reidel.

Popper, K.R. (1976). *Unended Quest: An Intellectual Autobiography.* London: Fontana/Collins.

Predebon, J. & Wenderoth, P. (1985). Imagined Stimuli: Imaginary Effects? *Bulletin of the Psychonomic Society* (23) 215-216.

Richards, N. (1977). Depicting and Visualising. *Mind* (82) 218-229.

Russow, L.-M. (1978). Some Recent Work on Imagination. *American Philosophical Quarterly* (15) 57-66.

Index

A

Abrams, M.H., 44
Affective Fallacy, 113
affective stylistics, 96, 139
AIDS, 66
Aletheia, 183
Allen Tate, 130
ambivalence, 112
Andrei Bely, 173
Anton Ehrenzweig, 194
Aristotle, 2

B

Bersani, 83
Biographical Criticism, 44
Blackmur, R.P., 110
Brice Wachterhauser, 12
Brook Thomas, 31

C

Catholic theology, 272
Cleanth Brooks, 119, 121
Code-naming, 55
Confucius, 54
Continental philosophy, 1
Cornel West, 90
Criticism, 57
  major scholars of, 26-53
Cultural,
  Literacy, 259
  Materialism, 152
  Materialists, 150
  Poetics, 51

E

Ecocriticism, 51
Edward Said, 41
Eliot, T.S., 4, 110, 119, 130, 269
Eric Voegelin, 134
Expressive Criticism, 44

F

Formalism, 46
Formalist critics, 272
Frank Lentricchia, 286
Franz Kafka, 26
Friedrich Engels, 36

G

Gadamer, 12
Gayle Rubin, 61
Gender,
  criticism, 54-91
  trouble, 62
Genre Criticism, 26

God, 4
Grecian Urn, 148
Greece, 2

H

Harold Bloom, 96
Hegemony, 155
Hillis Miller, J., 44
Hirsch, E.D., 259
Historical Criticism, 50
Historicizing Sexuality, 66

I

IMHO, 45

J

Jacques Derrida, 27
Jakobson, 272
James Joyce, 45
John Crowe Ransom, 119, 130
Jonathan Culler, 96
Julia Kristeva, 194

K

Kolodny, A., 51
Kubla Khan, 45

L

Language, 226-251
Lawrence, D.H., 194
Leavis, F.R., 119
Kesbian, 63
Lesslie Newbigin, 18
Literary,
  criticism, 258
  theory, 1, 2, 3, 8
Lodge, 104
Longinus, 2
Louise Rosenblatt, 92
Lukács, 37
Lyrical Ballads, 260

M

Maybe Mallarmé, 277
Mikhail Bakhtin, 26, 31
Minus feminism, 56
Moderate schism, 86
Monroe Beardsley, 113, 121
Moral Criticism, 45

N

New Criticism, 13, 97, 98, 111, 114, 132, 269, 286
New Historicism, 150, 151, 153, 289
Norman Holland, 96

P

PCE, 128
Postcolonial criticism, 41, 42
Post-modernism, 9
Potential space, 194
Professional Boundaries, 87
Psychoanalytic Criticism, 34, 188-

Q

Quant au Livre, 286
Queer Theory, 53

R

Raymond Carver, 104

Reader-Response Criticism, 31, 92-109, 289
Rhetorical Criticism, 42
Richards, I.A., 13, 44, 110, 118, 121
Robert Penn Warren, 119, 121
Rosenblatt, 33
Russian,
  Formalism, 7, 46
  Orthodox theology, 272
  schools of thought, 160-187
  tradition, 251

S

Samuel Taylor Coleridge, 112
Sergei Bulgakov, 177
Sigmund Freud, 34
Socio-Political Criticism, 49
Specifying Sexuality, 70
Stanley Fish, 44, 100, 103, 104
Stephen Greenblatt, 151
Structuralism, 39

T

Terry Eagleton, 12
The Art of Reading, 100
Thinking Sex, 61

U

United States, 3

W

Westphal, 71
William Empson, 44, 119
William K. Wimsatt, 110
William Shakespeare, 36
William Wimsatt, 113, 121
Winnicott, D.W., 35
Wittgenstein, 22
Wolfgang Iser, 32, 93, 96, 100
World War II, 111